More Praise for *Next*

The biggest climate and development challenges are too big to ignore.
Jorisch offers a hopeful glimpse into the inspiring minds behind the
innovations that embody our better future.

> — **Henk Ovink**, Special Envoy for International Water
> Affairs, Kingdom of the Netherlands; Sherpa to the
> United Nations High Level Panel on Water

Avi Jorisch has demonstrated once again that he is one of the most
incisive and far-sighted thinkers on our planet, offering us not just
a glimpse into what's next over the horizon but a lodestar to where
we *should* be going to ensure a better future for us all.

> — **Afshin Molavi**, Senior Fellow, Foreign Policy
> Institute, Johns Hopkins University School
> of Advanced International Studies

Next offers a thought-provoking narrative: in the coming decades,
the world will change to such a degree that today's science fiction
is tomorrow's science.

> — **Rodolphe Barrangou**, Distinguished
> Professor, CRISPR Lab Lead, North
> Carolina State University

Next compellingly builds upon the case for a sustainable existence
for our species both on and off planet through pioneering innovation,
thrillingly captured in this storied chronicle.

> — **Yvonne Cagle, MD, PhD**, Aerospace
> Mission Specialist

D1527952

next

A BRIEF HISTORY
OF THE FUTURE

next

A BRIEF HISTORY
OF THE FUTURE

AVI JORISCH

gefen
publishing house בית תורצאה לאור גפן
JERUSALEM ◆ NEW YORK Est. 1981

Cover Design: Lisa Mendelow
Cover illustration: Lisa Mendelow
Typesetting: Raphaël Freeman MISTD, Renana Typesetting

ISBN: 9798372691070

1 3 5 7 9 8 6 4 2

Gefen Publishing House Ltd.
6 Hatzvi Street
Jerusalem 9438614,
Israel
972-2-538-0247
orders@gefenpublishing.com

Gefen Books
c/o Baker & Taylor Publisher Services
30 Amberwood Parkway
Ashland, Ohio 44805
516-593-1234
orders@gefenpublishing.com

www.gefenpublishing.com

Printed in Israel

Library of Congress Control Number: 2021912928

For Eiden, Oren and Yaniv –
the greatest gift the universe has given me.
The future belongs to you.

I don't regret any of my dreams.
My only regret is not having dreamed more.

– Shimon Peres, No Room for Small Dreams

Contents

Preface   The Future Is Now   xi

Chapter 1   Space: Print Me Up, Scotty!   1

Chapter 2   Learning: The Internet Academy   11

Chapter 3   Shelter: Let There Be Light   23

Chapter 4   Environment: Water World   33

Chapter 5   Hygiene: There Will Be Blood   43

Chapter 6   Medicine: Playing God – Genetic Editing   53

Chapter 7   Disaster Resilience: The Ring of Fire   69

Chapter 8   Energy: The Electric Slide   81

Chapter 9   Prosperity: The King of Microfinance   93

Chapter 10   Food: Green Meat   105

Chapter 11   Water: Every Last Drop   117

Chapter 12   Governance: The Digital Republic   127

Chapter 13   Security: Google's X-Man   141

Afterword   Humanity 2.0   153

Acknowledgments   157

Endnotes   161

Bibliography   197

About the Author   235

The Future Is Now

The best way to predict the future is to create it yourself.

– Peter Diamandis, Singularity University

What's Next?

In March 2020, a few weeks before the coronavirus roiled America, my three young sons and I piled into the Washington Convention Center in DC for an AIPAC policy conference. I wanted them to see how technology can help solve the world's most intractable problems, from groundbreaking advancements in water preservation to novel new methods for recycling plastic. You know, the kind of stuff small children love.

As we wandered through the crowd, we bumped into my friend Eli Beer, the founder of United Hatzalah, an Israeli nonprofit that has revolutionized emergency care. There are few people I admire more. Over the past twenty years, Eli has brought together volunteer EMTs – Jews, Christians, and Muslims, among others – to save thousands of lives. One of his best innovations is an Uber-like app that connects anyone who needs emergency care with available EMTs nearby. These volunteer emergency workers often travel by "ambucycle," motorcycles refitted to function as mini-ambulances, which are nimble enough to weave through traffic. In Israel and elsewhere, Eli and company have helped drastically cut down the response time for people in need. (Little did we know that Eli himself would soon be in dire need, as he faced a life-threatening case of COVID-19 himself soon after our meeting.)

My kids gave Eli a hug, and he showed us around his booth. All three boys – Eiden, Oren, and Yaniv – strapped on virtual reality goggles to experience what it's like to work as a United Hatzalah volunteer. As their faces lit up, I felt optimistic not just about the future but about the ability of technology to make the world a better place. "When I get older," Eiden, my oldest, told me, "I don't want to drive a car. I want to ride an ambucycle and save lives."

I couldn't have been prouder. As we walked away, my middle child, Oren, grabbed my hand and pulled me down to his face. "But what's next, Baba?"

He didn't mean our plans for the afternoon.

A few weeks later, my sons and I were quarantined together around a screen in our living room. A SpaceX aircraft was about to launch from pad 39A at the Kennedy Space Center. The boys watched open-mouthed as mission control gave the order: "Three, two, one, blastoff." We tracked the spacecraft continuously for nineteen hours as it hurled itself toward the International Space Station. When the Crew Dragon docked, and the astronauts emerged smiling from their capsule, they made history: it was the first private spacecraft to berth with ISS, carrying cargo under commercial agreements with NASA.

"What's next?!" Oren asked me again. My kids were even more eager for me to tell them what the future is going to look like and what scientists and innovators are doing today to address the earth's scariest problems. I told them stories about *Star Trek*–loving inventors who 3D print spacecrafts in orbit, vegan researchers who replicate the composition and chemical structures of meat in a lab, and mad scientists who save humans from terrible disorders by cutting and pasting genes as if they were letters in Microsoft Word. Then, as much to satiate my own curiosity as theirs, I found myself looking for more. Who are the most impressive innovators out there today, shaping the history of the future?

In this present moment, imperiled by hunger, pollution, and global warming, human beings are at a critical juncture, closer than we've ever been to driving ourselves to extinction. But we're also in an era of abundance – and remarkable wealth – that's fueling the kind of innovation that could allow us to fundamentally change our destiny: curing the sick, feeding the hungry, eradicating poverty, and healing the planet.

Next tells the story of thirteen game-changing innovations that are poised to transform our species from a society of takers to a society of givers. Call it Humanity 2.0. Each venture featured in the following pages – together with the ideas and doers behind them – is already having an outsized impact on human history. In the coming decades, what's next will be dictated by our growing ability to leverage exponential thinking to bring about truly extraordinary innovations that are far beyond our current imagination – technologies that will, if used for good, allow us to make the world a far better place.

An Eruption of Disruption

More than half a century ago, long before the invention of the personal computer, engineer-turned-entrepreneur Gordon Moore received a letter from the editor of a trade publication called *Electronics*. Moore, the cofounder of a then unknown semiconductor firm called Intel, was delighted to learn that the magazine wanted him to write a piece for their thirty-fifth anniversary. The topic: how changes in the circuits that power computers would impact society. Moore was so excited, he scribbled a giant note to himself at the top of the letter: "Go-Go."

"I find the opportunity to predict the future in this area irresistible,"

Moore responded, "and will, accordingly, be happy to prepare a contribution."[1]

What Moore came up with would radically change the tech we use and the way we live. The power of microchips running our computers, he concluded, will double every year. And as he pondered what that might mean for the world, he also managed to predict the invention of home computers, cellphones, self-driving cars, and smartwatches – all of which would become cheaper over time. As *New York Times* columnist Thomas Friedman once joked, "The only thing he missed . . . was microwave popcorn."[2]

By 1975, Moore's hypothesis had already been proven true, but he believed the pace of growth was accelerating, so he updated his prediction. "Moore's Law," which posits that the power of microchips will double roughly every two years while their cost remains about the same, has held up ever since.

We feel the impact of this phenomenon every day. It's why our technology is almost unrecognizable compared to what we were using just two decades ago. Smartphones, social media, and GPS have all become commonplace in the past twenty years. And it's not just about the gadgets. We've seen a true revolution in science and technology, from crops genetically engineered to yield more food to advances in microfinance that have helped lift millions out of poverty.

Ray Kurzweil knows a lot about these changes. He's not only Google's director of engineering, he's the preeminent inventor of the flatbed scanner and reading machines for the blind. Using Moore's Law, he foretold some of the most amazing technological changes in the modern world. In a 2010 report on the 147 predictions Kurzweil made over thirty years, 115 turned out to be entirely correct, twelve essentially correct, seventeen partially correct, and just three wrong. Among other things, Kurzweil predicted the fall of the Soviet Union, computers with no moving parts, facial recognition software, voice-activated typewriters, robotic prostheses that allow paraplegics to walk, and a fully mature cloud-computing network.

In his 1999 book *The Age of Spiritual Machines*, Kurzweil used Moore's framework to analyze human history, arguing that exponential growth isn't a recent phenomenon, but something we've seen for thousands of years. He called it the Law of Accelerating Returns. By the nineteenth century, he wrote, technological change was happening at a rate faster than the previous nine hundred years combined – and included innovations such as the steam engine, the electric telegraph, and gas lighting. The first few decades of the twentieth century saw more technological advancement than the entire previous century – from cars and airplanes to radio transmission.

Kurzweil makes an utterly convincing case that the rate of global technological progress will continue to be exponential. "We won't experience 100 years of progress in the twenty-first century," he says, "it will be more like 20,000 years of progress."[3] He predicts the next few decades will see radical technological changes cut from the pages of science fiction novels.

According to Kurzweil, humans will be able to cure most diseases by the end of this decade. We'll be able to reverse-engineer the brain and use nanobots to treat debilitating illnesses, including neurological disorders like Parkinson's and Alzheimer's. And as a result, our lifespans will increase dramatically.

His predictions about energy have equally far-reaching implications. "In 2030 we will have [total] renewable energy," Kurzweil says, "and it will be inexpensive."[4] Solar, he maintains, will satisfy the total demand of humankind, likely meaning cleaner air and fewer wars.

His most shocking predictions involve virtual reality and artificial intelligence. Kurzweil believes that by 2029, computers will exhibit intelligent behavior equivalent to or indistinguishable from that of humans – including the capacity for love, romance, and humor. Artificial intelligence will eventually respond to the personalities and preferences of human users, and we'll build real human-computer relationships. But this is also the moment that AI surpasses us, as super intelligent machines gain the ability to conceive of ideas no human has ever thought of.

By the early 2030s, Kurzweil thinks we'll be able to copy a human brain and reproduce it in electronic format. Humans at this point will no longer need flesh, blood, or bones, and we won't die in the traditional sense. We'll just 3D print fresh organs. "When we change from an older computer to a newer one, we don't throw all our files away," he says. "Rather, we copy them and reinstall them on the new hardware."[5] The same will go for our bodies.

Even greater changes will come by 2045, though we can hardly comprehend them, because our brains are wired to believe that the future will evolve linearly and predictably, rather than exponentially. By that year, Kurzweil famously posits, we'll have achieved what's known as singularity, a period when humans will multiply their effective intelligence a billion-fold by merging our brains with artificial intelligence. This is the point in time when human civilization experiences unforeseen changes due to uncontrollable and irreversible technological growth – which will fundamentally impact how humans learn, work, recreate, and wage war. "This leads to computers having human intelligence, humans putting them inside our brains, connecting them to the cloud, expanding who we are," he says.[6]

That Kurzweil's reassuring predictions sound more like *Star Trek: The Next Generation* than *The Terminator* is not lost on futurists like Nick Bostrom, who believe that when singularity arrives, there's a strong possibility that machines will either enslave or destroy human beings. Bostrom envisions an AI that will "annihilate Earth-originating intelligent life or permanently and drastically curtail its potential."[7] The Rand Corporation, a US defense think tank, warns that the use of AI in military applications could give rise to a nuclear war by 2040.[8]

Even Elon Musk, the founder of SpaceX and Tesla, two of the

most innovative companies of the twenty-first century, has called artificial intelligence "more dangerous than nukes." He, too, believes the rate of improvement in AI is exponential, and that it's "capable of vastly more than people really understand."[9] As he once put it on Twitter, "competition for AI superiority at a national level [is the] most likely cause of World War III."[10]

Whether or not we're headed toward utopia or dystopia – or something amorphous in between – will rest on the decisions humanity makes over the coming few years.

The Paradox of Progress

As a species, we have thousands of years of experience grappling with new technology and making a mess of it. In the Bible, Genesis tells the story of early man using bricks to climb higher and higher into the sky, hoping to achieve God-like status. Seeing that society has lost its way, God decides to confound human speech so we can't understand each another, then scatters us across the globe. Or so the story goes. Either way, the moral of the Tower of Babel remains: human beings shouldn't play God. And if even a fraction of Kurzweil's predictions come true, things are about to get extremely biblical.

The past fifty years alone have put the promise and perils of technology in stark relief. Our lifespans have more than doubled, per capita income has tripled nearly everywhere, and the cost of food and energy has dropped thirteen- and twenty-fold, respectively. But our world has also changed at such a rapid pace that we've struggled to adapt, and in the trade-off for progress, we've been all too willing to accept or ignore the more sinister ramifications. Using genetic engineering to cure diseases also gives drug cartels the ability to synthetically alter organisms and create illegal narcotics. The same platforms that democratize free education have also taught criminals to rob banks with a single keystroke. The computer technology that has allowed us to get from one place to another autonomously will also inevitably allow a terrorist to remotely coordinate a suicide attack.

In 2020, social media allowed us to stay connected during a pandemic and, among other things, was instrumental in documenting police abuses, but it also continued to fester with propaganda and misinformation, which if left unchecked could portend a future of social engineering on a grand and terrifying scale. We also continued to allow the unfettered collection of our personal data, which is bought and sold to ends we don't yet fully understand and is all but guaranteed to have far-reaching implications for society. And the technology many countries used to stop the epidemic in its tracks – connected wearables, location tracking, facial recognition – was also abused to invade our privacy, break up protests, and racially profile.

"The ability of one to affect many is scaling exponentially," says Marc Goodman, author of *Future Crimes: Everything Is Connected, Everyone Is Vulnerable and What We Can Do about It.* "It's scaling for good and it's scaling for evil."[11]

But compared to the existential problems the earth is facing, the downsides of technology are the least of our worries. In 2020, the Paris-based research organization Future Earth released a report on climate change that combined the insights of more than two hundred leading scientists from more than fifty countries. They concluded that the challenges confronting humanity – extreme weather events, the decline of life-sustaining ecosystems, food insecurity, and dwindling stores of fresh water – compound one another. On their own, they're devastating enough, but taken together, they may wind up destroying our cities, our countries, our planet, and ultimately us.

Extreme heat waves increase global warming by releasing planet-warming gases from natural resources while intensifying water and food shortages. And the loss of biodiversity weakens our natural and agricultural systems, putting food supplies at even greater risk. "Our actions in the next decade," says Amy Luers, the group's executive director, "will determine our collective future on Earth."[12]

There's agreement across the board that the time to act is now. "We have only a very small window," says World Economic Forum president Børge Brende. "And if we don't use that window in the next 10 years, we will be moving around the deckchairs on the Titanic."[13]

We Choose to Go to the Moon

To meet the moment, we're going to have to take more moon shots than ever before. When President John F. Kennedy announced the Apollo program in 1962, landing a man on the moon seemed all but impossible. And if anyone was going to do it, all bets would have been on the Soviet Union, which had already launched the world's first satellite, Sputnik, and the world's first man, cosmonaut Yuri Gagarin, into orbit. America was losing the space race, and Kennedy wanted our astronauts to do something earth-shattering, to show people all over the world how remarkable the United States was – and by implication our system of capitalism and liberal democracy. "We choose to go to the moon in this decade and do the other things," Kennedy famously declared, "not because they are easy, but because they are hard."[14]

Not even seven years later, on July 16, 1969, Neil Armstrong, Buzz Aldrin, and Michael Collins blasted off into space on the Apollo 11 spacecraft. With more than half a billion people watching on television, when Armstrong climbed down the ladder onto the Sea of Tranquility, he couldn't have said it better: it was one small step for man, one giant leap for mankind.

The Apollo program remains one of the greatest mobilizations of resources and manpower in human history. The cost was about $22 billion, or $260 billion in today's dollars.[15] But it was worth the benefits – and not necessarily for the reasons Kennedy intended. NASA had to develop the world's biggest rocket, along with the smallest, fastest, and most nimble computer. The device was among the first to use integrated circuit computer chips and ultimately helped accelerate the silicon chip revolution. Kennedy's moon shot also jump-started the development of a high-speed data network, spacesuits, space food, heat shields, and numerous fireproof materials, among other products.

Well after the mission was complete, the impact of the investment continued to reverberate in new technologies, including the CAT scanner, originally developed to enhance images of the moon; the ear thermometer, first used to detect the birth of stars; and even invisible braces for teeth, which got their start as a material that could detect cracks in aircraft.

The world has changed dramatically since the Kennedy era. And while the United States is still considered to be a great problem solver, the federal government is no longer at the forefront of innovation. Few expect government spending on moon shots to increase in the near future, in part due to partisan gridlock in Washington. Fortunately, venture capitalists and entrepreneurs have taken an increased interest in moon shots, sometimes quite literally: with their help, the United States has announced it intends to send humans back to the moon by 2024, if not sooner. Water has now been found on this celestial body, which will deeply impact the future of lunar bases – both as a source of drinking water and fuel – and further the exploration of deep space.

Governments are no longer the only entities that can play a meaningful role in tackling seemingly intractable global challenges. Corporations, research institutions, and DIY innovators with few resources and little manpower, alongside a generation of techno-philanthropists like Bill Gates, who are spending billions of dollars of their own personal wealth, are now capable of achieving moon shots on their own.

If we're going to meet the challenges of this century – from climate change to food scarcity – governments, companies, and entrepreneurs from around the world will need to work together and use the type of bold, creative thinking that got us to the moon. As Astro Teller, the director of Google x, a research and development facility that creates radical new technologies, explains: "Moonshots live in the gray area between audacious projects and pure science fiction."[16] It is, he asserts, "almost more an exercise in creativity than it is in technology."[17]

Many are already embracing this mindset. Among them are Peter Diamandis, futurist and chairman of the X Prize Foundation, a nonprofit that funds public competitions to encourage technological development that benefits humanity. In 2008, he and Kurzweil founded Singularity University, a school that focuses almost exclusively on "moon shot thinking," where the world's greatest scientists, inventors, engineers, and technologists come together with entrepreneurs, investors, and philanthropists to help solve the world's most pressing problems.

The university doesn't strive to achieve singularity, nor does it give out degrees. Its goal is to teach students about advances in biotech, nanotech, artificial intelligence, robotics, neuroscience, and energy systems. More than a million people from more than 150 countries have attended the school's programs since it was founded. (I had the privilege in 2018.) And it not only gives people the knowledge they need to think boldly about the future, but in many cases access to the money they need to make their ideas a reality. Everyone who takes part is asked to focus on a central question: How can I positively impact the lives of at least one billion people and solve a grand global challenge?

Too Big to Ignore

Interviewing the innovators in this book and diving deep into their stories fueled me with a tremendous sense of faith and optimism that we'll be able to conquer the daunting obstacles that lie ahead. Today, advances in air travel and the internet have shrunk our world to the size of a fist: we now wield more processing power in a single smartphone than the entire Apollo 11 guidance system. There's always the risk of stumbling toward dystopia, but as Kurzweil says, "This is by far the best time in human history."[18]

The transformation the world is currently undergoing is profound and will far supersede the impact of the Industrial Revolution. Above all, three mega-trends are the driving forces behind the issues tackled in *Next*: the growth of a global middle class, rapid urbanization, and increased physical and technological connectivity. By the end of the decade, the world's population will reach 8.5 billion, the majority of which will be part of the economic middle class. And though half the world's population is now considered urban, by 2030 a full two-thirds of it will be. Many will live in a mindboggling forty mega-cities with populations of more than ten million people each.

"These powerful economic drivers will continue to dramatically transform our world over the next several decades," says Afshin Molavi, senior fellow at the Johns Hopkins SAIS Foreign Policy Institute, "lifting millions more out of poverty, reshaping global trade patterns, altering geopolitical alliances, creating new centers of innovation, and posing new and previously unimaginable challenges to societies and states."[19]

The innovations featured in the chapters that follow address thirteen critical areas outlined by the United Nations as key Sustainable Development Goals: space, learning, shelter, the environment, hygiene, medicine, disaster resilience, energy, prosperity, food, water, governance, and security. Many of the people behind the innovations were inspired by the likes of Kurzweil and Diamandis. Some of these visionaries have attempted to solve problems so big, most of us wouldn't know where to begin. *Next* offers readers a look at the key decisions – and failures – behind the process of turning an idea into a real-world breakthrough. And though each of their success stories is unique, collectively they reveal a blueprint for what it takes to tackle the impossible. All have required moon shot thinking.

Among them are Jun Sato, one of Japan's most renowned architects, who explained to me how his country builds structures to withstand natural disasters – and who has become a global pioneer in both seismic engineering and society-level planning in the bargain. During our interview, a magnitude 5.4 earthquake hit. Sato shrugged it off. "That wasn't so bad," he laughed. "The really big one is yet to come."[20]

You'll hear from Toomas Hendrik Ilves, the former president of Estonia, who helped transform his country into the world's first fully digital society, providing hundreds of social services from the cloud, including voting. From the Netherlands, where a significant portion of the population lives below sea level, you'll learn about the colossal efforts of water specialists like Henk Ovink, who are showing the rest of the world how to keep rising oceans at bay. And you'll read about revolutions already taking hold across the spectrum, from the electric and autonomous vehicles reshaping transportation to the difference-makers like Salman Khan reinventing education and Muhammad Yunus combating poverty through microfinance.

You'll sink your teeth into lab-grown meat that could save us all and get a closer look at earth-shattering technologies like CRISPR gene editing, which are set to transform medicine – and nearly everything else. You'll also discover how two solar panels, a refrigerator, and a simple water pump connected to a computer thousands of miles away can entirely transform a starving African village, and how Sivan Yaari is proving it, one project at a time, impacting the lives of millions. And you'll find out how a tiny wrench produced by an experimental, zero-gravity 3D printer could soon unlock a quantum shift for the human race, on our own planet and beyond.

These technologies and the new realities they present to humanity are *already* here now – they are firmly embedded in some places, and spreading. All of these ideas offer a glimpse at what's next for humanity. But above all, if I've done it right, they will also give readers hope about our lives. About our future as a species.

As the science fiction writer William Gibson once put it: "The future is already here. It is just not evenly distributed."[21]

CHAPTER 1

Space: Print Me Up, Scotty!

The Earth is the cradle of humanity, but
mankind cannot stay in the cradle forever.

– Konstantin Tsiolkovsky, from a 1911 letter

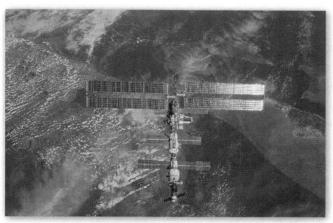

International Space Station over Miami, Florida (NASA)

Big Dang Deal

In November 2014, Barry Wilmore, a NASA astronaut, looked out the small window of the International Space Station and worried about what he was going to tell his boss. Weeks earlier, he and two Russian cosmonauts, Aleksandr Samokutyayev and Yelena Serova,

1

had arrived at this outpost about 220 miles above Earth – the only off-planet home for humankind. Almost immediately, they began conducting experiments ranging from disaster relief to how the human eye changes during space travel. As they worked, however, one of Wilmore's tools – a ratcheting wrench – drifted away in the spaceship.[1] "It's not uncommon for things to disappear in space," he says. "You just don't have gravity keeping stuff in place."[2]

If an emergency occurs or something breaks down, the consequences of losing tools can be calamitous. Which is why the space station spends millions on spare parts and backups, most of which will never be used. Unfortunately, the astronauts on his mission could not find another wrench.

Frustrated, Wilmore radioed mission control back on Earth. The NASA engineers on the other end of the line were concerned, but they quickly came up with a solution. They contacted a company called Made in Space, a California-based startup that was trying to prove that 3D printing could work without gravity.

A few weeks prior, NASA had sent one of their devices to the astronauts on a cargo spacecraft. The timing was fortuitous.

Invented by Charles Hull in 1984, 3D printers are similar to their ink-and-paper predecessors. The difference is they can make three-dimensional objects. "The ink is now plastic," says Jason Dunn, Made in Space's cofounder. Or an acrylic-based material known as photopolymer. When UV laser beams hit this material, the portion exposed to light turns into a solid piece, which the printer molds into a 3D shape. As Dunn explains: "We're melting it just like a hot glue gun out of a nozzle."[3]

Thanks to 3D printing, companies can now test designs without having to make a huge upfront investment. Today, industries across a broad range use this technology, from construction to aerospace. In space, 3D printing could revolutionize travel, telecommunications, and other industries. But the devices require gravity – a problem the company knew they had to solve. If every single belt, cog, and pulley isn't secured, once you remove the downward force ever-present on Earth, the printing mechanism fails or leads to strange results.

By the time Willmore lost his wrench, Dunn and company had been developing their printer for years. If they succeeded, the tool would be the first designed on Earth and made in space.

Back at Silicon Valley's Ames Research Center, the company's engineers produced several wrenches to ensure they met the proper specifications. After five days of work, mission control sent the digital file to the space station. After two hours of printing, mission control asked Willmore to go over to the box-like device about the size of a small microwave. He opened the door and pulled out a wrench. "[It's] a game-changer," he said. "Or as we say in Tennessee, it's a big dang deal."[4]

One small tool for human beings, one huge leap for humankind.

The Vomit Comet

Dunn's interest in space began when he was a child growing up in Florida. He was fascinated with exploring the world, from the oceans on Earth to the planets beyond it. The first time he saw the Space Shuttle launch from the nearby Kennedy Space Center at Cape Canaveral, he watched what looked like a little star moving up in the sky and was amazed that there were people on it disappearing into space.[5]

As he grew up, Dunn's interest in space increased. At the University of Orlando, he studied aerospace engineering and worked on NASA's shuttle program through an internship at Boeing. He got involved in a college club called Students for the Exploration and Development of Space, where he met Peter Diamandis, the Singularity University cofounder, who became his mentor.

In 2010, NASA announced it was going to stop flying into space. "I felt a little heartbroken and very confused," says Dunn, "because the whole reason I was doing this was to work on the space shuttle."[6] But Diamandis encouraged Dunn to join the Singularity University graduate studies program in Mountain View, California. There, Dunn met two entrepreneurs – Aaron Kemmer and Mike Chen. All three had a lot in common. They were obsessed with *Star Trek* and space, and they had pursued college degrees in either engineering, computer science, or philosophy.

Kemmer played a major role bringing the cofounders together. He grew up in the Florida panhandle and watched space shuttle launches from his home. He was mesmerized by the shuttles, by the fire, the smoke, and the chance to explore life beyond Earth. And from an early age, he knew he wanted to be an astronaut. He remembers jumping up and down on his bed when he was five years old, holding his Hot Wheels Space Shuttle. He tripped and fell and cut open his forehead, but wouldn't let go of the toy. "That's when I got my Harry Potter scar," Kemmer says. "Going into space was seared into my forehead."[7]

As he got older, his obsession with space didn't wane. And after graduating from the University of Florida and starting a news aggregation website, he kept thinking about what he could do that was bigger than himself – and for him, that meant a space venture. When he was twenty-five, he enrolled in Singularity University, hoping to learn all he could from Diamandis.

When he met Dunn and Chen in the program, he quickly realized they all had a common interest in 3D printing and its potential in outer space. NASA, they learned, had experimented with 3D printing in the 1990s, but the agency decided the technology wasn't ready. That changed in 2005, when Congress designated the US segment of the International Space Station as a national lab to encourage experiments that would improve life on Earth.[8]

After finishing the Singularity program, the three men decided to start a company along with Michael Snyder, a close friend of Kemmer. They alternated between calling themselves the Teenage Mutant Ninja Turtles (each one was assigned a character based on their personalities) and the four Jedi.[9] As they decorated their office, they filled it with science fiction posters from *Star Wars*, *The Tholian Web*, and *Mirror Mirror*. They also have a life-sized cardboard cutout of Mr. Spock in the reception area. "We are creating the technology of *Star Trek*," says Dunn, "building the replicator and transporter all in one with 3D printers."[10]

Shortly after forming their company, Kemmer and Dunn traveled to Alabama to NASA's Marshall Space Center where they pitched the idea of putting a 3D printer in space. It went well, and NASA eventually connected them to academics and government agencies, and let them conduct experiments on its reduced gravity aircraft. Known as the "Vomit Comet," it's a converted passenger jet that flies in the same way a roller coaster moves. With every nosedive, passengers get about twenty seconds of weightlessness. This allowed them to start testing a variety of 3D printers to see if they would work outside Earth's gravity.

Made in Space quickly got to work. From July through September 2011, the company performed more than four hundred tests on ten flights. "The feeling of zero gravity is impossible to explain," says Dunn. "It's entirely new. Outside of when you're an infant, you don't really have any new sensations or feelings."[11]

On the first nine flights, the company's printers failed. Because of the anti-nausea pills and the new floating sensation, the team had to automate every part of its experiments. Making real-time decisions was impossible. At first, everything the team printed turned to mush. Heat transfers differently on Earth than it does in space – it rises in gravitational environments, which is obviously impossible where "up" doesn't exist – and that impacts the melting and cooling of the plastic.

Made in Space had one chance left, and it had to design a new printer to make it work, an arduous task. The team spent days redesigning the device. The four eventually decided to try adjusting the printer's surface tension to make the layers of plastic stick together. They boarded the flight far from certain that their work would pay off. NASA, in the face of hitherto unproductive test flights, was not going to give them any more flight time. "We were down to our last chance to ever figure this out," Kemmer recalls.[12]

The pilot counted down from ten, then pulled back on the joystick controlling the aircraft. It climbed a kilometer into the sky. Then the pilot cut the engines. The plane began to drop. The team fired up the printer. Goo oozed from the device. The team waited a moment – and then it happened: the goo hardened. Everyone pumped their fists. "It was this amazing moment," says Kemmer.[13]

The tests proved that Made in Space had created a product that could actually work in zero-gravity environments like the moon or the surface of Mars. "In my heart, I always knew these were the guys to figure this out," says Yvonne Cagle, a NASA astronaut and the Singularity University instructor who served as their liaison to the space agency. "They had the passion, the drive, and determination to solve this challenge no matter what."[14] NASA soon offered them a contract to build a 3D printer that the agency could send to the space station. And after two years of trial and error, Made in Space's dream became a reality with Willmore's wrench.

Today, the company's devices can help reduce the risk of missions by fixing tools, or creating new ones in real time. And in the future, Dunn says, humans will be able to 3D print larger objects at the space station. That could mean we'll be able to travel deeper into the universe and live full-time in space or on other planets. As Dunn puts it: "We need to make it so that going to space is as safe as getting on an airplane."[15]

Life beyond Earth

In 1998, the United States, Russia, Japan, Europe, and Canada created the International Space Station, a research laboratory where astronauts study how to launch long-term missions to the moon and Mars, among other things. The driving force behind this project is to preserve life on Earth and build colonies in space.

It's an important mission – and one that could be existential. Today, most experts believe there are not enough resources on our planet for every person to have a standard of living equal to those in the Western world. If we fail to explore planets beyond Earth, we may become extinct. "There's an intrinsic limit to how much energy production we can produce and consume, how much CO_2 we can keep putting into the atmosphere, how much food we can produce as long as we are a one-planet species," says Dunn. "It's not about leaving Earth, but expanding and saving it."[16]

Already, entrepreneurs and governments see the moon, asteroids, and other planets as vast, untapped resources that humans can use to sustain ourselves – from water and gold to cobalt and iron. "The expansion of humanity into space will unlock unlimited potential for economic and population growth from the billions to trillions," says Bernard Kutter, the chief science officer of United Launch Alliance, a US space service provider that is a joint venture between Boeing and Lockheed Martin.[17]

Ramin Khadem, the former chairman of the board of trustees of the International Space University, agrees. "The moon is our eighth continent," he says. "Among its many important elements, it has water ice in its permanently shaded regions that humans will eventually use not only for their habitat and sustaining life beyond planet Earth, but also for creation of propulsion fuel to explore the universe beyond."[18]

Some of the top minds in the field are working to permanently settle humans beyond Earth. Elon Musk's company, SpaceX, wants to turn Mars into a vibrant green home. Jeff Bezos's Blue Origins believes humans can live in free-floating, cylindrical space colonies.

When we will leave the cradle of planet Earth remains to be seen. Some, such as Brian Weeden, the director of program planning for Secure World Foundation (a US-based organization dedicated to the sustainable use of space), notes that there are significant challenges ahead, from building the structures needed to sustain us to understanding how space may impact the human body.[19] But most experts agree that deep space exploration is not a question of if, but when. "What was impossible only a decade ago," says Yonatan Winetraub, cofounder of SpaceIL, the venture that launched the Bereshit robotic lunar lander and lunar probe, "is now a reality. If you dream big, technology will eventually catch up."[20]

Right now, the main obstacle is cost. Space travel is incredibly expensive. NASA spent about $100 billion to build the International Space Station, and it spends $3 to $4 billion a year to maintain it.[21] Meanwhile, a rocket to the moon costs as much as $1.6 billion per launch.[22] All of the private companies on the market are focused on cheaper ways to leave Earth – from larger or reusable rockets to solar propulsion.

Made in Space's cofounders began their journey by asking a different question: What if we didn't need to launch anything at all?[23] Both Kemmer and Dunn envision a future in which 3D printing will manufacture an entire spacecraft at the station, eliminating the constraints of traveling from Earth. "By taking one tiny step, they have fundamentally caused a quantum shift in thinking," says Chris Stott, a space entrepreneur. "This completely changes the equation for the human race."[24]

If we want to live on the moon or Mars, we'll have to learn how to manufacture basic items beyond Earth. Aside from creating tools and vehicles, Made in Space has started working on future space colonies by 3D printing bricks made of a special polymer that simulates regolith – the fine powdery material found on the surface of the moon and Mars.[25] Eventually, the company will begin to experiment with the actual material. By sending 3D printers to the moon, Mars, or anywhere else in the universe, NASA could build roadways, landing pads, and other structures humans need to sustain themselves – all from Rego brick. "Most of the technology is actually here, right now," says Michael Potter, director of the award-winning space documentary film *Orphans of Apollo*.[26]

Space and satellite expert Carol Goldstein agrees. "The combination of technology advances across a number of disciplines, including rockets, robotics, communications, and 3D printing technologies, to name just a few, makes it possible to see building a permanent presence off-planet in the foreseeable future."[27]

Over the next ten years, Kemmer predicts that space will also be home to factories that orbit the earth, much like oil platforms floating in the ocean. And that could mean big business. Morgan Stanley, Goldman Sachs, and Bank of America have estimated that by 2040, space-related products and services will reach $1.1 trillion.[28] "This venture represents the . . . next huge industrial revolution," says Peter Garretson, a former US Air Force officer and now a senior fellow at the American Foreign Policy Council.[29]

Universal Quality of Life

This revolution can also help improve life on Earth. Today, there are more than 50.1 billion devices online worldwide, used by almost half the world's population. Some analysts predict the amount of data we use will grow by 61 percent to 175 zettabytes by 2025.[30] If we stored this amount of data onto Blu-ray Discs, we would have a stack that goes to the moon twenty-three times.[31] This increase in data also means we need new equipment to handle the additional bandwidth.

One of the strongest candidates: ZBLAN optical fiber, which is used to build high-speed internet, transoceanic telecommunications, and medical devices.[32] When these fibers are produced in a zero-gravity environment, they are ten to one hundred times more efficient.[33] Starting in 2018, Kemmer, Dunn, and company began manufacturing ZBLAN in space. Eventually this business could generate billions in revenue. "The new space economy is the catalyst that will fundamentally transform life on Earth," says Stephen Eisele of Virgin Orbit, a Richard Branson–owned company that provides launch services for small satellites. "We are on the brink of opening space for everyone."[34]

And yet companies should proceed cautiously in all their space-related endeavors. Without thoughtful planning, unchecked industry and mining in space could be harmful and tarnish the natural beauty of planets, moons, and the universe. Humanity's record of protecting our planet is abysmal – from pollution to deforestation. But space offers us a second chance to change our relationship with nature.

"Our solar system, the moon and planets are pristine," says Dr. William R. Kramer, a lecturer at the International Space University and retired official at the US Fish and Wildlife Service. "Before we begin to settle, exploit, and dramatically alter these places of stark beauty and incredible scientific value, we would benefit from considering what is worth protecting. Should we repeat the same mistakes we've made on Earth?"[35]

Kemmer, Made in Space's cofounder, agrees. He wants his company and others to help humanity safely explore the universe without repeating the mistakes our species has made on planet Earth. "It's a unique challenge, a unique opportunity," he says – and one that other experts believe will save humanity.[36]

As Christian Sallaberger, the CEO of Canadensys Aerospace Corporation and chairman of the board of the International Space University, told me: "It is the first time ... our species has come together to design things that benefit our entire society and improve the quality of life for all on Earth."[37]

CHAPTER 2

Learning:
The Internet Academy

No schooling was allowed to interfere with my education.

– Grant Allen, *Rosalba: The Story of Her Development*

Salman Khan at 2011 Ted Conference
(Steve Jurvetson, CC BY 2.0)

Tiger Cousin

In August 2004, Salman Khan was living in Boston and working for a hedge fund when he and his wife, Umaima Marvi, hosted a family visit that would change his life – and the lives of millions around the world.[1] That weekend, Khan's twelve-year-old cousin Nadia Rahman visited from New Orleans and shared that she was having trouble with pre-algebra. Her school had placed her in the less advanced class, and Khan didn't think her parents realized the repercussions – that it might set her on a path of underperformance and low expectations. "I want to work with you," Khan told his cousin, "if you are willing."[2]

Khan understood the importance of getting an education; until much later in life, he didn't have the opportunity to attend good schools. Khan was raised in Metairie, Louisiana, a town best known for electing white supremacist David Duke to the state legislature.[3] His parents – both from Bangladesh – divorced in the 1970s, and his father left when Khan was two. They only met once more, a decade later, before his father died of a heart attack.[4] "He never sent child support," recalls Khan, "because he didn't have money despite being a doctor."[5] To feed her family, Khan's mother worked at convenience stores.[6] They were poor, he says, but they always had food on the table.

Khan attended Grace King High School, an unexceptional but diverse public school that influenced his approach to education. Most of the attendees were minorities, half were poor, and "a few classmates were fresh out of jail," he recalls. Others were college bound and took advanced placement classes.[7] Part nerd, part punk-rock rebel, Khan sported wild hair and pierced ears but was known for his keen mathematical mind. He was so sharp that he even got a perfect score on the math portion of the SAT and became his high school's valedictorian.[8]

For college, Khan was accepted to MIT, where he earned degrees in math, electrical engineering, and computer science. (He also became the lead singer of Malignancy, a heavy metal band.)[9] Because his family was poor, he qualified for financial aid but still had to take out $40,000 in loans to cover the rest.[10] He later got his MBA at Harvard, where he claims his main goal was to get married. "I'm dead serious," Khan says. "Silicon Valley in the late '90s was the absolute worst place to find a wife or a girlfriend."[11]

He succeeded – and met Marvi, who was attending Harvard Medical School and later became a physician. When the two hosted Nadia that weekend in 2004, Khan wanted to see her succeed just as he had. When she returned to New Orleans, he started tutoring her by phone, carving out time between his work and her soccer practice. "I became what I like to call a 'tiger cousin,'" Khan says.[12] Two months later, she had made so much progress that Khan called the school and asked them to test Nadia again. After the exam, her teacher moved her into more advanced math classes.[13]

Soon, Khan's extended family learned about Nadia's success – and they wanted help, too. "I found myself working on the phone with about fifteen cousins," he says.[14] Most of their basic math skills were poor – even when it came to simple division. Khan was shocked and wanted to help them improve. But it was hard working with so many different family members at once. To make it easier, he created a website to allow his students to practice problems and track their progress.

About two years later, Khan explained to a friend what he was doing for his family.

"How are you scaling your lessons?" the friend asked.

"I'm not."

"Why don't you make some videos of the tutorials and post them on YouTube," the friend suggested.

"That's a horrible idea," said Khan. "YouTube is for cats playing piano. It's not for serious mathematics."[15]

The more Khan thought about it, however, the more he was

inclined to take his friend's advice. In November 2006, he started recording YouTube videos out of his closet, "a kind of monk's cell," he recalls, "without distractions or the temptations of too much comfort."[16] His only equipment: a desktop, a microphone, Microsoft Paint, some free photo software, and a very basic recording camera.[17] The total cost: $1,100.[18]

Khan quickly discovered that his cousins liked him far more on YouTube than in person. They found his explanations more valuable when they could have him on demand. "The worst time to learn something," he says, "is when someone is standing over your shoulder going, 'Do you get it?'"[19]

Others felt the same way. Not long after he began posting videos, Khan learned that many people who weren't related to him were watching his videos, too. By 2008, thousands of people were watching his videos every month.

He had stumbled into a new career – entirely by accident.[20]

It Was Very Strange

Every year, America spends $1.3 trillion on education – more than any other nation.[21] And yet only about a quarter of fifteen-year-olds in the United States can use math in their daily lives. About a fifth of them don't have basic competency in science, according to the US President's Council of Economic Advisors.[22]

Khan wanted to change these unfortunate statistics, but doing so would require him to quit his job at the hedge fund and devote himself full-time to his online learning platform. He was torn. "I was very happy and satisfied," Khan recalls.[23] He loved his job and his boss and was doing well financially. But in 2009, he quit and created a nonprofit, using his savings to expand his video operations. The experience was terrifying but oddly liberating. "It was very strange for me," he said, "to do something of social value!"[24]

By then, his platform, Khan Academy, was attracting an even larger audience, in part because he allowed students to work at their own pace. Users could only move to the next level after mastering the previous one.[25] Students wrote to Khan, thanking him for his help; because of it, they were able to pass difficult subjects such as algebra and trigonometry. Teachers sent him emails saying he had saved their students from dropping out of school.

Khan's concept was simple but has proven to be effective. Studies show that everyone learns at a different pace. Some grasp a subject faster and are able to rapidly move to the next subject, while others lag behind and struggle. When children are given the appropriate time to master concepts, they will eventually move on. But most classrooms test kids at the same time, at the same pace. "It is not just about zeroes and ones," says former astronaut Nicole Stott, an advocate for STEM (science, technology, engineering, and mathematics). "The Khan Academy opens the world of knowledge to learners of all ages, giving them critical tools and the confidence to learn any subject, anytime they want."[26]

Khan's goal isn't to replace teachers, but to help them and their students inside or outside school. "[Khan Academy] can be a useful tool in the hands of a thoughtful teacher, as long as the ultimate goal is not to deliver information to a passive group of students, but instead to spark their critical thinking and build their problem-solving skills" say Aleta Margolis, founder and president of Center for Inspired Teaching, a nonprofit based in Washington, DC.[27]

He's also hoping to change the way people learn, whether they live in Minnesota or Brazil. Khan doesn't believe students fail math because it's too difficult or because they aren't bright. He likes to provide the following example: Two students in seventh grade learn exponents, then take a math exam. One gets a 70 percent and the other 80 percent. Both children get passing grades, and the teacher moves on to teach the next-level subject, negative exponents. But doing so becomes much harder, because they never learned the previous lesson. The same goes for algebra and calculus. Each lesson builds off the previous one, so if students fall behind, and no one is helping them, they never catch up.

"There are not enough skilled teachers in the world to meet the demand for quality STEM teaching and learning," says Robert Murphy, a former senior Rand Corporation education technology expert. "Especially in emerging economies, rural areas in the developed world, and among refugee populations. Khan Academy provides a free, effective instructional program with timely targeted feedback for learning that can be used to help fill these major gaps, particularly when there are no viable alternatives."[28]

By the end of 2009, Khan had a growing audience and had gotten some press, but he still hadn't secured major funding. His savings were nearly gone, and he had no idea how to continue to expand his audience and make money.[29] He would often meet with venture capitalists who loved the idea but challenged his basic premise that the videos should be free. "This you need to pay for," they would say. "You need to put in ads."[30]

But filling his platform with ads didn't seem right to him. If kids wanted to learn algebra, they should be able to do so without any distractions. Khan felt somewhat delusional for being so stubborn, considering he was still recording videos out of a walk-in closet. But he refused to budge. "It was stressful," Khan recalls.[31]

He was getting five- and ten-dollar contributions, but that wasn't enough to sustain him. He was about to give up. "I'd realized I had less tolerance for digging into my savings than I thought," he recalls. "[There is] nothing like burning $5,000 a month out of savings while having a toddler in the house to put a strain on marriage."[32]

And then something miraculous happened.

It's Raining Math

In early 2010, just as he was thinking about closing down the academy, Khan got a PayPal donation through his website for $10,000. He emailed the donor, Ann Doerr, to thank her, and when she learned he knew her husband, John, a well-known Silicon Valley investor, she invited him for lunch. She was surprised to learn he was struggling. Because he had been on a number of major TV news shows, "[I] assumed he was set financially," Doerr recalls. "Then I found out I was his biggest contributor."[33]

As they ate lunch, Khan shared that he was about ready to quit and get a "real job." Twenty minutes after they said goodbye, Khan pulled into his driveway. He looked down at his phone and saw a text from Doerr saying she was going to send him $100,000 right away. "I almost crashed into the garage door," he wrote.[34]

A few months later, in July 2010, Khan received a text message from Doerr, who was attending the Aspen Institute Ideas Festival. "Bill Gates is talking about your stuff on stage," she said. Khan was surprised to learn that Gates used the academy to teach his children. He immediately downloaded the video and promptly "shit a brick," Khan recalls.[35] There was Gates, the world's wealthiest and arguably most charitable man, telling the audience that he was using Khan Academy, a relatively unknown platform, to teach his children math and science. "Today if you are motivated to learn," he said, "this is an amazing time for everyone…this one guy is doing some unbelievable fifteen-minute tutorials.…I think you just got a glimpse of the education of the future."[36]

Suddenly, the money started pouring in. Gates followed up with an in-person meeting in Seattle and gave Khan several donations totaling $5.5 million. Others were just as generous. Google gave Khan $2 million.[37] The O'Sullivan Foundation gave him $5 million. Reed Hastings, founder of Netflix, donated $3 million. Intuit cofounder Scott Cook and his wife donated $1 million; and Mexican business magnate Carlos Slim (then the richest man in the world) gave him $317 million.[38]

As Khan put it: "It felt epic."[39]

Teachers Were Blown Away

With the money from all those donations, Khan quickly started hiring engineers, programmers, and developers to build out the back end of the website and provide teachers and parents with data on what students were accomplishing.[40] "Teachers were blown away," says Ben Kamens, one of the programmers, "every time. They were completely shocked, as if this had never existed before."[41]

And while Khan continued producing all the math and science videos, he hired a team to create lesson plans for dozens of other subjects – from world history to SAT prep. Today, the academy has delivered well over several billion combined lessons and exercises.[42] The official platform is available in eighteen languages, and outside volunteers have translated part of the content into an additional twenty-six languages.[43] Khan Academy has even partnered with famous institutions such as the Metropolitan Museum of Art, the British Museum, and the American Museum of Natural History, providing them the platform to deliver their own educational content. "Over a billion people around the world now have access to a high-quality free math education," says Supriya Tripathi, a New Delhi–based Hindi content creator for the Khan Academy. "The fact that this content is available in so many languages fundamentally changes the destiny of an untold number of global citizens who want and deserve better lives."[44]

In July 2018, Khan Academy launched Khan Academy Kids, a free mobile app primarily for children ages two to six. With society's youngest students exposed to a significant amount of screen time, researchers from the Early Academic Development Lab at the University of Massachusetts-Amherst found that Khan Academy Kids boosted early literacy skills across the socioeconomic divide. "This app nailed it," says Professor David Arnold, who led the study. "It is engaging, targets the right subject matter, and scaffolded the material so that it wasn't too easy or over the kids' heads."[45]

Yet there are educators who are critical of Khan's approach, who think he's simply feeding children the educational equivalent of Chicken McNuggets.[46] Gary Stager, a veteran teacher who has worked with students on six continents, is one of them. He believes that criticizing students' performance without questioning what they are being asked to perform does little to prepare them for an uncertain world. "Sal Khan may be helping students do marginally better at an unchallenged traditional school curriculum. That's fine, perhaps even laudatory," he says. "[But] since Kahn is profoundly incurious about how learning occurs or about the history of education, he reverts to a toxic 'only I can fix the education system' worldview shaped by those who got lucky on Wall Street or in Silicon Valley."[47]

Karim Ani, founder of Citizen Math, agrees. "Khan Academy bills itself as providing a 'world-class education.' It is a helpful resource, but hardly transformative. It offers exactly the same experience teachers have provided for generations; the only difference is that it's online."[48]

Sylvia Martinez, the coauthor of *Invent to Learn: Making, Tinkering, and Engineering in the Classroom,* feels similarly, adding that any discussion on Khan's platform must start with the question "How do you believe people learn?" "The things they're doing are really just rote," she says. "Students 'fumbling around' is actually where the learning happens, and there's no shortcut for this process."[49]

And yet Khan claims that his program allows teachers and students to do more fumbling around, precisely because it frees up time for creative activities during the school day, including art, games, and collective brainstorming. "It'd piss me off, too," says Khan, "if I had been teaching for 30 years and suddenly this ex-hedge-fund guy is hailed as the world's teacher."[50]

Gates is even more blunt. "It's bullshit," he says of the criticism against Khan. "If you can't do multiplication, then tell me, what is your contribution to society going to be?"[51]

Both Gates and Khan acknowledge that for subjects such as writing and history, there is no easy way to automate learning. So what happens if a student becomes so advanced in math but is still functioning like a normal kid when it comes to writing, history, and social studies? There is no good answer – at least not yet. But Khan hopes to figure it out – and believes that in the future, people will look back at education today and think of it as the Stone Age.

Nothing Seemed to Work

In the fall of 2017, after a battery of tests, I learned that my six-year-old son, Eiden, had a serious learning disability. Professionals recommended I sign him up for an extensive tutoring program, which I did. But part of me struggled to accept the diagnosis (and as it turned out, he simply had attention deficit disorder, a far more benign disability than they originally thought). And so a few weeks after his initial diagnosis, while I was at a conference in San Francisco, I had a conversation with a colleague about Eiden's struggles that changed the way I thought about education.

As we boarded a ferry and stared at the sun setting over Alcatraz Island, he told me his daughter had just finished calculus.

"Oh, yeah?" I responded. "How old is she?"

"She's twelve."

I couldn't believe it. Most kids in America don't learn calculus until they're seventeen. And that's when he explained she had been doing online learning with Khan Academy – and that it was free.

Up to that point, I had never heard of Khan or his platform, but when I got back to Washington, DC, I downloaded the app and tested my son. He really was about two and a half years behind his peers in math.

We decided to try the program to improve his skills. He started working diligently, at first under my supervision, and after a few weeks, completely on his own. Within three months, he had caught up with his friends. After a year, he was a full grade ahead of his class. What really turbocharged Eiden's learning was the ability to watch the videos as many times as he needed to understand the concepts, then take tests that didn't allow him to move on until he got everything right. Not only did his self-confidence improve, he had learned one of the most valuable life lessons: there is nothing he couldn't teach *himself* as long as he applied determination and grit. He quickly became interested in the other subjects Khan Academy offers, including history, economics, and art.

I was so excited about his success, I started having my other kids take the courses. Khan Academy proved especially important as we all went into lockdown during the spring of 2020, as the coronavirus pandemic spread. The virtual learning program my children's school offered was good, but far from perfect. I supplemented it with Khan courses to make sure they continued to learn. Doing so was incredibly hard, but yielded tremendous results. It was clear that this was a wonderful and important supplement to – though not a replacement for – traditional classroom education. But in the long term, Khan's courses had transformed Eiden from a poor student into someone well above average.

Other Khan students may experience similar transformations – and at a critical time. In 2020, as the world battled COVID, many classrooms around the world attempted "Zoom school" with various degrees of success. In the United States, research shows that this switch wiped out academic gains for many students and widened racial and economic gaps.[52] Those using the Khan Academy appeared to do better, especially among minority groups who historically have had fewer opportunities. Survey data shows that African Americans, women, and economically disadvantaged students were among the heaviest users of the Khan Academy's official LSAT program, and there is at least anecdotal evidence of their success as a result.[53] "This achievement demonstrates Khan Academy's "groundbreaking commitment to helping [minority] students prepare for the LSAT," says Kent Lollis, vice president and chief diversity officer of the

Law School Admissions Council, a Pennsylvania-based nonprofit that promotes quality, access, and equity in law and education.[54]

Nadia, Khan's niece, also succeeded as a result of his classes. More than a decade after their tutoring began, she has grown up to be an impressive young woman. In 2014, she graduated from Sarah Lawrence College and later received two master's degrees from the Icahn School of Medicine at Mount Sinai and the New School. Today she is a research coordinator at the New York University Langone Medical Center.[55]

As Khan wryly puts it: "So far, so good."[56]

CHAPTER 3

Shelter: Let There Be Light

Namaste: The inner light in me
recognizes the inner light in you.

– Sanskrit greeting

Sivan Yaari bringing solar energy panels to African village
in Karamoja, Uganda (Lior Sperandeo, CC BY-SA 3.0)

Heart of Darkness

As Sivan Yaari's white SUV rumbled over the dirt road into the tiny village of Karamoja, Uganda, the horror started to spread through her limbs. It was March 2017, and for weeks, Yaari had read the reports of death and starvation, as a quarter of Uganda's forty million people faced the specter of acute famine. As the head of Innovation: Africa, an aid organization that brings water and electricity to remote areas of the continent, she was no stranger to suffering. But this sight was unlike anything Yaari had encountered before.

When she and her team arrived, they were confronted by emaciated children caked in mud. Rail-thin women who had bound their stomachs with rope to fight off hunger pains were wailing. People of all ages were on their hands and knees drinking cow's blood out of a soiled bowl for sustenance. No rain had fallen in three months, and the region was in the grips of catastrophic drought. Many of the villagers hadn't eaten in days.

Yaari and her staff gave the people whatever food and water they had. Then they got down to work.

Within days, they returned with truckloads of food and equipment. To the cheers of hundreds of villagers who came to help, they unloaded bags of beans and corn and enough solar panels to provide desperately needed energy to pump enough water for six surrounding villages. Heavy drilling machines also rolled in on big blue rigs with pipes long enough to reach an aquifer 130 feet down. And when the fresh water began to pump through the newly installed taps, throngs of men, women, and children erupted in joy.

"God bless you," they shouted as they lined up to hug Yaari and her team. Drinking water from a tap was unlike anything they had experienced before – it was the first time the village had access to free-flowing water. The singing and dancing lasted for days.

"It really warms your heart," says Yaari, "to see how such a simple solution can change the lives and futures of so many people."[1]

Few of us will ever be in a position to make such a direct and singular impact on the lives of so many. Sivan Yaari has done it thousands of times.

Where Is Madagascar?

As unlikely as it sounds, it was in the service of fashion, not people, that Yaari's relationship with Africa first began more than twenty years ago. Yaari was just nineteen and fresh off a tour with the Israel Defense Forces in 1998 when she got the job she now credits with changing her life. Though born on the outskirts of Tel Aviv, Yaari had spent her teenage years in France, and her fluency in the language made her a perfect candidate for a position in quality control at a Jordache jeans factory in Madagascar. When she interviewed in Tel Aviv with the company's cofounder, Rafi Nakash, she had to ask him where the country was. He had barely said "Africa" before she offered an enthusiastic yes.

Yaari grew up in a family of modest means, but it wasn't until she got to Africa, she says, that she discovered what it really means to be poor. When she arrived in Madagascar, she was deeply unsettled by the number of people – and children in particular – who were without shoes and clothing, looked sick and malnourished, and who didn't have access to clean water, basic medical facilities, or schooling. She visited a medical clinic in the countryside where she saw scores of people waiting outside for help and getting none. When she asked if there was anything she could do, the nurse said thank you, but no. There was nothing to be done. "I don't have vaccines or medication," the nurse told her. "They all went bad, because we don't have electricity or refrigeration."[2]

Yaari quickly came to understand that the lack of electricity created even deeper problems. Her colleague took her to a nearby secondary school, but by the time she got there, it was after dark. The classrooms were full, and the students were using gas lamps. The children from the best-off families sat in the front rows near the light, because they were the ones paying for the kerosene. Those less fortunate sat in the back in near darkness.

The dearth of light was also a major issue for nurses in the village, who were doing things like delivering babies with one hand while holding kerosene lamps in the other. It came as no surprise to anyone, Yaari says, that so many mothers and babies didn't survive.[3]

When Yaari began traveling to Jordache's six other factories around Africa, she found the same despair wherever she went. "It took me time to understand why this was happening," she says,[4] but one thing seemed clear. "If we could just bring energy, it would be so much better."[5]

Yaari was still in her early twenties, and after working in Africa for a few more years, she moved to New York to get a degree from Pace University and a master's in international energy management from Columbia's School of International and Public Affairs. But Africa was never far from her mind.

As a grad-student volunteer for the United Nations' Energy Bureau, she traveled to Senegal to inspect how machines were being used in villages to grind wheat and corn – and concluded it did not work very well at all. Because villagers had no money for electricity or the diesel fuel it takes to run machines, she says, "I understood I needed to find a completely different solution."[6]

Yaari consulted with her professor, Philip LaRocco, who specializes in renewable energy.[7] "It is quite simple," he told her. "All you need is two solar panels."[8]

Just Add Water

Approximately half the citizens of Africa are without electricity, but what the continent lacks in power, it makes up for in sunshine. A single pair of solar panels can generate enough energy to power an entire medical center, twelve light bulbs, and even a refrigerator. They're also low maintenance, easily installed, and can last for thirty years. Nearly every roof in Israel has a solar panel. Yaari wondered if the same could be done in Africa.

By 2008, Yaari had set up her first project in the village of Kidigozero, Tanzania. For $4,270, she was able to install two solar panels and a refrigerator in the local clinic. On the very first day the lights came on, residents were being vaccinated. For many, it was also the first time they had seen light at night. Within a few weeks, a doctor agreed to move to the village.[9]

"It is so simple," says Yaari. "And yet it makes such a big difference. I felt like we had to do more of it, village by village. Until we cover the entire continent."[10]

Back in New York, she officially registered Innovation: Africa (originally called Jewish Heart for Africa) as a nonprofit to bring Israeli solar and water technology to the continent, and immediately started raising funds.

"It was as if she was struck by lightning," recalls LaRocco.[11]

By 2009, Yaari had installed her second set of solar panels at a primary school in Putti, Uganda, which had just ten classrooms for eleven hundred students. The lights enabled the children to complete their homework at night and study for national exams. But there was a problem: the school couldn't afford to pay for new light bulbs when they burned out. The only sustainable solution was to find a way for the villagers to raise the money themselves.

Though many in Putti didn't have shoes or clothes, almost everyone had mobile phones. "There is one guy who collects all of the cell phones and walks eight miles to another village where there is also no electricity, but there is a car," says Yaari. "People were paying ten cents to use the car's battery to charge their cell phones."[12]

To help schools, medical centers, and orphanages raise money, she decided to let people use the solar system to charge their phones for ten cents a shot. Pretty soon, Yaari recalls, "They had more money than they needed."[13]

All of Innovation: Africa's installations are now maintained through this pay-per-use model, which generates the funding required for villages to replace light bulbs and batteries – and is infinitely replicable and scalable.

But the biggest lesson Yaari learned from her early work in Putti was much more elemental. When she returned a few months after the installation to check on the school project, the headmaster told her they weren't using it. "The students are too weak to walk to school," he explained. "There is no water." Putti was experiencing severe famine.[14]

Yaari learned that the average African woman spends over three hours a day collecting and carrying water. This is 1,095 hours per year, or the equivalent of 136 full American workdays. And the water they do manage to bring home is often unsanitary, causing more than 80 percent of the developing world's deaths and diseases. Women and children in Putti were fetching water instead of working or going to school, standing on long lines for the privilege of digging into holes with their hands to fill jerricans with filthy, disease-ridden water.

Without electricity, access to basic education and health care becomes nearly impossible, but far more fundamentally, it also means you can't pump water from the ground. Electric light and refrigeration alone was never going to make a dent.

"I realized we were fixing the wrong problem," she says. "People were weak and unhealthy because the water was making them sick."[15]

Yaari had always assumed that Africa didn't have much water, but she soon found out it has plenty, in deep underground aquifers. It's directly beneath the feet of those who need it most, anywhere from sixty-five to 650 feet down, all across the continent.

"What people need is energy to pump it up," she says.[16]

In 2009, Yaari returned to Putti to carry out what would become the first of hundreds of Innovation: Africa aquifer projects, all of which follow the same basic playbook. Yaari hires a geologist to survey where and how deep to drill, then brings in a drilling company and local contractors to do the rest, which includes installing a pump and water tank and working with the community to decide where to locate the taps.

After the Putti project was complete, the villagers were able to pump twenty thousand liters of clean, safe water per day to use for cooking, drinking, and livestock. And in the aquifer projects that followed, Yaari decided to install an extra tank that would provide water to drip irrigation pipes, a technique developed in Israel in the mid-1960s that's far more effective than traditional flood irrigation and sprinkler systems, regardless of the plants or location. Drip irrigation uses just a third of the water and doubles the crop yield.

With electricity, clean water, and drip irrigation in place, the villages touched by Innovation: Africa began to thrive. Children were able to bathe and receive an education; adults were able to use the water to start businesses, earning income that paves the way toward healthier, happier, and financially independent lives. Many started by selling the extra fruits and vegetables they produced; others made bricks or launched bakeries.

"What amazed me was the entrepreneurial spirit in the village," recalls Yaari of what she discovered in Putti. "We saw water as the color blue. They saw it as green."[17]

Cloud Backup

To date, Innovation: Africa has completed over three hundred solar and water projects, transforming the lives of more than two million people in ten African countries, including Cameroon, Ethiopia, Malawi, Tanzania, Senegal, South Africa, the Democratic Republic of the Congo, and Uganda. And with each project, the organization has proven that it takes the "innovation" part seriously.

IA's chief engineer, Meir Yaacoby, created a custom-designed monitoring system that collects data from each solar array they install, which is uploaded to a server that can be accessed anywhere in the world. The technology allows Yaari's Israel-based team (and her donors) to stay up to date on the water output and energy consumption at every site. It also uses artificial intelligence and advanced algorithms to predict problems before they start. When there's an issue at any location, Yaari's team in Tel Aviv and local project managers receive an alert on their phones.

"It's off-grid, remote monitoring, so, at any point, we are able to know how much water we're pumping into every village," says Yaari. "If something breaks, meaning a pump hasn't pumped water in 24 hours, we are notified by the system."[18] The platform won the United Nations Innovation Award in 2013.

"IA's impact far surpasses much larger, less focused NGOs," says Gil Haskel, head of Israel's Agency for International Development Cooperation. "The secret to their success is the focus on specific technologies that transform lives."[19]

IA has also launched a new technology they call the Energy Box, a single container that includes everything needed to bring a school or medical center on line, including LED bulbs, batteries, and a human-machine interface (HMI), which serves as a dashboard that connects a person to the device, along with the remote management system.

IA has done all of this with a modest annual budget, all of which is raised through private donations. "One hundred percent of it goes to Africa – and to the Israeli companies whose technology and equipment are purchased," says Yaari. "Not a penny of it is spent on the running of the NGO. All our salaries and overhead are paid through foundations."[20]

"Yaaris model blows me away," says billionaire businessman and philanthropist Natie Kirsh, who has invested both his time and money in helping the organization scale. "It will get it done."[21]

IA's projects not only save lives, they also create jobs for locals who are trained by Israeli engineers to do the work in their own communities. And above all, the efforts teach local community leaders, project managers, and engineers how to be self-reliant and maintain the technologies on their own.

"Africa has among the highest levels of global inequality around the world," says Stephen Koseff, the former CEO of Investec, Africa's largest investment bank and a member of IA's board. "IA is making a meaningful dent at reducing this disparity and bettering the lives of millions."[22] David Arison, fellow board member and VP of global business relations at Miya, agrees. "In my experience, I have not encountered any other person alive who has made more of an impact on the quality of life in African villages."[23]

Yet Yaari still feels she has not done enough. "It is only a drop in the ocean," she says.[24] There are currently over 600 million people in Africa without energy, and 350 million people searching for water every single day. And the problem is only going to get bigger.

It took 200,000 years for the earth's human population to hit one billion at the turn of the nineteenth century – and just two hundred more for us to multiply to the 7.9 billion we number as of this writing. In just thirty years, that total will increase by two billion more, and half of them will be born in Africa – competing for the same food and water.[25] Yaari plans to reach at least a thousand villages by 2025. We're just going to need a lot more Yaaris.

"The solution is simple because the technology exists, and the impact is priceless," she says. "It just has to be done. The simplicity of the solution is what keeps me going."[26]

CHAPTER 4

Environment: Water World

God created the world, but the Dutch
created the Netherlands.

– Dutch saying

Henk Ovink (left) with Peruvian politician and engineer Reynaldo
Hilbck Guzmán (right) in a helicopter flying over the Piura River
after the flooding (Embassy of the Netherlands, Lima, Peru)

New Amsterdam's Looming Water Crisis

Six weeks after Hurricane Sandy ravaged the New York region in 2012, Shaun Donovan visited the Netherlands to learn how the tiny country so successfully keeps the ocean at arm's length. Then secretary of housing and urban development, Donovan had been tapped by President Obama to lead a task force to rebuild in Sandy's wake, but also to explore radical new ways to address America's insufficient infrastructure in the context of climate change. His guide was Henk Ovink, the Netherlands' director general of spatial planning and water management, who drove Donovan around in a small minivan, opening his eyes to a Dutch water-management system that's the envy of the world. For the first time, Donavan understood what was possible when a society's engineering and culture actually merge for the greater good.

When Donavan's plane landed back in Washington, he saw an email from Ovink that was short and to the point: "I hope this isn't too forward, but could I come work with you?" Donovan replied before the plane reached the terminal. "You're just forward enough," he wrote. "When can you start?"[1]

By the end of this century, scientists predict that the ocean will rise by as much as four feet across the globe. In New York City, according to many climatologists, that could mean storm surges of twenty-four feet. Miami Beach will almost certainly be entirely under water. But far sooner than that – within the next five years – almost two-thirds of the world's population will already be living in coastal areas vulnerable to increased ecological problems, including harsher storms, flooded deltas in winter, parched deltas in summer, and salt water infiltration of underground aquifers.[2] Large parts of Vietnam will be underwater at high tide, with over twenty million people affected. Bangkok will face massive water threats, as will most of Shanghai, one of Asia's most important cities. India's financial capital of Mumbai is at imminent risk of being completely wiped out by water, along with Alexandria in Egypt and Basra in Iraq.[3] The list goes on.

"Time is running out," says Stefan Rahmstorf, professor of physics of the oceans at Potsdam University. "It is time to end fifty years of dithering and finally act decisively to avert a looming planetary catastrophe. Otherwise, rising sea levels will flood large coastal cities and destroy entire island states."[4]

Henk Ovink agrees. "We will feel the impact of climate change all over the world," warns the planet's leading flood expert, "most profoundly through water."[5]

In August 2013, Shaun Donovan and the Hurricane Sandy Rebuilding Task Force issued its report, which leaned heavily on the Dutch "resiliency" model and Ovink's policy recommendations. These included building dunes and undersea barriers, overhauling wastewater treatment plans and the weakest links in the electrical grid, constructing storm-surge bulwarks, and building purpose-designed affordable housing.

"Water, floods, and climate change have not been a policy issue in the US," observed Ovink. "Your vulnerability to massive rains, stronger hurricanes, and longer droughts make water *the* policy issue of today."[6]

Malcolm Bowman, head of the Storm Surge Research Group at the State University of New York at Stony Brook, frames the matter even more urgently. "My middle name is Noah," he says. "The Flood's coming, you'd better build an ark, get everybody aboard."[7]

Swamp People

The Dutch have been battling the sea for centuries. Two thousand years ago, the area's first inhabitants were drawn to its peat swamps. The moist forests have waterlogged soil that prevents dead leaves and wood from fully decomposing, resulting in abundantly rich clay. Roughly the size of Connecticut and Massachusetts, the Netherlands literally means "lower countries," with half of its flat topography at less than three feet above sea level – and 27 percent fully below it. More than 60 percent of the tiny country's population of seventeen million lives in this area. Dutch water authorities are mandated to ensure that the risk of death as a result of flooding never rises above one in 100,000. (By comparison, your chance of dying on an airplane is one in eleven million.) If a mega-storm ever breaks through, it could flood thousands of square miles and paralyze one of the most important economies in the world.

"There is nothing inherently distinct about the Netherlands," says Jos Dijkman, a retired member of the Deltares Water Institute. "What is special is that due to the setting of the country – one-third below sea level – there is a high societal priority for flood protection, and unlike most of the world, we abide by the very real law of 'thou shalt take into account sea-level rise.'"[8]

For the last decade, the Dutch government has worked with the Intergovernmental Panel on Climate Change, which won the Nobel Prize in 2007, to figure out what it will take to climate-proof their country for the next two hundred years.

The group predicts that the North Sea will rise by almost a foot and a half by 2050, between two and four and a half feet by 2100, and up to thirteen feet by 2200. The government takes no part in the debate on whether climate change is real or not. It simply accepts that water is rising, that extreme weather conditions cause massive flooding, and the possible effects of both. "It is an adaptive strategy because we are not certain what will happen in the next decades," says Jan Hendrik Dronkers, director general at the Dutch Ministry of Infrastructure and the Environment. "The secret of our new program is that if the sea level changes, we expect we will be able to deal with that."[9]

In 2007, the Dutch parliament put together the Delta Committee to implement that goal. Their plan calls for aggressive measures, including extending the coastline, building massive surge barriers, and fortifying levees. The commission estimates it will cost $1.5

billion annually for the next hundred years to defend the country and its people against high water.[10]

And perhaps more than any other country on the planet, Holland is fully prepared to make the investment. For the better part of the last century, it has been building and refining complex systems to protect its population from the regular havoc caused by the ocean and flooding, which once destroyed so many of its homes and crops. When it comes to stemming the tides of nature, the country already leads the world. And for the most part, it owes its position to the vision of one man: Cornelis Lely.

The Mother of All Dikes

Schoolchildren around the world are taught about the fictional Little Dutch Boy who saved his country by putting his finger in a leaky dike. The boy in the Mary Mapes Dodge novel *Hans Brinker, or the Silver Skates* stays up all night in the cold so the adults can make the necessary repairs in the morning. The Dutch built dikes for centuries, until it became clear to just about everyone that they couldn't go on simply plugging leaks. As Holland became an international powerhouse for goods, commodities, and shipping, they knew they needed bigger ideas and more effective, long-term solutions to keep the water at bay.

In 1913, Holland's minister of transport and water management, civil engineer Cornelis Lely, put before the Dutch cabinet a revolutionary plan to permanently close off the Zuiderzee Bay and protect it from floods with a massive hybrid structure known as a dike dam. The cost of building it would be roughly equal to the country's entire annual budget. But to help the project partially pay for itself, Lely's design called for the land inside the area of the dam, known as a polder, to be pumped dry to mine its clay and then be used for extensive agriculture.

For years, lawmakers weren't interested. But two major events eventually changed their minds. World War I made food scarce for millions of Dutch and Europeans, and vast amounts of farmland were needed to grow more. (Building the dike dam would eventually turn Holland into the second-largest exporter of food in the world.) But more importantly, a huge flood hit the Netherlands in 1916, breaking many of its dikes and destroying massive numbers of homes. Several Dutch counties went bankrupt trying to repair the damage, and government officials were reminded once again how vulnerable the country was to flooding.

Two years later, the Dutch parliament passed the Zuiderzee Act, which sought to protect Holland from the potentially calamitous effects of the North Sea, increase food supply through the development of new agricultural land, and convert the Zuiderzee into a freshwater lake to help manage water. Effectively closing off the entire bay, the Zuiderzee Works became one of the largest land reclamation and water drainage projects in history, with its main dam and enclosure dike, the Afsluitdijk, being the largest ever built until 2006. The American Society of Civil Engineers proclaimed the project to be among the seven wonders of the modern world.[11] "It is an extraordinary feat of Dutch engineering," says Bas Jonkman, professor of hydraulic engineering at Delft University of Technology. "Along with other impressive structures on Earth, like the Pyramids of Giza, [it] can be seen from space."[12]

Constructed from 1927 to 1932, the Afsluitdijk is so huge and ambitious in scope, it's almost impossible to imagine how humans were able to build it. Starting in four locations, tens of thousands of workers began by creating two giant islands in the middle of the sea, dropping twenty-three million cubic meters of sand and thirteen million cubic meters of glacial sediment via ship every day. Heavy stones were then dropped on the inland side and boulder clay placed on the ocean side. Brushwood mattresses, in turn secured by boulders and old concrete, kept the material in place. Both a dike and a dam, with water on both sides, the Afsluitdijk was raised twenty-five feet above sea level with sand and clay, over which grass was planted. A road three hundred feet wide and twenty miles long was then built on top, connecting Northwest and Northeast Holland. The dam also turned the southern sea into a lake, named the Ijsselmeer for the river that feeds into it. Sluices were built to let the water flow out from the lake into the ocean, converting the seawater into freshwater.

The next step in Lely's plan was to create polders, a word that comes from the Old Dutch for "dry land," which has been adopted by thirty-six languages around the world. Poldering is an engineering marvel whereby water is drained from a large body of water, uncovering fertile land below it. The first polders were created in Holland in the eleventh century – and by 1961, with more than four thousand polders, roughly half of the country's total land area was made up of ground reclaimed from the sea. They even have a saying for it: "God created the world, but the Dutch created the Netherlands."

According to Cornelis Lely's instructions, after portions of the Ijsselmeer were dammed off, engineers built ten miles of dikes around what was once the southern sea and pumped the water out using windmills. The best land was used to grow various grains such as rye, wheat, barley, and oats, while the less fertile land was forested.

The Afsluitdijk was finally put to the test in 1953, when one of the most severe storms in history hit the country. In the south, where the dikes were less sophisticated, 340,000 acres were flooded, forty-seven thousand buildings were damaged or destroyed, thirty thousand livestock were lost, and almost two thousand people were killed. In the area protected by the Afsluitdijk in the north, there was no damage. On a single night, the massive investment had paid off in lives and money saved. The area was no longer vulnerable to flooding. Lely died in 1929 having never witnessed the success of his master plan.

"Water is a double-edged sword," says architectural historian Marinke Steenhuis, a member of the Afsluitdijk quality team. "On the one hand, it is the black swan that can wreak havoc, displace people, and decimate cities. On the other, it is the basis of life and prosperity to every living creature on Earth."[13]

For the next thirty years, the Dutch continued to invest huge amounts of time, effort, and money into bolstering their defenses. More storm-warning systems, more dams, dikes, locks, sluices, and levees, and more storm surge barriers. In the Rotterdam port, the Oosterschelde and Maeslant barriers each have giant arms that cost $500 million to build and are nearly the size of the Eiffel Tower; these can close the mouth of the city's waterway in the event of a major storm. But building bigger, better, and higher, the Dutch eventually came to understand, could only get them so far.

Let the River Run

In the mid-1990s, Holland's Rhine, Meuse, and Scheldt Rivers swelled to unprecedented levels, forcing the evacuation of 250,000 people and a million farm animals – along with a dramatic change in the country's approach. "We were shocked," says Dutch water official Martin Hoenderkamp. "We thought we were prepared for everything. We thought evacuation was for other countries."[14]

By 2006, the Netherlands approved a multi-billion-dollar plan called Room for the River, which aimed to restore the natural floodplains of Holland's rivers and protect areas most likely to flood. "The Dutch had strayed too far away from the environment and over-engineered nature," says David Waggonner, a leading architect and founder of the Dutch Dialogues, a collaborative effort bringing together US and Dutch water experts. "They knew they needed a more sustainable solution based on landscape."[15] The government course-corrected, ultimately concluding that they could preempt future catastrophe by working with the rivers rather than trying to control them. "With the sea barriers, we sealed off our front door," one official said. "Alas, we've been caught off guard through the back entrance."[16]

With more frequent and intense rainfall and less area to actually work with, the country's rivers were discharging too much water, putting millions of lives at risk. Dutch officials put together a revolutionary proposal to expand the space for rivers at high water capacity. "It's no longer a war on water," says Tracy Metz, Holland-based journalist and author of *Sweet and Salt: Water and the Dutch*. "Holland's engineers and policymakers undertook the unprecedented, mind-bending exercise of lowering the dykes instead of raising them."[17]

In the end, the program implemented thirty-four measures that also included deepening floodplains, widening rivers, and moving two hundred families to drier areas. Work began in 2007 in thirty-nine separate locations and lasted for twelve years. Plans called for the demolition of farms and moving citizens out of harm's way. "The farmers were angry at first. We talked to them literally around their kitchen tables," says Hans Brouer, a senior rivers expert who worked on the project. "Half of them said they wanted to retire or try their luck in Australia. The other half wanted to build new farms for the future."[18] Ultimately, the government bought the land for market value.

As Henk Ovink explained to me, it's projects like Room for the River and the new Delta Committee that best encapsulate the success of the Dutch approach. The idea is that water mitigation is about much more than just engineering. It involves good governance, innovation, openness to new ideas and ways of thinking, and realizing that when the common good is in danger, individuals must rise to the occasion and put their interests aside.

Dealing with water intelligently isn't a luxury, but a matter of survival. And as the threat of climate-driven water catastrophe looms, the world will need to follow Holland's lead. Or hope for an email from Henk Ovink offering to help.

In March 2019, New York mayor Bill de Blasio announced a ten-billion-dollar climate-focused infrastructure project that implements many of Ovink's recommendations from the Hurricane Sandy Rebuilding Task Force. They include elevating parks, constructing a five-mile seawall around Staten Island and sand dunes around the Rockaways, and installing removable flood barriers around Lower Manhattan that could be used in the face of massive storms.

"It's a choice in the end, and our best opportunity," says Ovink, who is now a special envoy for the Kingdom of the Netherlands. "Nothing is too big to confront. We can close our eyes and do nothing and let the worst happen, see more assets and people lost, or think about that future as an opportunity. I choose the latter."[19]

CHAPTER 5

Hygiene: There Will Be Blood

Don't wait for a girl to become a woman to empower them. Empower a girl's life by giving them sanitary pads. With pads, we give them wings.

– Arunachalam Muruganantham,
aka the Pad Man, personal correspondence

Arunachalam Muruganantham (http://
bharathbalasubramanian.com/, CC BY-SA 4.0)

Rag Time

Arunachalam Muruganantham was on the couch when he noticed his wife hiding something behind her back. On confronting her, he discovered it was a bloody rag. The twenty-nine-year-old Muruga-nantham had seen these rags in the family outhouse when he was growing up in a small village in southern India, but he had never known what they were for. His new wife Shanthi revealed that the rags were for menstrual blood, and that many women used rags, leaves, sand, sawdust, mud, or even ash to absorb the discharge.

Muruganantham asked his wife why she didn't just use pads that could be thrown out after each use. Shanthi explained that while she understood all the benefits of sanitary pads, using them would mean "we will have to cut down the family's milk budget."[1]

Muruganantham decided to go to the local pharmacy, where the cashier seemed horrified by the purchase. "He gave it to me as if it were contraband,"[2] recalls Muruganantham with a laugh. "I don't know why – I didn't ask for a condom."[3] It was 1998, and the 20 rupees (about 50 cents) the napkins cost him could have fed the family for several days.

When he inspected one of the pads at home, Muruganantham was shocked to discover that it was filled with nothing more than compressed cotton. Why were raw materials of such minimal value being sold for such an exorbitant amount of money? The son of a handloom weaver had a thought. He could make inexpensive pads of his own.[4]

Addicted to Sanitary Pads

Muruganantham knew his way around fabrics. The next day, he went looking for the softest cotton he could find at one of the textile mills in his village. But when he sewed it together for his wife to try out during her next menstrual cycle, she wasn't impressed. She told him his pad was no good and that she would stick to the rags, thank you very much.[5]

Muruganantham was undeterred. For the first time, he understood that women who couldn't afford sanitary pads were far more susceptible to disease and infection, and he was determined to change the situation. He started developing various pads based on different materials and gave them to his wife and sisters to test, but the cultural taboos against discussing anything connected to the subject were so strong that they'd never offer much feedback. Muruganantham briefly attempted to take on the testing himself, at one point tying a soccer-ball "uterus" filled with goat's blood to his hip, with a tube that ran down to his underwear. During the course of his day, walking or bicycling around town, he'd periodically press the ball to simulate squirting blood and discovered very quickly that his pads didn't work very well.[6] Muruganantham's undergarments were constantly wet, and the experience gave him a newfound respect for the strength of women. "Doing this for a week will make you sick and give you fever," he says. "Having wet genitals is really terrible."[7]

Muruganantham eventually got permission to expand his pool of test subjects with some female students at a local medical college. But because of deeply baked cultural norms, these women proved equally embarrassed when it came time to share their opinions. And then the rumors began to spread. "Under any circumstance, approaching female students for their used sanitary pads would be extraordinary," says Indian entrepreneur Vishal Gondal. "But in conservative rural India, this is simply unprecedented."[8]

While his wife Shanthi knew about her husband's ambitions to create a more cost-effective pad, Muruganantham never told her about his new test subjects. When she confronted him about it, he lied and told her he had gone to the local college to repair their main gate, suspecting she wouldn't understand. Shanthi decided to go back to her parents for a few days, then after a few weeks decided not to come home. "My wife thought I was a psychopath and decided to leave me after she saw me looking at sanitary pads," says Muruganantham. "Nobody understood me. People started to avoid me entirely."[9]

Soon after, a divorce noticed arrived. "My wife tried everything she could to make me stop doing research and bring me back to my senses," recalls Muruganantham. "But I was obsessed."[10]

Like Magic

Muruganantham was determined to figure out the exact material used in standard pads, which he surmised was some kind of unusual cotton, and he spent two and a half years calling American and European companies, hoping to get answers.[11] Calling from a local kiosk, often after midnight India time, he spent a small fortune on phone charges. He'd tell anyone who'd listen that he owned a textile mill and was considering entering the sanitary products business, and eventually he found a helpful female representative whom he convinced to send him a sample of the exact fabric they were using.[12]

When he opened the package a few weeks later, he was totally flabbergasted. He expected to find cotton, but instead he found something more like cardboard. Muruganantham had no idea what to do next. Eventually his dog scratched the material – and almost by happenstance, Murugantham discovered the fiber inside. Muruganantham determined that the cardboard was compacted cellulose manufactured from pine bark.[13]

It was immediately clear that one of his biggest challenges would be keeping costs in check – multinational companies mass produce sanitary pads with machines that cost millions of dollars. Muruganantham set about designing a low-cost machine that would allow people to make sanitary pads from the comfort of their homes or in small industrial centers.

When his wife left him, Muruganantham was forced out of his ancestral village after his neighbors decided that his quest to create a pad was keeping the protective goddess away from their community. He rented a room in downtown Coimbatore, sharing an apartment with five other tenants, and turned his living quarters into a laboratory workshop. His neighbors came to believe his spirit had been taken over by demons and that he had turned into a pervert. "We thought he had become a vampire who drank women's blood," recalls S. R. Ramesh, a fellow Coimbatorian and handloom weaver. "Many of the villagers wanted to chain him to a tamarind tree and hang him upside down."[14] Others thought he was doing "abnormal things," says Sashi Anand, vice president of the Coimbatore Women's Welfare Organization. "No one knew he was doing serious research. People thought he was doing black magic."[15]

When he wasn't working on his innovation, Muruganantham took roofing jobs to get by. But he was determined, and often staying up all night, Murugantham eventually created a pair of devices capable of producing sanitary pads at a much lower cost. The first, originally made of wood and iron, looks like a large meat grinder and is able to break up compacted cellulose. "It was beyond amazing to see the board transform itself into fluff," recalls Muruganantham, "I was so happy. I felt like a magician."[16] The second machine, which resembles a drill press, compacts the pulp into pads.

The whole process takes approximately two minutes and can be mastered in less than an hour of training. First the cellulose is ground into fluff, which is then placed into a metal compartment and pressed by plates into a hard, half-inch layer. The material is wrapped into a soft, gauzy cloth and sealed with a heating machine. At around $1,000, Muruganantham's machines are vastly less expensive than those used by multinational companies, which can run in excess of $1 million.[17]

With his new pad in hand, Muruganantham went back to the medical college in late 2004 to test his samples. "When I use your pad," said one of the volunteers, "I don't even think about my period."[18] After eight and a half years, Muruganantham knew he had finally done it.

His pad soon earned recognition and press coverage. In 2006, Muruganantham visited India's Institute of Technology in Madras to show them his invention, and they were so excited that they registered his pad for the National Innovation Foundation's Grassroots Technological Innovations Award.[19] Against 943 entries, he won first place for the Best Innovation for the Betterment of Society, an award granted personally by the president of India, Pratibha Patil. Suddenly Muruganantham was in the national spotlight.

Following a television interview, his ex-wife Shanthi phoned to express her congratulations.

"Do you remember my voice?" Muruganantham asked. "Why couldn't you understand what I was doing?"[20]

"I left you so you could follow your dreams,"[21] Shanthi replied.

He asked her to come back. Shanthi agreed, and they are still together to this day.

100 Percent Napkin-Using Countries

There are approximately 350 million women of menstruating age in India,[22] and when Muruganantham created his machine, just 12 percent of them were using sanitary pads. Today, that figure has climbed to about 57 percent, in large part because of Muruganantham's pad.[23]

Still, more than 20 percent of Indian girls drop out of school when they hit puberty because their menstruation cycles force them to miss so many days each month.[24] India's Ministry of Health estimates that because of unclean menstruation-management practices, 70 percent of women are at risk of severe infection. And in urban India, somewhere between 43 and 88 percent of women still use reusable cloth for their period.[25]

When Muruganantham finally figured out how to make his low-cost sanitary pad, he didn't set out to make money. "This has to be

introduced to the world," he told Babu Yogeswaran, a close friend
and filmmaker. "I must create a self-sustaining social revolution
for those who need it most."[26] Muruganantham wanted to give the
world's poorest communities the ability to make and distribute pads
for themselves.

For about eighteen months starting in 2006, he built about five
thousand machines and made thousands of trips to small villages
across India,[27] in many of the poorest and least developed states,
such as Bihar, Madhya Pradesh, Rajasthan, and Uttar Pradesh, sometimes called by the acronym BIMARU, which means "sick states." In
places where women often walk for miles just to get water and where
menstruation can cause further financial hardship, he sought out
women who might be interested in making their own pads. In many
of these villages, men resisted because of their traditional patriarchal
traditions. But after months of Muruganantham's repeated visits and
pleading, fathers and husbands eventually relented and allowed the
women in their families to use his machine.

Over the next few years, female-run cooperatives and nonprofits
around the country began adopting Muruganantham's model en
masse. Women understood that using rags wasn't good for them,
and once they had a low-cost way of getting pads, they were all too
willing to use them. Many of these groups buy Muruganantham's
machine, train over the course of one day, and immediately start
producing about a thousand napkins daily.[28] And if they need
financing, they often secure bank loans that can be paid off with the
money earned from their sales.[29]

Murugantham owns the patent rights to his machine, but he gives
away the right to produce pads with them free, so those who use
the machines can profit off them – and enfranchise their ultimate
customers. While Muruganantham's workshop also produces pads,
the women around the country who purchase his machine to start
pad-making centers produce their own versions of the pad, packaged

under various labels. There are now more than twenty-one hundred local brands making his pads.[30]

Traditional pads costs around eight rupees – those made on Murugantham's machines sell for as little as three. Each machine provides jobs for ten to fifteen women, who are able to produce pads for thousands.[31] There are currently machines in over fifteen hundred Indian villages in all twenty-nine Indian states,[32] and the model has spread to at least thirty other countries around the world, including Bangladesh, Kenya, Mauritius, Nigeria, Nepal, Rwanda, the Philippines, and Zimbabwe, to name just a few.[33] His success will mean the transformation of an untold number of lives, and by extension of society at large.

Muruganantham has plans to expand the production of his machines around the world.[34] And Muruganantham turned down big multinational companies that approached him for help getting their expensive sanitary pads into local markets. He doesn't want to sell his innovation to big companies, preferring instead to empower women to produce sanitary pads themselves. "Muruganantham has succeeded where multinationals have failed," says Venkatesh Mahadevan, chief information officer of Dubai Investments. "He brought affordable sanitary napkins to those who need it most. He will go down in history as a true visionary and innovator."[35]

Muruganantham hopes to increase pad use among Indian women to 100 percent, while also giving those in the lowest socioeconomic strata an opportunity to earn a living selling pads produced at local centers – and facilitating a more effective feminine hygiene regime in communities that desperately need it. His priority is for sanitary pads to eventually be used everywhere around the world.

"The Pad Man is a god-sent angel," says Dr. Sujirtha Beena, an alternative medicine doctor in Coimbatore. "Above all, Muruganantham has succeeded in changing the culture of India's rural society. Young girls and women can now openly talk about and learn how to practice clean hygiene."[36]

His work has also encouraged a new generation of innovators. "Muruganantham's life story inspires millions of Indians like me," says Dr. Rengaraj Venkatesh, chief medical officer of Aravind Eye Care System, the largest primary eye care facilities in the world, "to reverse-engineer solutions to significant problems facing the entire developing world, and not just those facing the field of gynecological hygiene."[37]

In 2014, Muruganantham was named one of *Time's* 100 Most Influential People in the World, and in 2016, he won the Padma Shri award, one of the highest civilian honors granted by the government of India. *Fortune* magazine listed him among the top fifty greatest leaders of 2019.

"On the one hand, I feel like a celebrity," says Muruganatham. "On the other, so many women are still using dry leaves, ashes, and sawdust powder during menstruation." He is keenly aware of how much more work is left to be done. "Many countries are trying to send rockets to the moon and Mars without empowering women," he says. "I love the idea of reaching the stars, but first let's make sure everyone on Earth who needs sanitary pads has them."[38]

CHAPTER 6

Medicine: Playing God – Genetic Editing

The unthinkable has become conveivable. We're
on the cusp of a new era in human history.

– Nobel Prize laureate David Baltimore,
personal correspondence

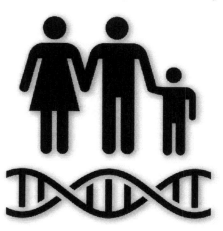

China's Dr. Frankenstein

It had been a little over a year since Chinese biomedical researcher
He Jiankui made the announcement that stunned the world. It was

December 2019, and the first scientist in history to successfully produce a genetically edited baby – three of them, in all – now found himself standing in front of a judge in Shenzhen, China, accused of conducting illegal medical practices and deliberately violating Chinese national regulations on biomedical research and medical ethics.

The verdict from the Nanshan District People's Court was swift. Jiankui, known to his friends as JK, was guilty. He was sentenced to three years in prison and ordered to pay a 3 million RMB fine (roughly USD $430,000).[1] The judge also found that JK had forged ethical review documents and misled doctors into unknowingly implanting gene-edited embryos in two women. The ruling was harsh, but in one sense it was just a formality. JK had already been tried and convicted by his peers in the global scientific community.

In November 2018, when Jiankui first broke the news about the birth of Lulu and Nana, twin girls whose embryonic genes he had modified in secret using a new technology known as CRISPR (an acronym standing for clustered regularly interspaced short palindromic repeats), the initial astonishment quickly curdled into a collective gasp. Within a few weeks, as the potential ramifications of what Jiankui had done came into focus, he was fired from his job at Shenzhen's Southern University of Science and Technology. In short order, the experiment was castigated in the BBC as "monstrous," and academic journals from the Lancet to Nature piled on with scolding headlines like "Do Not Edit the Human Germ Line."[2] Revered bodies such as the National Institutes of Health condemned the work unequivocally, and hundreds of JK's fellow Chinese scientists issued a joint statement in resolute opposition, calling the study "crazy" and "a huge blow to the global reputation and development of Chinese science."[3] But the harshest rebukes came from renowned researchers in his own field, such as stem-cell biologist Kathy Niakan of the Francis Crick Institute, who denounced JK's endeavor as "highly irresponsible, unethical and dangerous," echoing the sentiments of so many of her colleagues.[4]

JK's crime was set in motion in June 2017, when he recruited a Chinese couple pseudonymously named Mark and Grace, who, along with six other couples he signed up, met the requirements of his experiment: a father infected with HIV attempting to have a baby with a healthy mother. JK offered the couples in vitro fertilization and gene editing so that their embryos – and offspring – would have innate resistance to HIV. The idea was that the technique could ultimately be used to reduce the high HIV/AIDS rate in places like Africa.

The hopeful parents all had similar fertility problems and signed informed consent forms. JK and his colleagues carried out the experiment in secret, taking the sperm and eggs from each pair and altering the genomes of the embryos using CRISPR-Cas9, a technology that enables geneticists to edit parts of a human genome by removing, adding, or altering sections of a cell's DNA sequence. In this case, however, unlike all the previous research done with CRISPR-Cas9, JK was editing the human germline – meaning whatever changes he made would be passed on to his subject's children, and their children's children, potentially forever altering the DNA of our species.

It was a red line no CRISPR scientist had yet dared to cross, and JK's gambit was deemed particularly premature and unjustified because of the exposure to risk in exchange for little, if any, upside. Critics of his editing method argued that Lulu and Nana, along with a third gene-edited baby later born to another set of recruits, could still be vulnerable to HIV with none of the purported benefits – and an even greater likelihood to develop cancer and heart disease, among other untold problems. Experts agree that there are other safer, more effective ways to prevent HIV in pregnancy.

What JK had done was let CRISPR out of the box – without

asking permission. And the world was left wondering if that genie could ever be contained again.

Opening the Genetic Floodgates

Humans have been modifying organisms for over thirty thousand years. While our ancient ancestors didn't have scientific laboratories, they manipulated DNA through what Darwin famously called selective breeding, or artificial selection. The process of choosing organisms with the most desired traits and mating them repeatedly over many generations yields significant genetic changes.

Dogs are generally considered the first organisms to undergo artificial selection.[5] As hunter-gatherers, early humans were a consistent source of food for East Asian wild wolves, who are thought to have first joined man as scavengers. Over time, they were domesticated, bred to increase docility and obedience, and eventually to manipulate specific traits such as size, hair length, and body shape. Today, they barely resemble their ancient wolf ancestors.

Humans have also been modifying food for nearly ten thousand years. Archeological sites in southwest Asia (in what is today modern Turkey) provide evidence that as far back as 7800 BCE, people were engaged in the selective breeding of corn, which before humans got to it had been a wild grass with small ears and few kernels.[6]

In 1973, scientists Herbert Boyer and Stanley Cohen produced the first modern genetically engineered organism by removing a gene that encodes antibiotic resistance from one bacteria and inserting it into another, conferring the same antibiotic fortitude upon the recipient. A year later, Rudolph Jaenisch and Beatrice Mintz became the first to introduce foreign DNA into mouse embryos. By 1974, scientists, governments, and global citizens were so concerned about the new technology that a universal moratorium was imposed for one year so that society could consider the potential ramifications. But in 1975, attendees of the Asilomar Conference established guidelines for genetic engineering that defined safety in order to mitigate risk, and with those standards in place, a new era of modern genetic research and development was ushered in.

The race to profit from this new industry was in full swing by 1980, when the US Supreme Court granted legal ownership rights over genetically modified organisms (GMOs) to their inventors. General Electric filed a patent on a bacteria used for spill mitigation that breaks down crude oil. The US Food and Drug Administration approved the first bacteria to synthesize human insulin, known as the drug Humulin, two years later. And in 1987, scientists successfully modified the DNA sequence of a Calgene Flavr Savr tomato to increase firmness and extend its shelf life.

The floodgates for genetically modified organisms have been open ever since, and over time, scientists have found ways to develop crops with increased nutritional value and bigger yields that are also drought resistant and easier and more efficient to cultivate. Critics have been challenging the safety of these organisms for decades, but the scientific community has by and large concluded that genetically engineered foods are just as safe as traditionally selected crops.

It was only a matter of time until humans began to gain control over our own DNA. But up until the last decade, gene editing was prohibitively labor intensive and inaccurate. Researchers would primarily load genes onto viruses that would take them to their target cells. "For a long time, people didn't really have a clue what these repeated DNA sequences in bacteria genomes really did,"[7] recalls Rodolphe Barrangou, a scientist who was working for the Danish food ingredient manufacturer Danisco in 2007 when he made a key discovery, thanks to your morning yogurt.

Barrangou was sequencing genomes from bacteria used as starter cultures and noticed that they contained DNA markers that played a role in infecting and destroying dairy cultures. These bacteria had repeating DNA sequences (CRISPRS) that confer a form of immunity to bacteria from invading viruses and ultimately keep dairy products from spoiling too quickly.[8] In nature, bacteria build up immunity from invaders by storing a small bit of a virus's DNA. And like a "most wanted" poster, the bacteria then relay that bad code to an extraordinary protein called Cas9, whose job it is to police the intracellular neighborhood for invading viruses. When Cas9 sees an exact match to the information on the poster, it cuts it out and kills it.

The discovery was extremely valuable to Danisco for manufacturing dairy cultures resistant to viruses. But once fully understood, the true value – to the future of the human race – was immeasurable.

Bigger Than Breakfast

In 2012, molecular biologists Jennifer Doudna and Emmanuelle Charpentier discovered that Streptococcus pyogenes, the bacteria that causes strep throat, had a kind of GPS that directed its Cas9 enzymes to a specific strand of DNA and sliced it in two. Cas9 could be sent anywhere in the genome in order to snip out mutated genes. A year later, in what scientists call the Great CRISPR Quake, Doudna and Charpentier announced that they had figured out a way to use the method on humans to target and edit human DNA.[9]

Published in *Nature*, their research, as Berkeley's Fyodor Urnov puts it, instantly became a "deservedly immortal science paper."[10] CRISPR-Cas9, or clustered regularly interspaced short palindromic repeats and the associated protein 9, "fundamentally allows us to change human evolution if we want to," Doudna explained. "It's that profound."[11]

Like a book that describes us, our genome is made up of three billion base pairs of DNA arranged in a variety of sequences, and their particular order dictates all human traits. Handed down from generation to generation, every cell in the body carries a copy of this code. By 2003, thanks to the Human Genome Project, computers had sequenced the entire genome, and for the first time were also able to identify the genetic mutations for diseases with no cure. But until CRISPR-Cas9, there wasn't a whole lot scientists could actually do with that information with any kind of efficiency.

"It's like having one typo in a book containing 3 billion letters," says Matthew Porteus, professor of pediatrics at Stanford and cofounder of CRISPR Therapeutics.[12] "[Before CRISPR,] we spent six years trying to repair one mutation." Now we have the genetic equivalent of Microsoft Word, allowing scientists to target, edit, and ultimately replace DNA as easily as cutting and pasting. CRISPR molecules have a pair of molecular scissors that can unzip DNA and snip off sections of the genome, and they can be programmed to find DNA that is either mutated or disease-prone. "It's often described as a kind of Swiss Army knife," says Emmanuelle Charpentier. "It's really a universal tool."[13]

CRISPR systems, according to science journalist Megan Molteniare, are "the fastest, easiest, and cheapest methods scientists have ever had to manipulate the code of life in any organism on Earth, humans included. It is, simply, the first technology truly capable of changing the fundamental chemistry of who we are."[14]

What many now call the eighth wonder of the world will impact us deeply as a species, in both the near and far term. And over the course of the last decade, there has been a flood of research and development to try to push forward CRISPR's potential.

"With CRISPR, we can do genetic experiments that would have been unimaginable just a few years ago, not just on inherited disorders but also on genes that contribute to acquired diseases, including AIDS, cancer and heart diseases," says Mark Mercola of the Stanford Cardiovascular Institute. "It's no exaggeration to say that CRISPR has been revolutionary."[15]

CRISPR could lead to previously unimaginable medical treatments and is already being used to cut out HIV and eliminate Huntington's disease from the brain. According to Dr. Daniel Kraft, founder and chair of Exponential Medicine, at a biomedicine and tech conference, ten years from now we'll have CRISPR-based xenotransplants from humanized pigs. "If you need a heart, liver, or a kidney, you can get one from a pig," says Kraft. "Might not be kosher, but you'll take it."[16]

Today there are thousands of scientists working with CRISPR on every conceivable organism, including dogs, butterflies, horses, wheat, and corn. And almost every major industry is investing tremendous amounts of money into exploring the technology's promise, putting us on the brink of what has already become a multi-billion-dollar DNA hacking industry. Pharma is researching all kinds of breakthrough medical applications, from cures for bacterial infections to cancer. Agriculture companies are trying to create crops capable of reversing climate change. Energy corporations are experimenting with algae that turn into biofuel.

Almost every week, the media churns out headlines announcing that CRISPR-enhanced products are going to help achieve humanity's greatest aspirations and horrors: everything from the mundane, like the ability to grow hair on command, to the miraculous, like an end to aging and pain – or to children programmed with bigger muscles and super intelligence who only need to sleep four hours a night. CRISPR not only has the potential to completely eliminate microbes that cause disease – and feed the world with sustainable and healthy new foods – it may even be used to resurrect extinct species. Yes, scientists are already working on bringing the wooly mammoth back.

"What sounds like science fiction today," says Rodolphe Barrangou, the first scientist to provide experimental proof of CRISPR, "will just be science in the next ten years."[17]

Working the Bugs Out

Almost immediately after the discovery of CRISPR, a debate began on whether the DNA sequencing of mosquitoes should be changed to render them incapable of harboring the parasites that transmit deadly diseases like malaria, ZIKA, and yellow fever. The mosquito is mankind's hunter king, killing about two million people annually – more than any other species does, including humans themselves. (By way of comparison, snakes kill fifty thousand of us annually, and sharks just ten.)

The female mosquito uses two serrated mandible cutting blades to slice open human skin and insert her proboscis, which acts as a syringe to extract human blood, which she needs to grow her eggs. Her saliva contains an anti-coagulant that shortens the amount of time she needs to do her job, decreasing the chances humans will detect her deadly act. And if she's carrying the malaria parasite, it gets injected into the bloodstream, too, where it spawns and attaches to our red blood cells, leading to chills, extreme fever, vomiting, yellow skin, spleen and liver enlargement, and often death.

Most scientists believe that the creature's only purpose is to control the human population. "Contrary to popular belief, the mosquito does not even serve as an indispensable food source for any other animal," explains Timothy Winegard, author of *The Mosquito: A Human History of our Deadliest Predator.* "She has no purpose other than to propagate her species, and perhaps to kill humans."[18]

In order to fight this assassin, humans currently spend in excess of $11 billion per year on shields, sprays, and other forms of protection. In 2016, the Bill and Melinda Gates Foundation donated $75 million to facilitate CRISPR mosquito research. Since then, one of the options being vigorously pursued by researchers includes making genetic edits that would wipe out only those mosquito species that carry parasites (roughly one hundred of the thirty-five hundred known), often referred to as an "extinction drive." The approach would mean eliminating through sterilization species such as the *Aedes,* a transmitter of diseases like yellow fever, Zika, West Nile, chikungunya, and Mayaro dengue, which kill over 700,000 people annually and account for 17 percent of all infectious diseases globally. "Countries seriously affected by dengue and Zika have shown real interest in testing this technology," says World Health Organization scientist Florence Fouque, who also points to the great potential for suppressing mosquitoes that are developing resistance to insecticides.[19]

Alternatively, researchers have been pursuing what's known as a "gene drive" approach, aimed at altering the DNA of mosquito species that transmit disease to prevent them from doing so. Using CRISPR, scientists at the Universities of California in San Diego and Irvine have engineered transgenic *Anopheles stephensi* mosquitoes that carry an anti-malaria parasite effector gene. "We know the gene works," says Anthony James, a professor of molecular biology, genetics, and biochemistry at UC Irvine and one of the first scientists to carry out a mosquito gene drive. "We now need the political will to put this disease into the history books."[20]

Mosquito-borne diseases, scientists predict, are just the beginning, as CRISPR's real-world potential to eliminate or alter other disease-carrying insects appears limitless – and imminent. Notable examples currently being considered include sand flies that transmit leishmaniasis, ticks that spread Lyme disease, and rats that decimate native bird and turtle populations in the Galapagos, among many others.

"This notion of permanently altering the genetics of an entire species – it goes against everything I was trained to think," says Todd Kuiken, a researcher at the Genetic Engineering and Society Center at North Carolina State University who served on the United Nations committee for gene drives. "What's hard to accept is that, at this point, it might end up being our best option."[21]

Beyond Hitler

For all its mind-blowing promise, CRISPR has put human beings on the precipice of playing god, and it's far from clear what this mighty power will unleash, either in the halls of science or writ large across nature itself.

"At a very instinctive level, there's a sense that these are things humans are not supposed to be doing," says Alta Charo, a professor of law and bioethics at the University of Wisconsin, Madison. "You can make that new animal, or you can wipe out that whole species. And if doing that turns out to have been a bad idea, it means you're going to have to deal with the consequences."[22]

The concern is nearly universal in academic circles. "When it comes to experiments on animals, plants and microbes, two things worry me," says Stanford bioethicist Hank Greely. "One is the intentional misuse of CRISPR. The other is that people with good intentions will inadvertently cause harm."[23]

In the near term, even in cases where the reward would seem to far outweigh the risk – like driving the extinction of mosquito species that have killed hundreds of millions of people – the unanswered questions remain daunting. What other species would step in and take their place? How would it impact the ecosystem and the equilibrium created by nature over millions of years? Would it provide carte blanche in other areas of science to engage in genetic engineering, leading us down that slippery slope to designer humans? And, perhaps most profoundly, should we even be doing this at all?

He Jiankui took it upon himself to answer the most difficult question for the rest of us – and the ripple effects of that decision will be felt for years to come.

Upon learning of Jiankui's experiment in 2018, Jennifer Doudna and the rest of the CRISPR community were outraged. "[I am] horrified, honestly," she said. "And disgusted."[24] It was the realization of Doudna and Charpentier's very worst fears, which they had outlined at the first International Summit on Human Gene Editing just three years earlier: that someone in the community would go rogue and conduct CRISPR experiments on human babies.

In a statement, Emmanuelle Charpentier and specialists from seven countries called for a "moratorium on all clinical uses of human germline editing," being careful to draw the distinction between JK's research, which involves gene edits that are both permanent and passed on to future generations, and genome editing that is limited to somatic cells, which only affect certain tissues and are not passed on. "That is," they clarified, "changing heritable DNA (in sperm, eggs or embryos) to make genetically modified children."[25]

Jiankui's experiment has now forced governments and scientists to grapple with how to regulate this powerful tool. And as with all new technologies, finding a global consensus on enforcement is unlikely, which means JK's CRISPR babies were the first, but not the last.

"Germline DNA is a public trust, just like freedom, equality, and ideas," says Dr. Tshaka Cunningham, a former scientific program manager at the US Department of Veterans Affairs. "It's like the air we breathe. And we should not alter it unless we are sure what the consequences will be. The train has left the station. We are going to have a take a side."[26]

The World Health Organization has called on all researchers to cease work on genome editing "until its implications have been properly considered" and created a global registry to track anyone conducting such research.[27] The United States, China, and other international organizations have also taken action.

American enforcement authorities are investigating Rice University's Michael Deem, a scientist suspected of knowledge of Jiankui's baby project. It also appears that two US-based companies were involved in supplying JK with some of the technology he needed. Massachusetts-based Thermo Fisher Scientific is alleged to have given JK Cas9, and the Bay Area's Synthego (whose cofounders worked as rocket engineers at SpaceX) is said to have provided the synthetic guide RNA – in other words, one company provided the tools and the other the manual.

In May 2019, China began drafting regulations that would hold anyone manipulating the human genome through gene-editing techniques like CRISPR responsible for any related adverse con-sequences. By then, the government had already begun the inves-tigation that would lead to Jiankui's conviction, calling his work a "shocking and unacceptable" breach of ethics and a brazen violation of Chinese law.[28]

But in many ways, the Chinese government is speaking out of both sides of its mouth. In a potential harbinger of nefarious outcomes ahead, China is turning the other cheek as its scientists genetically engineer a wide variety of creatures, including dogs to have more muscle and humans to become biologically enhanced super soldiers.[29]

CRISPR, Russian president Vladimir Putin ominously presaged, "may be more terrifying than a nuclear bomb."[30]

The primary fear is that JK's research put a recipe out into the world that can't be unwritten, a first domino in what ultimately leads to a dystopian future of eugenics. Originally developed by English scientist Francis Galton in the late nineteenth century, the term, which outlines a method to increase certain desired heritable characteristics in an effort to improve the human race, fell into disfavor after being adopted by the Nazis, who used it as a pretext for monstrous ends.

Even Jennifer Doudna, the godmother of the CRISPR movement, which won her and Charpentier a Nobel Prize in 2020, is kept up at night by the thought. Over the years, she's had a series of disturbing dreams in which she walks into a room to find the silhouette of a man sitting in a chair with his back to her. As he turns around, she realizes with horror that it's Adolf Hitler, who leans over and whispers, "So, tell me about how Cas9 works." Doudna says she wakes up shaking and thinks, "Oh, my gosh, what have I done?"[31]

Putting aside the worst-case scenario, there is the very real concern that genetic editing could lead to tremendous societal inequality – exponentially greater than anything we have faced previously. The strong possibility exists that the rich will become genetically superior by paying to live longer, healthier lives. "Once you start creating a society in which rich people's children get biological advantages over other children, basic notions of human equality go out the window," says David King, founder of Human Genetics Alert, an independent watchdog group that opposes certain outcomes of genetic engineering. "Instead, what you get is social inequality written into DNA."[32]

Still, for all those sounding the alarm, there are just as many who are unapologetically bullish about the idea of improving the human condition, hypothetical pitfalls be damned.

Stephen Hsu, founder of Genomic Prediction, a company that develops technology for advanced genetic testing, insists that equating CRISPR and genetic testing with Nazism is "not just stupid but actually insane." Hsu believes that fifty years from now, people will look at the way we currently conceive children as old-fashioned. "Sex is for recreation," says Hsu, "and science is for procreation."[33] He is pushing for a general population that is smarter, healthier, lives longer, and has a decreased number of people with genetic disorders such as Down syndrome.

Many scientists are calling for a global debate on whether we should go in this direction, essentially turning reproduction into production – and our babies into consumer products.

"My grandchildren will be embryo-screened, germline-edited," says Daniel MacArthur, director of the Centre for Population Genomics at the Garvan Institute. "[It] won't change what it means to be human. It will be like vaccination."[34]

Some in the field believe that the same goes for humanity's relationship with nature. "We have been messing with nature ever since we came out of the trees," says Stanford law professor Hank Greely, who likes to remind people that corn used to be a grass and that tomatoes were once bitter berries. "Geneticists changed that. [But] we called them farmers."[35]

The history of the medical establishment is replete with examples of advances that were initially rejected but later widely adopted, including procedures that seemed impossible and in hindsight became the standard of care. Up until the middle of the nineteenth century, physicians ridiculed Ignaz Semmelweis for advocating hand washing in order to reduce contagious diseases. His critics forced him into a Viennese insane asylum, where he was beaten to death. For the first few decades after newborn incubators were invented, they could only be found at amusement parks and sideshows. Even Gregar Mendel, the father of the laws of genetic inheritance, was marginalized for most of his life as a "simple" monk from a provincial town in what is today the Czech Republic – and only proven correct decades after his death.

Whether He Jiankui is ultimately judged a crackpot or a pioneer, or maybe something in between, depends on the telescope of time. Some prominent CRISPR scientists, including Harvard's George Church and George Daily, believe that if JK's babies are healthy, they might be viewed more like Louise Brown, the first infant born through in vitro fertilization, as opposed to Jesse Gelsinger, the first person to die in an early gene therapy experiment in 1999.

"The fact that the first instance of human germline editing came forward as a misstep should not let us stick our neck in the sand," says Dr. George Daley, dean of Harvard Medical School, who has called for an end to the debates about ethical permissibility so that a path toward clinical research can be cleared. "It is time to move forward."[36]

CHAPTER 7
Disaster Resilience: The Ring of Fire

You can run, but you can't hide.

– Joe Louis, world heavyweight boxing champion

緊急交通路
EMERGENCY ROAD
地震災害時、一般車両通行禁止
CLOSED IN THE EVENT OF MAJOR EARTHQUAKE
東京都・警視庁

Emergency Road Sign in Suginami, Japan, 2012 (Abasaa)

Paper Houses

In January 1995, a young architect named Shigeru Ban traveled to Kobe, Japan, to witness the aftermath of one of the most destructive earthquakes in history. The magnitude 7.2 Great Hanshin-Awaji Earthquake and its ensuing seventy-four aftershocks killed 6,433 people, destroyed nearly 400,000 buildings, numerous roads and rail bridges, and the majority of the quays in the port. About three hundred fires raged in the city, disrupting water, gas, and electric lines.

Residents of Kobe told Ban about the violence that rattled them out of their beds in the predawn hours. For twenty seconds, the world was filled with the sound of glass breaking, roof tiles falling, and the shrieks of old wood bending. When the living began to venture outside, what they found seemed to defy reality. Shattered windows. Crushed cars. Collapsed buildings. And dead bodies everywhere. Seismologists later determined that the focus of the quake was located on the east-west strike-slip fault line where the Eurasian and Philippine plates meet. In all, it caused more than $100 billion in damage.

Ban was among the staggering 1.2 million volunteers who poured into the Kobe region to provide relief and assistance. As an architect, he felt that too many of his colleagues in the profession hadn't been doing enough to help the thousands of people who had lost their homes in natural disasters, including himself. "We [were] not working for society," he recalls. "[We were] working for privileged people, rich people, government developers."[1]

Ban knew what he needed to do to improve the situation. After seeing one of the local Catholic churches completely destroyed, he approached the priests with a radical proposal.

"Why don't we rebuild the church out of paper tubes?" he asked.

The interaction was as short as it was awkward. "Oh, God," the skeptical priests replied. "Are you crazy? After a fire?" They turned him down flat.[2] Which person of sound mind would agree to a building made out of paper?

Undeterred, Ban recruited volunteers and forged ahead with his plan to build houses for those in Kobe who needed them most – using recycled paper tubes. As a construction material, they proved strong, cheap, and durable in the face of moisture and termites, and, perhaps most surprisingly, also water- and fireproof. His temporary units, called Kobe Paper Log Houses, provided warm, safe shelter for thousands of displaced refugees. The structures rested on foundations of donated beer crates loaded with sandbags, and for insulation, Ban employed waterproof sponge tape backed with adhesive, inserted between the paper tubes of the walls. Each unit cost less than $2,000.

After Ban built fifty homes, the priests finally relented. "As long as you collect money by yourself, bring your students to build, you can do it,"[3] they told him. So Ban spent five weeks rebuilding the Takatori church, which would later become internationally known as the Paper Church. Meant to last three years, it was universally beloved and remained in Kobe for more than a decade. Eventually it was dismantled and shipped to Taiwan, where it serves to this day as a permanent house of worship, primarily serving victims of the island's various earthquakes. Ban's easily constructed paper homes are now routinely used all over Japan – and around the world – when natural disasters strike.

X-Day: Apocalypse

Experts say it isn't a question of if, but when. Government officials call it X-Day: the moment Japan's 125 million inhabitants experience the unthinkable, a catastrophic earthquake that strikes at the populated heart of the country and wreaks untold havoc.

The Land of the Rising Sun is one of the most vulnerable places on Earth to natural disasters like earthquakes, typhoons, and tsunamis because of its location in what's known as the "Ring of Fire," a twenty-five-thousand-mile horseshoe-shaped area defined by a series of oceanic trenches, volcanic arcs, and belts – all perched on four precariously shifting tectonic plates. With over 450 volcanoes, the Ring hosts more than 75 percent of the world's active and dormant volcanoes, and 90 percent of all earthquakes.

Though as many as two thousand earthquakes hit Japan each year, for the most part, the country has remained relatively lucky in terms of *where* they have struck for about a century.

The last seismic mega tremor to hit Tokyo was in 1923. Described by residents and escapees as "hell on earth," it killed 143,000 people and destroyed 695,000 homes across Tokyo and Yokohama.[4] The Great Kanto Earthquake measured 7.9 on the moment scale, an updated version of the Richter scale that measures energy at the epicenter of an earthquake. Experts predict that there's a 70 percent chance that the next magnitude 7 earthquake will hit Tokyo before 2050. And there's an even greater chance of a magnitude 9 quake in the Nankai Trough off the Pacific coast, which could inundate cities like Tokyo – and the entire island of Kyushu – with sixty-five-foot-plus waves.

Tohoku University's Yuichi Ono, a professor of disaster science and former UN official, puts it bluntly. "Japan is a ticking time bomb."[5]

Kobe was in many ways a wake-up call. Within moments of the disaster, thousands were dead, "crushed by buildings that Japanese engineers were amazed – and ashamed – to see crumple like cards," writes David Pilling, former Tokyo bureau chief for the *Financial Times*.[6] The Hanshin Expressway collapsed, and thousands of buildings erected before 1981 toppled.

"Earthquakes don't kill people," Shigeru Ban observed. "The collapse of buildings kills people. And that is the responsibly of architects."[7]

In the decades since Kobe, bold Japanese architects and engineers like Ban have proven themselves equal to the challenge. In the quake's immediate aftermath, officials tightened regulations – and then continued to tighten them again and again until the country had one of the world's most advanced building codes. In an unprecedented marshalling of resources, talent, and public policy, it has put in place a system that integrates design thinking and innovation, which has already saved an untold number of lives. After investing billions of dollars in technology and infrastructure, Japan is now the most-prepared country on the planet to protect its citizens from earthquakes and tsunamis – and no doubt will be well into the future.

"Following every natural disaster, the Japanese study carefully what happened in order to improve building design so that above all, we are able to better protect people's lives," says Keio University professor Rajib Shaw. "That is the very minimum requirement."[8]

Japan's buildings must now be designed to withstand smaller earthquakes unharmed, without a single repair. For major quakes (defined as larger than the magnitude 7.9 quake that hit Tokyo in 1923), preserving the building is secondary to the protection of human life. Among other techniques, Japan uses reinforced walls and foundations of a certain thickness. In many cases, buildings rest on massive rubber shock absorbers or Teflon-coated pegs embedded into the foundation, which essentially allow buildings to float, decoupling them from the ground so they can move semi-independently. "When the structure can absorb all the energy from the earthquake, it will not collapse." says Jun Sato, a structural engineer and associate professor at the University of Tokyo. "Great nature is our best teacher."[9]

For high-rises and skyscrapers, architects use multiple sophisticated techniques that allow for strong yet flexible structures that sway, including hollow walls that hide metal plates and fluid-filled shock absorbers that deploy thick oil in the opposite direction of movement. "It's like a yardstick when you bend it – it snaps back without any damage," explains John W. van de Lindt, a civil engineering professor at Colorado State University.[10]

According to the University of Tokyo, 87 percent of the city's buildings are now either retrofitted or constructed according to anti-seismic standards.[11]

In the process, Japan has also pioneered an entirely new and innovative industry. "What Japanese architects have done in the last twenty years is the envy of the world and nothing short of astonishing," explains Tokyo Institute of Technology's Toru Takeuchi. "We have pioneered an entire industry that manages to marry seismic engineering requirements with functional and elegant design."[12]

Many of Japan's most iconic buildings employ high-level seismic design, including Tokyo's Mori Tower, a fifty-four-story mixed-use skyscraper reinforced with steel piping that rests on 192 oil-charged shock absorbers. Tokyo's Skytree radio tower, the second tallest building in the world, relies on a core vibration system, an idea that originated in Japan's rich architectural history of five-story traditional wooden pagodas. "It's an incredible energy dissipating system," says Sigrid Adriaenssens, a civil and environmental engineering professor at Princeton University, of the highly innovative feature. "It allows for independent movement of the tower itself, which counterbalances and suppresses the swaying caused by earthquakes."[13]

Still, for all the levitating buildings and paper houses, the Japanese are well aware that their future safety can never rest solely on the promise of miraculous feats of engineering and technology. On a societal level, their most impressive achievement might be the successful mobilization of an entire populace toward readiness.

"While Japan is renowned internationally for its resilient infrastructure and its seismic technologies," says Meri Joyce, a Tokyo-based specialist in disaster preparedness and response, "where the country really excels is its preparedness at the community and individual level."[14]

There's a Plan for That

Every day at five in the evening, hundreds of loudspeakers across Tokyo and other parts of Japan boom out a children's song called "Yuyake Koyake," encouraging children and workers to go home. The melody announces the end of the day, but more importantly, it also tests an emergency system designed to save lives when an imminent disaster is approaching. If an earthquake is about to strike one of the biggest and most important metropolises in the world, the loudspeakers blare the real-time early alarm, an eerie noise similar to the *Godzilla* theme song. TVs and radios blast it, too, and cell phones erupt in a series of long beeps.

"These warnings are terrifying," admits Dr. Satoru Nishikawa, a professor of disaster resilience at Nagoya University and former senior Japanese cabinet official. "It makes my blood freeze as I brace for safety."[15] And that, of course, is the intended effect.

For all the energy it has channeled toward engineering and design innovation, the Japanese government has sunk that much or more into meticulous planning and preparation. It has spent over a billion dollars to build a seismic alert system that can detect earthquakes eighty seconds before they arrive, giving residents enough time to turn off gas mains, step away from windows, and make their way down from high floors. If a tsunami follows, citizens are directed to the closest defense bunkers.

Were a magnitude 7 earthquake to strike the northern Tokyo Bay, the effects would be calamitous: an estimated ten thousand people killed; almost 150,000 injured; over three million in need of immediate evacuation; over five million stranded; and at least 300,000 buildings destroyed.[16] The government would aim to restore power within a week and the water supply within a month.

"We know from experience that critical infrastructure such as electricity, gas, and water gets hit hard as a result of disasters," says Takeshi Komino, a disaster management expert who has worked all over the world. "It is baked into Japanese culture to prepare ahead of time for the inevitable and do what it takes to get basic lifelines up and running as quickly as possible."[17]

Tokyo's 338-page *Disaster Preparedness Tokyo*, issued in multiple languages, outlines what people should expect when disaster strikes – with zero sugar coating. A comic strip depicts a forlorn figure navigating falling objects, derailed trains, crashed vehicles, collapsed buildings, and a lack of power and cell service. Advice includes "accepting death."[18]

"This is not a 'what if' story," the manual warns. "In the near future, this story is sure to become reality."[19]

Every September 1, drills take place in workplaces and schools across the country to inculcate the need to seek refuge in safe places. The government instructs residents to use L-shaped brackets to fasten furniture, and anti-slip pads to secure cabinets, chairs, and tables. Citizens are also encouraged to be vigilant about storing extra canned food, water, flashlights, medicine, and batteries.

Tokyo also has the world's largest fire brigade trained to deal with earthquake-sized natural disasters. "Japanese firefighters are often regarded like members of the Tokkotai," says Mikio Ishiwatari, a senior advisor at the Japan International Cooperation Agency, referring to the revered kamikaze pilots of WWII. "They are prepared to sacrifice everything in order to save lives in the face of tsunamis, earthquakes, and volcanic eruptions."[20]

In Tokyo, preparedness is so much a part of the culture, it's quite literally everywhere you look. Like an architect's plans, every last detail has been carefully thought through and anticipated, which is one of the reasons the *Economist* Intelligence Unit now ranks Tokyo as the safest city in the world.[21] Major roads marked with large blue catfish – the mythological Namazu, causer of earthquakes – are specifically designated for fire trucks and rescue vehicles. Over a dozen of Tokyo's parks and three thousand of its schools and community centers have been fully prepped as evacuation centers.

Manhole covers across the city are designed to be quickly removed and refitted with special seats and privacy tents, turning them into emergency toilets. Benches double as cooking stoves. Solar-powered charging stations are ubiquitous for electric bikes and smart phones. And city officials have built in enough underground water reservoirs and food stores to allow entire districts to survive the first seventy-two hours.[22]

A Global Shake-Up

In 2011, Tohuko was hit by a magnitude 9.0 earthquake, the fourth most powerful in the history of seismology, and Japan learned once again that no matter how precisely it plans, the country still has significant vulnerabilities.[23] The earthquake was so fearsome, it knocked the earth six and a half inches off its axis and moved Japan thirteen feet closer to America. And the tsunami that followed wreaked mayhem and unspeakable disaster. Over 130 feet high at their peak, the giant waves killed eighteen thousand people, and more than 120,000 buildings were destroyed. The devastation only mounted when three reactors of the Fukushima Daiichi Nuclear Power Plant melted down, spreading radiation in the worst nuclear accident since Chernobyl. Tohuko soon became the most expensive natural disaster of all time, causing more than $235 billion in damage.

But, as with so many of the rude geo-seismic awakenings that preceded it, Japan absorbed the lessons, adapted, and improved – and is now that much more prepared in the bargain. On the whole, the earthquakes that have hit Japan over the last two decades have only proven the effectiveness of its regulations and push toward technological innovation. Even though the epicenter of the quake was 230 miles from Tokyo, the city experienced extended shaking. But the buildings did exactly what they were supposed to do: sway like trees in the breeze. Not a single building fell in Tokyo, despite the record-breaking magnitude of the quake – a testament to the high level of engineering used in the construction of the city's structures.

At the time of the disaster, twenty-seven Shinkansen high-speed trains were on the move. As a result of advanced seismographic technology placed throughout the country, they detected the earth's tremors ahead of time. This allowed the train conductors to put on the emergency breaks a few precious moments before the most violent movements took place. No passengers lost their lives – or were even injured.[24]

Despite extensive damage to the track network and infrastructure, bullet train service resumed just forty-nine days later. "The speed of restoration was incredible," says Takeshi Fukayama, senior consultant and expert in railway development at Mitsubishi Research Institute.[25]

When Typhoon Lan reached landfall in 2017, Japan had even more proof that its redoubled efforts were paying off. Despite a storm surge of nearly ten feet, not a single home flooded. The ten-foot surge caused by 1949's Typhoon Kitty, by comparison, flooded nearly 140,000 homes.

The Land of the Rising Sun has indisputably set the bar for the rest of the world, and to varying degrees, countries such as Chile, China, Italy, Mexico, Peru, and Turkey are adopting seismic technologies innovated in Japan. Unfortunately, too many are lagging behind in this regard, including the United States, which has used the methods sparingly, with a few notable exceptions (such as Apple's new headquarters in Silicon Valley). Safety advocates argue that it's a huge missed opportunity to save billions in reconstruction costs after an inevitable earthquake hit.

"Short-term thinking is absolutely the biggest villain," says Evan Reis, a cofounder of the US Resiliency Council. "People are willing to roll the dice."[26]

The urgent need for long-term, low-cost systemic solutions has never been greater. It is only a matter of time before the next large earthquake or tsunami hits one of the world's major population centers on a fault line or near the ocean. "The next ten years will witness extreme levels of climate change and disaster risk," says Keio University professor Rajib Shaw. "Except these risks will no longer be 'extreme.' Extreme events will be the new normal."[27]

Though the cost of disaster mitigation has come down significantly in the last few decades, the reality for most countries is that the price is still too high. Engineering and planning at such a high level requires tremendous investment – Japan now spends $46 billion annually to maintain, repair, and manage water mains, ports, airports, and other large assets that make up its disaster resilience program.[28]

"If you need evidence of why earthquakes are political and economic, almost as much as natural," observed the *New Yorker*'s Amy Davidson after Tohoku's magnitude 9 monster in 2011, "look at the pictures from Japan. Then remember the ones from Haiti."[29]

The magnitude 7.0 quake that hit Haiti in 2010 completely decimated the country's ill-prepared infrastructure, flattened Port au Prince, and killed hundreds of thousands of people.

Once again, Shigeru Ban got on a plane to lend a hand. Together with local professors and university students, he built fifty shelters made of paper tubes and local materials that cost less than $300 each.

"These natural disasters will continue happening," said the Pritzker Prize–winning architect. "More problems are coming. I need to solve them one by one."[30]

CHAPTER 8

Energy: The Electric Slide

If we keep pulling death from the ground,
we will reap death from the skies.

– Van Jones, *The Green Collar Economy*

A Charge to Keep

When entrepreneurs Martin Eberhard and Marc Tarpenning sold their e-book business, NuvoMedia, for $187 million in 2000, the partners weren't sure what they wanted to do next. With backgrounds in computer science and electrical engineering, both had become obsessed with the pernicious effects of fossil fuel dependence. Tarpenning had spent his formative years after college working for the conglomerate Textron in Saudi Arabia. "If you want to see what oil does to a local economy, and where our treasure ends up going," Tarpenning says, "spending six years in Saudi Arabia is quite illuminating."[1]

Eberhard didn't need any convincing. "Somewhere along the way, I started thinking that this global warming thing was not a hoax," he recalls. "Maybe the wars we were having in the Middle East were at least somehow involved in oil, and I decided that we needed to do something different."[2] Eberhard also happened to be recently divorced. "I was thinking that I should do what every guy who gets divorced does and buy a sports car," he says. "But I couldn't bring myself to buy one that got eighteen miles to the gallon."[3]

The car he really wanted didn't exist, so Eberhard created a spreadsheet that modeled out the various power sources available, including gasoline, diesel, natural gas, solar, wind, fuel cells, and batteries. "The results were startling," he recalls. Eberhard discovered that hydrogen was just as bad as gasoline, and that even under the best circumstances, it was only about 20 percent efficient with the technology available. "Your hydrogen fuel-cell car will require three to four times as much of whatever your source fuel is per mile compared to electric vehicles," says Eberhard. Lithium batteries, on the other hand, are about 95 percent efficient. "We were surprised to learn that electric cars were head and shoulders above everything else," he says.[4]

At the time, GM had already sunk more than $1 billion into the development of the EV1, the first modern electric car from a major manufacturer, before infamously repossessing and crushing the entire line because the cars were unprofitable. When the two engineers started digging into why the EV1 failed, they concluded it was the battery type and business model. And before long, the pair had convinced themselves they could do better.

Early EV1 models used lead-acid batteries, which yield a range of up to a hundred miles. But throughout the 1990s, the battery industry was rapidly changing, and Eberhard and Tarpenning felt that lithium-ion batteries, which today yield over four hundred miles of range, presented a huge opportunity. The battery itself was a real disruptor in the market – in terms of both cost and performance, it improved by about 7 percent each year. "It was so much better," says Eberhard, "that it was stunning to us that nobody else was doing it."[5]

In 2003, Eberhard and Tarpenning decided that the most effective way to battle climate change and reduce the world's reliance on oil was to start their own electric car company. But they didn't jump in blindly. "We had no experience making cars," recalls Eberhard, "and we had a lot to learn."[6]

For months, they struggled to come up with the perfect name for their new venture. One night, Eberhard was eating at the iconic Disneyworld restaurant Blue Bayou, overlooking the Pirates of the Caribbean, when it struck him. "What do you think about the name Tesla Motors?"[7]

The very engine they intended to use in their car, known as the AC induction motor, had been patented by the legendary Serbian-American inventor Nikola Tesla in 1887. In July 2003, the pair incorporated the company and rented office space in Menlo Park, California, which still had the sign from the previous tenant: "Bushtracks African Expeditions." They flipped the sign over and wrote "Tesla Motors" on the back.[8]

Zero Hour

Early on, to get a sense for the market, Eberhard drove around Palo Alto trying to figure out who their ideal customer might be. He snapped a lot of driveway pictures and noticed that he often saw an old BMW or Porsche parked next to a Prius. And that's when it hit him: "Someone who likes a fun-to-drive hot car," says Eberhard, "but also feels bad about the gas mileage and oil consumption."[9]

Eberhard and Tarpenning started working on their go-to market plan. Up until then, Eberhard recalls, electric cars "had been given such a black eye in the marketplace. People thought about them as punishment cars, dork-mobiles, just ugly golf carty things."[10] Their plan was to innovate on a successful business model that was already common in the tech industry: first create a high-end product that commands high prices, then produce a mid-market product with higher volume, and eventually leverage the skills, economy of scale, and price reductions to secure the mass market.

The two engineers started tinkering with a model car. One afternoon, Eberhard called an old friend, Malcolm Smith, who was a Silicon Valley product designer. "I can't tell you what we're doing," Eberhard said, "but why don't you come check out this car I have."[11] When Smith arrived, Eberhard showed him their business plan, then said, "Let's go for a ride."[12]

They jumped into a small yellow two-seater with a decal on the side that read "tZero," a reference to the mathematical symbol that means the beginning of time within a system. As the two turned slowly onto Sand Hill Road, Eberhard asked Smith to try to touch the dashboard. Just as he reached out, Eberhard hit the accelerator, and Smith's hand never made it – the sheer force of the acceleration drove him straight back into his seat. The car had an AC propulsion motor with a lithium-ion battery that allowed the tZero to go from zero to sixty in less than four seconds.

"I get it," Smith thought. "This isn't a nice little science experiment."[13] He eventually became one of Tesla's first employees.

"The tZero will be remembered as the father of all modern electric vehicles," says Seth Weintraub, founder of the popular news site Electrek. "It changed the world and ultimately became the modern Tesla."[14]

In the fall of 2003, Eberhard and Tarpenning started speaking to potential investors in the Silicon Valley ecosystem. But at first, they only pitched people they knew would never invest, so they could hone their pitch and not burn their chances with serious investors.

At the time, they acknowledged that building a high-performance electric car "sounded impossible," recalls Tarpenning.[15]

They eventually decided that the only model that made fiscal sense would be to sell directly to consumers, as opposed to going through traditional car dealerships. They also concluded that they shouldn't try to build their own car from scratch. Instead, they'd build on top of an existing car they could customize, eventually settling on Lotus, a British auto manufacturer known for their sexy sports cars. Eberhard and Ian Wright, the company's first employee, both drove Lotus Europas.[16]

With the pitch honed and the business plan complete, they went back out to raise money in earnest. And though they got a bit of capital from friends and family, no one seemed willing to step up with a big investment – until they reached out to one man who was willing to give them a shot.

"We would love to talk to you about Tesla Motors," wrote Eberhard in a short email on March 31, 2004. "Particularly if you might be interested in investing in the company."

Elon Musk sent a note back that very night. "Sure," he wrote.[17]

Eberhard and Ian Wright flew down to the SpaceX office in Los Angeles. "He gave me half an hour to make a presentation, which turned into two hours," recalls Eberhard. "And by the end, we had a handshake deal that he would lead the investment in the company."[18]

Musk shared their passion for building a superior electric car that could change the world. At their second meeting in LA, Tarpenning joined Eberhard to make the final pitch. "He liked the idea and peppered us with questions," Tarpenning recalls. And just like that, "He said, 'I'm in, you convinced me.'"[19]

In April 2004, Musk invested $6 million and became the company's largest investor.

Off to the Races

By the summer of 2004, Eberhard had a rough idea of how he wanted his first car to look. The engineer turned businessman-carmaker knew he needed a sports car, not just to play against the stigma that electric vehicles (EVs) were for crunchy environmentalists, but also because sports cars have higher margins. Top-tier buyers are traditionally less price sensitive, which meant they'd need to sell fewer cars to become profitable.

According to Tarpenning, their initial call for design submissions came back "terrible."[20] Yet no matter how hard they tried, they couldn't communicate to designers what they wanted. All except for one.

In the fall, Eberhard turned to his long-time friend and next-door neighbor Bill Moggridge, one of the cofounders of the world-renowned design firm IDEO and a longstanding faculty member of the Stanford Design School. Over wine, Moggridge peppered him with questions.

"OK, let's consider this axis, from retro to futuristic," Moggridge said. "Where would you want your car to be on that axis?" Retro was Eberhard's preference.

"Here's another axis, masculine to feminine," Moggridge said. "Where do you imagine your car on that axis?" Eberhard wanted something in the middle.

"Curvaceous or boxy?" Moggridge asked. "You could look at the classic old Ferraris, which are very curvaceous, and the modern Lamborghinis, which are very boxy."

"Somewhere in between, but closer to the curvaceous end," Eberhard replied.[21]

Moggridge, Eberhard recalls, was able to take his preferences and turn them into "magic." "He spoke the language of designers," recalls Eberhard, "but knew me well enough as an engineer to understand my vision."[22] The engineer was then able to go back to his designers and explain exactly what they wanted for their first car.

Around Christmas, Eberhard hosted a small house party for Tesla's employees, their families, and company advisors. He put the design sketches up on the wall and asked each guest to vote with green or red Post-it Notes. At the end of the night, there was one sketch covered in green. It was the car designed by Barney Hatt from Lotus Design Studio: the Roadster.

Problem Child

On July 19, 2006, the Tesla Roadster was unveiled to an elite group of Hollywood who's whos at the Barker Hanger in the Santa Monica Airport. Guests were told that the first one hundred people to pre-order the $100,000 two-seater would get an engraved plaque inside their cars. Within two weeks, Tesla had sold 127 Roadsters, with a first batch of customers that included George Clooney, Google founders Sergey Brin and Larry Page, inventor Dean Kamen, Hyatt heir Nicholas Pritzker, and sportswear designer Julie Chaiken.[23]

In short order, the Roadster received rave reviews from the *New York Times, Fortune, Wired,* CNET, and the *Washington Post,* which declared, "This is not your father's electric car."[24]

Yet from the start, the Roadster was plagued with bugs that would significantly delay its delivery date. "We have a tremendous number of difficult problems to solve just to get the car into production," Eberhard wrote to Musk in November 2006. "I stay up at night worrying about simply getting the car into production sometime in 2007."[25]

Slowing the production was what's known as the "elegance creep" phenomenon. The company kept customizing their car, making it as beautiful as possible and enhancing the user experience. Tesla started with five subassemblies – and eventually had hundreds. Over time, the Roadster barely resembled the Lotus Elis it was meant to be based on, and the two cars shared only 7 percent of their common parts. The cost to produce the first Tesla skyrocketed. Both investors and employees worried it would choke the company to death.

Between the Roadster's launch and the date customers actually got their cars, Tesla's leadership underwent significant changes. By August 2007, Eberhard had resigned as CEO, though he remained president and a member of the company's board of directors. A short time later, Eberhard was forced out. In the year that followed, the company hired and fired two more CEOs – until Musk finally took over in October 2008. By that time, Musk had already invested more than $55 million, and many feared the company was on the fast track to bankruptcy.

"I've got so many chips on the table with Tesla," Musk explained. "It just made sense for me to have both hands on the wheel."[26]

In his first year as CEO, Musk made drastic changes. In addition to firing 25 percent of his employees, he sold 10 percent of the company to Daimler AG for $50 million, raised an additional $40 million of debt, and secured a $465 million loan from the US Department of Energy.[27]

In fall 2008, a full year after its promised summer 2007 delivery date, the Roadster finally started going out to buyers. "We had incredibly supportive customers who stayed with us, " recalls Tarpenning, "I don't think anyone cancelled their reservations – it was craziness."[28]

That same year, Tarpenning decided it was time to leave the company.

Bigger, Stronger, Faster

On June 29, 2010, Elon Musk and members of the Tesla team walked into the NASDAQ exchange and rang the opening bell. Tesla officially became the first American carmaker since Ford in 1956 to go public. Musk secured $226 million, giving the company the capital infusion it needed to grow. The problematic Roadster was discontinued in

2012 after the company sold approximately twenty-five hundred cars.

To capture a larger share of the total auto market, Musk knew he needed to pivot. To do that, Tesla would need to develop advanced electric drive components and produce low-cost, high-energy-density lithium-ion batteries. He focused his energy on the Model S, a full-sized luxury car the company had been developing since 2007, which went to market in June 2012 and very quickly won multiple accolades. The National Highway Traffic Safety Administration called it "the safest car ever tested," *Consumer Reports* deemed it the "best car ever tested," and *Road & Track* rated it "the most important car America has made in an entire lifetime."

In 2013, Tesla announced its plan to build its multi-billion-dollar Gigafactory with the aim of bringing the cost of lithium batteries down by at least 30 percent. Located near Reno, Nevada, the $5 billion structure became the largest building in the world by footprint, with 5.8 million square feet of space roughly equal to a hundred football fields. The factory is also powered entirely by green energy, including solar, wind, and geothermal sources.

A year later, the company achieved a major milestone. For the first time, Tesla released an autopilot car, which gave the Model S semi-autonomous driving and parking capabilities.

In 2015, Tesla released its falcon-winged luxury crossover SUV, the Model X, to near universal acclaim. And a year later, it launched the Model 3, a cost-effective sedan targeting the mass market. The entry-level sticker price was $35,000, which led to a staggering half million pre-orders. Over the previous six years, Tesla had only sold about 200,000 cars – a figure many car manufacturers sell in a month.

Today, Morgan Stanley calls Tesla "the world's most important car company." With a valuation of more than $460 billion, it's also the seventh most valuable company in America. In 2020, it was added to the S&P 500.

The Future of Sustainable Energy

"When something is important enough," says Elon Musk, "you do it even if the odds are not in your favor."[29]

Tesla's official mission statement is "To accelerate the world's transition to sustainable energy,"[30] and to achieve this end, the company has moved well beyond electric cars. For homeowners and businesses, Tesla has developed a range of products that allow customers to produce, manage, store, and consume their own renewable energy. The ecosystem includes solar panels and solar roofs that provide 100 percent sustainable energy, which can then be stored in a Powerwall that both makes electricity available during peak hours and provides power when the grid experiences outages.

"In the next few years, we'll reach a decisive point," says Lawrence Burns, author of *Autonomy* and former vice president at General Motors. "That's the amazing moment when the technology works, the people want it, the price is low enough to make it work, and the companies can make money selling it."[31]

When Tesla launched, there were no viable electric cars on the market. Today, there are about three million on the road globally, including over a million Teslas.[32] To date, Teslas alone have driven about ten billion miles, saving the planet more than four million metric tons of CO_2, the equivalent of the annual emissions of one million cars.[33]

"Elon has managed to take it further than I could have imagined," says Tarpenning. "To see so many on the road and people really loving them just feels great."[34]

In the last few years, Musk has also unveiled the Tesla Semi, an electric hauling truck. (He says driving diesel-powered trucks is "economic suicide.")[35] And in the near future, Tesla intends to design autonomous mini-buses for mass transit.

"The transition is just getting started and there is no turning back," says Daniel Sperling, founding director of the Institute of Transportation Studies at the University of California, Davis. "Both the automotive industry and international policy leaders are committed to EVs, which represent the single most important transportation strategy to slow climate change."[36]

Every major car manufacturer now produces electric vehicles, and there are a significant number of world leaders now calling for an eventual ban on cars with internal combustion engines. Industry analysts predict that in the coming years, the market for EVs will explode as their prices decrease at an inverse proportion to their increase in range, and more government policies support their mass adoption.

"Regulation drives innovation," says Roland Hwang of the National Resources Defense Council, who points to California's zero-emission vehicle credits program, which incentivizes manufacturers to produce a minimum number of electric vehicles per year, as one of the prime movers of Tesla's success. "For decades, automakers have repeated one line: 'It can't be done.' Tesla is proof positive they were wrong."[37]

In 2017, China adopted its own New Energy Vehicle Regulation, based on California's program, and the country is now the largest market for EVs in the world, with well over a million sold in 2019 alone.[38] China has traditionally battled terrible smog in its larger cities, but it has also grown increasingly concerned about importing more than 70 percent of its oil from abroad. In EVs, it sees a golden opportunity to "leapfrog other countries in the auto sector as an industrial policy," says Yunshi Wang, director of the China Center for Energy and Transportation at the UC Davis Institute of Transportation Studies. "China is engaged in self-enlightened interest and is poised to dominate the clean car economy for a very long time to come."[39]

In Norway, which provides huge tax incentives for electric cars – not to mention exemptions from bridge tolls and free public parking – nearly 60 percent of all new car sales are EVs.[40] The government has decided to completely phase out the sale of new internal combustion engine cars starting in 2025, and many other European countries have proposed similar phase-out plans.

"When the industry combines electric drive and autonomy, we will witness the most profound change since the industrial revolution," says Robbie Diamond, founder of Securing America's Future Energy (SAFE), an organization based in Washington, DC, committed to combating the economic and national security threats posed by dependence on oil. "And it will happen faster than people think."[41]

In the coming decades, both Martin Eberhard and Marc Tarpenning envision a green revolution around the world, driven by electric vehicles and solar energy, that will significantly reduce the harmful emissions we are putting into the atmosphere. Eberhard likes to cite the late Saudi oil minister Ahmed Zaki Yamani, who once said, "The Stone Age did not come to an end for lack of stones, and the oil age will not come to an end for lack of oil."[42] What it will take is vision. "Progress is not foreordained," says Tarpenning. "It is created by people."[43]

The founders of Tesla have proven it.

"If you get up in the morning and think the future is going to be better, it is a bright day," Elon Musk says. "Otherwise, it's not."[44]

CHAPTER 9

Prosperity: The King of Microfinance

As long as poverty, injustice and gross inequality persist in our world, none of us can truly rest.

– Nelson Mandela

Nobel Peace Prize winner Muhammad Yunus at a summit hosted by the University of Salford, May 2013 (University of Salford Press Office, CC BY 2.0)

From Loaner to Laureate

On a frigid evening in December 2006, Muhammad Yunus walked jubilantly up the red carpet into Oslo City Hall and waved to the cheering crowds. It was the 105th anniversary of the Nobel Prize, and hundreds of dignitaries, government officials, and royals had already made their entrance, along with nine women from the villages of Bangladesh.

The excitement was palpable as Yunus made his way to the dais, with their Majesties the King and Queen of Norway following shortly behind. Wearing a tan *kurta* and matching *salwar* trousers, he smiled as he looked out at the attendees, who were there to award him the prestigious Nobel Peace Prize for pioneering the concepts of microcredit and microfinance. In large part because of his lending program, Bangladesh's poverty rate had dropped by more than 10 percent since Yunus launched his venture.[1] All told, the World Bank estimates that millions of people are either direct or indirect beneficiaries of the economic platform he brought to life.[2] Yunus had proven that even the poorest of the poor, unable to qualify for traditional bank loans, have the ability to work to bring about their own development.

"I firmly believe that we can create a poverty-free world if we collectively believe in it," he told the crowd. "We can put poverty in the museums."[3] The auditorium rose to its feet.

"I can't believe that this has really happened," the laureate said as he made his way off the stage.[4]

If receiving such an honor seemed implausible to Yunus, it would have been entirely inconceivable to him as the young and disillusioned economics professor who had set out thirty years earlier to try something different to alleviate poverty. What's even more incredible is that the world-changing financial system he eventually sparked started out with a simple bamboo stool.

A Step Up

It was 1976 when Yunus first walked into Jobra, a multiethnic village in southern Bangladesh where Muslims, Hindus, and Buddhists live side by side. The country was still reeling from the impact of a famine that had begun two years earlier, and the head of Chittagong University's economics program was at a professional crossroads. Since his return from the United States, where he completed his PhD at Vanderbilt University, Yunus had seen too many dead bodies, and too many of his countrymen "simply lay down very quietly on our doorsteps, wait[ing] to die."[5]

Yunus had begun to dread his own lectures. "What good were all my complex theories," he asked himself, "when people were dying of starvation on the sidewalks and porches across from my lecture hall?"[6] Nothing he was teaching was making a difference. The poor kept getting poorer, and life was getting worse for the majority of Bangladeshis.

"I needed to run away from these theories and from my textbooks and discover the real-life economics of a poor person's existence," he recalls. "To become a fugitive from academic life."[7]

To create a rural economic assistance program that actually worked, Yunus knew he would have to become a student all over again. "The people of Jobra would be my professors," he decided.[8]

To better understand the root of the poverty cycle, the young academic began visiting the poorest households in Jobra and spending time with the villagers. One morning, he stopped at a house with crumbling mud walls, where he saw a woman squatting on the dirt floor, gripping a half-finished bamboo stool between her knees. The mother of three was twenty-one-year-old Sufiya Begum, whose fingers were black and callused from her daily work turning strands of cane into Bengali mudda stools.

Sufiya told him she survived almost entirely on credit. She would buy five taka (about twenty-two cents) worth of raw materials from a *paikar* middleman and repay the loan by giving him finished stools. Yunus was stunned to learn that her income worked out to fifty poisha a day, or about two cents.

To acquire materials, Sufiya and the other villagers also had the option of going to local moneylenders, who were more than happy to dole out usurious loans. They charged anywhere from 10 percent a week to 10 percent a day. In every scenario, the poor would eke out a meager subsistence and almost certainly remain impoverished for the rest of their lives. Neither Sufiya nor her children were likely to ever break the cycle. Her kids didn't go to school, and Yunus couldn't see how Sufiya would ever be able to shelter, clothe, or feed them properly. "It seemed hopeless to imagine that her babies would one day escape this misery," he recalls.[9]

"I was angry," he says. "Angry at myself, angry at the economics department and the thousands of intelligent professors who had not tried to address this problem and solve it."[10] The professor was convinced that Sufiya's children would be condemned to a life of hand-to-mouth survival and penury, and that her income would be kept so low that she'd never be able to save or expand her economic base. Moneylenders made sure that their borrowers paid a price that barely covered the cost of the materials, earning them just enough to stay alive. Sufiya was living as a bonded laborer, but she might as well have been a slave. "It seemed impossible to me, preposterous," he says.[11]

Yunus wondered whether he should just reach into his pocket and give Sufiya the small amount of money she needed. "That would be so simple, so easy," he says. "But I resisted the urge."[12] Giving her money wouldn't address the root of the problem, and Sufiya wasn't asking for charity.

The professor made a list of the forty-two villagers who were dependent on moneylenders and tallied up how much each of them needed to buy their raw materials. "My god, my god," he said, as he calculated the modest figure that would help them shake the yolk of exploitation. "All this misery in all these families for the lack of twenty-seven dollars."[13]

Sufiya and those like her weren't poor because they were lazy or stupid. They worked long days full of tremendous physical exertion. But traditional financial structures weren't set up to provide the credit they needed. If Yunus personally lent the twenty-seven dollars to the villagers of Jobra, they could sell their products to anyone and get the highest return for their labor. They wouldn't be suffocated by the usurious rates they were being charged, and they could repay the traders and keep the profits themselves. He distributed the loans and told the villagers to pay him back whenever they could, with no interest.

From Untouchable to Huggable

The next day Yunus got into his white Volkswagen Beetle and drove to a local branch of the government-owned Janata Bank, Bangladesh's largest financial institution. He knew that for his plan to work on a larger scale, he would need to charge interest, and a bank would ultimately need to act as his partner in lending money to the poor. As Yunus explained his vision, the bank's manager laughed and listed all the reasons it wouldn't work, including the fact that preparing the documentation alone would cost more than the loan itself. "The bank is not going to waste its time on such a pittance,"[14] the manager told him. Besides, the people would need to be literate in order to fill out the forms and sign them, and the bank would need collateral, which the most destitute would almost certainly not have.

Yunus wasn't just up against the Janaa Bank, but rather the entire banking system, which was set up to service only those with money. "Poverty is not created by the poor," Yunus says, "but by the institutions built and the policies adopted."[15] Yunus continued to push, and after six months of haggling with the bank's head office in Dhaka, the loan was finally formalized in January 1977. The bank agreed to lend his project three hundred dollars, as long as he acted as the guarantor. Yunus and his colleagues would distribute the loans to Jobra's "banking untouchables" personally, in order to spare them the indignity of dealing with the bank, which required Yunus to sign for each and every request.

Out of a strong desire to solve a real-world problem, Yunus had cast aside the most central premise of banking – collateral – and become a moneylender himself. He had no idea what he was getting himself into. But he knew he needed to take his untouchables and make them "touchable, even huggable."[16]

Over the next two years, he planted the seeds of what would become an entirely new economic system. "I tried a great number of things," Yunus recalls. "Some worked. Others did not."[17] To his great surprise, over 98 percent of his initial loans would come to be repaid, a rate that far exceeded those backed by secured assets. And, as Yunus puts it, what started out as an attempt "to relieve my guilt and satisfy my desire to be useful to a few starving human beings" soon became much more.[18] By 1979, he had established Grameen Bank, which means "rural" or "village" in Bangla – "the bank for the poor."

After studying the loan operations of other banks, Yunus made it his mission not to repeat their mistakes. Grameen does not require borrowers to put up collateral for a loan, nor does it ask them to sign legal documents, since it does not want to take anyone to court.[19] "We have no guarantee, no references, no legal instrument," says Yunus, "and still it works. It defies all the conventional wisdom."[20]

Yunus also did away with the lump-sum payment most banks require at the end of a loan period. He felt this was psychologically trying for borrowers, who often try to delay repayment as long as they can – as the loan grows bigger and bigger – leading a significant percentage to eventually give up on paying it back. It also leads borrowers and bankers to ignore problems as they arise, in the hopes that they will go away as the loan is due.

To solve this problem, Yunus implemented a weekly repayment

program. The loan payments were so small that borrowers would not miss the money. And to make things extremely simple, loans were paid back fully after one year. So if you borrowed 365 taka (about sixteen dollars), you repaid at a rate of one taka a day (about four cents).

Seeing how crucial support groups were to success, Yunus required each loan applicant to join a group of like-minded individuals with similar economic and social circumstances. The groups not only provided succor, they also made borrowers much more reliable – because of peer pressure. All members had to approve the loan requests of the others in the group, building in a collective moral responsibility.

"The underlying genius of Yunus's model is the premise that relationships matter and provide a critical form of collateral," says Brown University professor Andrew Foster. "You are far less likely to fleece your friends and family, which helps ensure borrowers pay back their loans."[21]

One of the reasons Grameen's system works is that it requires the groups to form – and manage – themselves. A prospective borrower must take initiative and explain the way the bank works to a second individual, often a friend or family member who might be terrified or skeptical, or forbidden by a husband to deal with money in the first place. Those two courageous people then work together to find a third, fourth, and fifth person to join them. The group of five presents itself to the bank, and loans are initially given to just two members. If these loans are paid regularly over the next six weeks, two more members get their loans. And only after all four of those loans perform as expected for another six weeks does the fifth member of the group get his or her loan.

It takes anywhere from a few days to several months for a group to be certified by Grameen, and only after all of its members undergo seven days of training on the bank's policies and pass an oral exam.

Applicants know that if they fail, they aren't just letting themselves down, but the entire group.

The same pressure applies when the group receives their loans. If a borrower can't or won't repay a loan, the whole group becomes ineligible for larger loans until repayment is made or a program is put in place to remediate the issue. While there is no joint liability – the repayment responsibility rests solely on the individual borrower – the group helps to ensure no one defaults.

Every group is also required to build up a special savings account they can access if they encounter hard times, or even in the event they see an additional revenue opportunity. Each borrower deposits 5 percent of his or her loan into this general fund, and any member of the group may take an interest-free loan from it, provided all members approve, and it doesn't exceed half the reserve's total amount. Year after year, these group funds are used for seasonal malnutrition, medical bills, school supplies, natural disaster relief, and dignified family burials.

But the group also has an additional fail-safe measure. Up to eight borrower groups form what's called a "center," a loose federation that meets once a week with a bank employee. It is during these meetings that all the loan repayments and deposits are made. A center chief is elected by all members to solve any problems the groups are unable to solve themselves. And by design, the meetings happen in the open, reducing corruption, mismanagement, and misunderstandings. They also keep Grameen workers, the center chief, and the group chairperson accountable to the borrowers.

The group structure is not without its critics, who argue that the process intimidates borrowers. But Yunus maintains the practice ensures that only those who are the most needy and serious step forward. "We want only courageous, ambitious pioneers in our microcredit program," he says. "Those are the ones who will succeed."[22]

A vast majority – 97 percent – of those pioneers happen to be female.[23] Prior to the establishment of Grameen, women represented less than 1 percent of all Bangladeshi borrowers, primarily because traditional banks excluded them entirely. Yunus saw that women – with the most insecure social standing in Bangladesh and around the world – experience poverty and hunger far more acutely than men. But he also found that they tend to adapt quicker, perform more consistently, pay more attention, and work harder to lift themselves out of poverty. Grameen operates on the premise that the more credit women receive, the faster society can change.

One Poisha at a Time

By 1982, just three years after Grameen launched, the bank had grown from five hundred initial borrowers to twenty-eight thousand and dispersed roughly $25 million. By 1999, that number jumped to $190 million, with a near-perfect repayment record. And by the time Yunus received his Nobel Prize in 2006, Grameen had dispersed close to $8 billion, of which $7.16 had been repaid, with $720 million in outstanding loans. Today, Grameen has distributed more than $20 billion to at least eight million people, most of whom are women, in over one hundred countries around the world. The repayment rate is still 98 percent.[24]

"The Nobel Committee summed it up well when they said that loans to poor people without any financial security had appeared to be an impossible idea," says economist Christian Ahlin. "Yunus trailblazed an unforeseen explosion in access to formal credit throughout the developing world."[25]

With more than twenty-five hundred branches serving around eighty-five thousand Bangladeshi villages, and a staff of almost twenty-five thousand people, Yunus's bank for the poor has been a driving force in making a meaningful dent in his county's poverty rate. More than 68 percent of Grameen borrowers and their families have crossed the poverty line.[26]

Around the world, at least 1.9 billion people lived in extreme poverty in 1990. By 2020, that number had shrunk to 705 million – meaning every single day for the last thirty years, at least 105,000 people crossed over the poverty line.[27] Many of them leveraged microfinance programs to build better lives for themselves and their families.[28] The sector as a whole now has a combined portfolio of at least $124 billion in loans.[29] And according to Bangladeshi World Bank economist Shahidur R. Khandker, more than two hundred million people are either direct or indirect beneficiaries of microfinance programs today.[30]

In terms of sheer impact, Brown University's Mark Pitt compares Yunus to Ghandi. "On the one hand full of wisdom, and on the other super practical. As an economist, he created a well-thought-out, brilliant program to meet head-on a failure in the credit markets for the most underserved segments of society."[31]

From across the political divide, the development industry has for the most part adopted Yunus's vision. Though critics like the University of San Francisco's Bruce Wydick argue that microfinance is "far from the poverty elixir its advocates touted it to be"[32] – not to mention that measuring the direct impact of such programs is difficult – most economists now conclude that they produce broad positive effects, raise wages, encourage entrepreneurialism, and promote human flourishing. And at the very least, but perhaps most importantly, they provide a desperate segment of the population with a liquidity tool to ride out periods of instability or a sudden shock to their income, which can often pose a greater threat than low income itself.

"There is no silver bullet to completely eradicate poverty," says Tufts economist Cynthia Kinnan. "But Yunus and Grameen proved that microcredit could successfully bring financial access to millions of poor households. And we now have evidence that, for talented but low-wealth entrepreneurs, short-term access to credit can indeed unlock their escape from a 'poverty trap,' where low incomes can be self-perpetuating."[33]

By necessity, Grameen is operated as a for-profit institution, and it has turned a profit in all but three of its thirty years in existence (the exceptions were 1983, 1991, and 1992). It now offers the same products traditional banks do, including dividends to its owners and interest rate loans – 20 percent for income-generating loans, 8 percent for housing loans, 5 percent for student loans, and interest-free loans for the impoverished – plus generous deposit rates of 8.5–12 percent. But Grameen pursues profit as a double bottom line: the social purpose is paramount, and the business efficiency is a means to an end, not an end unto itself.

Still, Grameen requires subsidies on a continuing basis and relies on the generosity of donors and socially conscious investors. Studies show that microfinance programs that target the poorest borrowers generate sufficient revenue to cover about 70 percent of their full costs.[34] Timothy Ogden, managing director of the Financial Access Initiative, a research center based at NYU, warns that the microcredit industry itself could be threatened unless investors and international organizations continue to subsidize it. But that just might be the cost of helping the poor. "The sacrifice that social investors make could take many forms, including lower or zero returns compared to alternative investments, higher risk, longer timeframes, or less liquidity," Ogden says.[35]

However microfinance evolves in the future, Yunus has built an enduring platform on the idea that getting credit is a human right, and that all human beings, including the poorest, are endowed with endless potential.[36] He's hoping to someday reach the estimated one billion potential micro-borrowers across the globe, but he's already improved the lives of millions.

When Yunus stepped off the stage that night in Oslo, he looked over at one of those people, Taslima Begun, a Bangladeshi housewife turned entrepreneur who was also awarded the Nobel Prize. She took her first loan in 1992 for fifteen hundred taka (about sixty-five dollars) to buy a goat, spun that into a *mishuk* (motorized rickshaw) business and a thriving watch store, and is now a member of Grameen's board.[37]

"My parents gave me birth," she said. "But Grameen Bank gave me a life."[38]

CHAPTER 10
Food: Green Meat

How many things, too, are looked upon as quite
impossible, until they have been actually effected?

– Pliny the Elder, *Natural History*

Beyond Meat CEO Ethan Brown,
2019 (Steve Jurvetson, CC BY 2.0)

Meat and Human Evolution

Twenty years ago, Tel Aviv University archeologists discovered a small cave in the Samarian foothills that completely upended our understanding of human evolution. Located near the Afek Industrial Park, where many modern-day Israelis work in tech, it contained the remains of Paleolithic-era *Homo sapiens* that lived in the area over 200,000 years ago. Geological shifts had sealed the underground limestone cavern shut, where the secrets of Qassem Cave remained lost to the world until construction workers widened a highway in 2001.

The inhabitants of the cave appeared to be the world's first industrial workers, producing thousands of knives and other tools for a mass-production line used for butchering and ultimately eating deer. Evidence suggests that these prehistoric humans stored bone marrow and consumed it as needed. Archeologists concluded that our human ancestors were engaged in nothing short of a robust food innovation business.

The story of human evolution has always been intimately tied to the consumption of meat. Using fire to cook animals gave humans more energy, which led to larger brains and bigger bodies. This shift produced increasingly sophisticated hominids and transformed our ancestors from scavengers into hunters. As a species, we are designed to love meat. Sociologists believe that when early humans came back from hunts with prey, they danced. This model worked well for millions of years and provided the necessary calories to grow the human race into the roughly 7.9 billion we number today. Over the last few centuries, as our population increased exponentially, we have leveraged science and technology to get more food output per acre and more meat per species of livestock. But feeding the modern world is a problem that is growing more complex – and dire – by the day.

Research now shows a direct correlation between animal protein consumption and epidemics of cancer and diabetes.[1] Medical evidence also suggests that eating a diet rich in red meat triples the levels of chemicals linked to heart disease.[2] But more urgently, meat production is currently responsible for 18 percent of the planet's greenhouse gas emissions – and takes up 70 percent of our arable lands. Each year, more than seventy billion chickens, pigs, cattle, and other livestock are slaughtered globally for human consumption. The toll that takes on our natural resources is devastating: it takes approximately fifteen hundred gallons of water to produce a single pound of meat. And as the population increases to approximately ten billion by 2050, the human demand for meat will double, along with the ramifications.

Google founder Sergei Brin, who has invested millions in both commercial and nonprofit ventures that empower social entrepreneurs to take on climate change, has suggested three possible outcomes for the human race when it comes to meat: we can do nothing and suffer continued environmental damage; we can all become vegetarians or use vegetable-based protein alternatives; or we can produce meat from cells rather than raise entire animals.[3]

Humans will not need to make a binary decision on whether to eat or abandon meat. But we will need to consider the origin of our meat. If we choose poultry, pigs, and cows, then our choices are limited. If, on the other hand, we choose to define meat by its composition and chemical structure – amino acids, lipids, trace minerals, vitamins, and water made to taste, feel, and look like meat – then we have unlimited innovative solutions.

For now, 75 percent of our food system is based on just twelve plants and five animals, which experts say is nothing short of a global crisis. "For the human race to survive," says Scott May, head of MISTA, an innovation platform for the food industry that was launched by Givaudan, "we must remove the large-scale animal practices while increasing biodiversity sooner rather than later."[4]

Ethan Brown, the founder of Beyond Meat, wants to do it with science.

"People love meat, and we've been consuming meat since before we were human," Brown says. "So I think the fix here is technological. We bypass the animal, agriculture's greatest bottleneck."[5]

High Steaks

There is nothing new about veggie burgers. The first commercial veggie burger was sold in a natural foods restaurant in London in 1982.[6] But these patties are infamous both for being tasteless and for having a strange texture.

Ethan Brown used to eat his favorite Double R Bar Burgers from Roy Rogers as often as he could get them, but around the time he turned thirteen, he started to lose his appetite for beef. His father owned and operated a dairy farm in rural western Maryland,[7] and Brown became attached to the livestock. "I can just remember thinking: 'This is like an orgy of animals I am eating,'" he says. "I started to feel different about it."[8]

Brown embarked on an intellectual and emotional journey that eventually led him to take up veganism and adopt Hinduism's deep respect for all living creatures. He came to believe that the human tendency to see ourselves as starkly different from the rest of life on the earth wasn't just convenient, but incredibly harmful. "You can't sort of say 'us-them' in a scientific way," he says. "The reason that you think that way is because you want to create something that is separate, because it's easier to exploit."[9]

Brown was deeply influenced by his father, Peter Brown, a geography and government professor who also owned a dairy farm as a hobby.[10] The elder Brown's primary area of focus is how humanity has contributed to the deterioration of the earth's life support capacity.[11] When Brown graduated from Connecticut College in 1994, his father asked him what he wanted to do with his life. Brown said he didn't really know. "Well, what's the biggest problem facing the world?" his father asked.

"Climate," Brown responded. "If we don't get climate right, nothing else matters."[12]

Brown enrolled at Columbia University to pursue a master's in business administration, then got a job at Ballard, a Canadian company that develops fuel cells, where he worked on developing a proton-exchange membrane that promised to help curb climate change.[13] But over time, Brown says he is becoming increasingly dumbfounded by the fact that the meat industry, not automobiles or power plants, is actually the single largest contributor to greenhouse gas emissions around the world.[14] "At these big conferences, MBAS and engineers would go on and on about fuel cells, and then go out and have a steak," he says.[15]

Brown invested in Worthington Foods, a company that had a significant ownership stake in Morningstar Farms, best known for its veggie burgers. Brown also started thinking about the kind of plant-based venture that would appeal to a mainstream fast-food consumer. "I wanted to create the whole thing," he says. "I wanted to prove that you could do it."[16]

Though his friends and family were skeptical, after eight years at Ballard, Brown quit to start a company that would create "meat" directly from plants. "Here was a chance to change the world," he says, by tackling the issues of climate change, natural-resource depletion, human health, and animal welfare with a single product. "It wasn't brilliant foresight," Brown likes to remind people. "It was being unable to tolerate not doing it."[17]

Prius for the Plate

Per pound, beef is far and away the largest single contributor to the world's greenhouse gases, producing seven times as much as the equivalent amount of chicken – and sixty times as much as peas.[18] Consuming less of it would mean less demand on land, feed crops, and water supplies. But the typical veggie burger was never going to appeal to beef's mass audience. The traditional stand-in for the meat-averse simply couldn't replicate the hamburger experience. With only 5 percent of the US population keeping a vegetarian diet, Brown understood that he'd need a different path to go after the trillion-dollar US meat and poultry market.[19] He identified three potential avenues: lab-grown meat, in vitro meat, or developing a process that used plant protein to make food taste and feel like real meat. Brown thought the latter would be the most palatable to consumers.[20]

"The thing that I think most people didn't capture that well is that meat is a completely knowable entity. You can unpack it. You can figure out what's in it. You can analyze it to death," says Brown. "And so, to do that and rebuild it was the approach."[21]

Brown started by investing in a vegan restaurant that served textured soy protein from Taiwan. The establishment did so well – even attracting a non-vegetarian consumer base – that he opened a business in Maryland importing the faux meat from Taiwan. He made one of his first deals with Whole Foods to distribute it throughout the mid-Atlantic region.[22]

But Brown knew that textured protein was never going to fool anyone into believing they were eating real meat. So he began looking for a substitute that had the same taste and consistency and came across researchers from the University of Missouri who were claiming amazing results. In 2009, he set up a visit and got a first glimpse at the technology that would eventually become the heart and soul of his company, Beyond Meat.

Food science professor Fu-Hung Hsieh and researcher Harold Huff had managed to transform powdery pea protein isolate and soy protein into something that tasted like fibrous protein. Using a sophisticated piece of equipment called an extruder, which is something like a pressure cooker crossed with a food processor, dry ingredients are mixed with water, kneaded and heated, then pushed through a specially designed cooling process that realigns the food's protein molecules in ways that give them a texture that closely resembles meat.[23] "It's never about taste," says Huff. "It always about fibrous structure. Mouthfeel is everything."[24]

Hsieh and Huff did everything they could think of to manipulate the moisture, pressure, and temperature of various ingredients to get the texture right. After making some significant progress, they began showing their product to a wide variety of individuals, including Ethan Brown. Luckily for Brown, he was the only entrepreneur who clearly saw the market potential and started the long process that eventually took Hsieh and Huff's food to local supermarkets.

The following year, Brown exhausted every resource he had to license the technology and launch Beyond Meat.[25] He started by sending emails to Silicon Valley venture capital firms, calling his pitch the "Prius for the Plate," but only got a few replies. "My inbox wasn't exploding," he jokes.[26]

There was no shortage of doubters and potential investors who thought the idea was "bizarre" or "gross." He'd respond by asking, "Have you ever seen how a piece of meat is made?"[27]

In the Wilderness

Eventually, he got a response from Raymond Lane, a partner at Kleiner Perkins, one of Silicon Valley's premiere venture capital firms. To satisfy his curiously, Lane got onto his private jet and flew out to Columbia, Missouri. When he tasted Brown's food, "It had a texture and a fiber that was meat-like," Lane recalls. "And then as I took the product and tore it apart it looked like chicken."[28]

Lane was sold, but he had to persuade his firm to invest. They had reservations about the food market and Brown's lack of experience. "There were all sorts of skeptics about doing this," Lane recalls.[29] But in April 2011, Kleiner Perkins invested $2 million.

Twitter cofounders Biz Stone and Evan Williams were also interested. "My first thought was, 'Oh boy, some kind of hippie guy who is going to preach about how mean eating animals is,'" says Stone, who's a vegetarian himself, of their first meeting with Brown.[30] After questioning Brown, they were impressed with his business experience and his strategy to get into supermarkets and restaurants. They decided to invest. "This was no novelty food thing that was going to go into the freezer section next to the silly products," says Stone. "This was a guy who from the beginning was saying, 'We are going to be in McDonald's.'"[31]

Eventually, other big players joined in, including Taiwan's Tsai family, Morgan Creek Capital, DNS Capital, and Honest Tea founder Seth Goldman. But at that point, money was still tight. Brown had already run through his 401K and savings accounts, and even sold one of his houses. "I was in the wilderness," Brown says. "For a couple of years, it was everything going into it. There is a lot of collateral damage that goes along with that."[32]

When Brown traveled to pitch Bill Gates, who eventually invested in Beyond Meat, he had a hard time paying for his hotel room, having maxed out his credit cards.

But that same year, Beyond Meat released its first product at Whole Foods: chicken strips. Bill Gates wrote a blog post about his experience eating a Beyond Meat chicken taco: "The 'meat' was made entirely of plants. And yet, I couldn't tell the difference. What I was experiencing was more than a clever meat substitute. It was a taste of the future of food."[33]

The company went on to introduce precooked frozen burgers and eventually their signature burger made from peas. And by 2016, Beyond had a giant breakthrough: Whole Foods decided to sell Beyond Burgers in the meat section. In short order, other major food retail stores followed suit. By now it was clear: Brown's products were not just speaking to vegans. Mainstream consumers were finally ready.

Is it Fake or Real?

Today, Beyond's products are available in over nineteen thousand retail stores and restaurants, to the tune of $250 million in annual revenue. The Beyond Burger can be found in the meat sections of more than five thousand grocery stores and on the menus of over four thousand hotels, college cafeterias, and restaurants, including TGI Fridays, Bareburger, Beggie Grill, and BurgerFi.[34] Brown wants to eventually rival JBS, one of the world's largest meat processors with $45 billion in revenue. "Our ambition is to literally be in every major continent changing the way people eat," he says.[35]

Every day, Beyond tests and develops products in its food lab in El Segundo California, called the Manhattan Beach Project Innovation Center. (Brown liked the atomic allusion.) The lab's scientists have made it their mission to take plants and transform them into burgers, sausages, and chicken that taste exactly like the real thing – with a significantly smaller environmental footprint and no cholesterol.

"Not only are food innovators trying to build a new kind of rocket ship to take us someplace that we have never been before," says culinary scientist Ali Bouzari, "but we are also trying to turn that vehicle into a Honda Civic and bring it to the mass market in a few years. It is the food industry's version of SpaceX."[36]

A recent study by the University of Michigan showed that the Beyond Burger generates 90 percent less greenhouse gas emissions and requires 46 percent less energy to produce than a beef burger.[37] They also need less water and land to produce.

In 2019, Beyond Meat went public, and shortly after, McDonald's announced that the company would be its Canadian plant-based burger supplier.[38] That same year, Dunkin' introduced its Beyond breakfast patty.[39] And as demand for meat alternatives increases across the industry, more and more food providers are either using Beyond products or adopting their own. Burger King has experienced record sales with one of Beyond Meat's largest competitors, Impossible Burger. Nestlé is trying to compete with its Awesome Burger.[40]

If Brown is right, in the not-too-distant future we will be able to buy plant-based burgers from most supermarkets and food establishments. "The consumer is turning so quickly," says Brown. "Once we break the code and get to the point where it's indistinguishable from animal protein, I think you will see that shift."[41]

"This is the first time in human history we are literally building food from the bottom up," says Nir Goldstein, managing director of Israel's Good Food Institute. "And this is just the beginning."[42]

For now, plant-based protein represents what Rusty Schwartz of food-innovation incubator KitchenTown calls "the tip of the spear for disrupting the meat industry."[43] And the industry has taken notice. In a tactic reminiscent of the milk industry's efforts to derail the exploding popularity of nut-based beverages, Big Meat is on the attack, lobbying for regulatory changes to ban the labeling of plant-based burgers as "meat." One meat industry–backed nonprofit called the Center for Consumer Freedom recently launched a national marketing campaign. "Fake meats grow on vines," reads one of its newspaper ads. "They're ultra-processed imitations that are assembled in industrial factories."[44]

Brown, for his part, is fighting back. "The automobile is not a fake horse-drawn carriage," he says. "It's just plain meat. We are building it from the same stuff, so we should be able to call it meat."[45] And to detractors who argue that burgers made by companies like Beyond Meat have larger carbon footprints than traditional veggie burgers, Brown has an easy answer. "How many people are eating black-bean burgers?" he asks. "That is like taking a Tesla, which does have a good environmental outcome relative to an internal combustion engine, and comparing it to a bike. It's just not relevant."[46]

If capitalism is a relentless march toward efficiency, the meat industry has plenty of cause for concern. "Plant-based protein and 'clean' meat is without a doubt the future," says vegan advocate and CEO of data. World Brett Hurt. "We can save our planet's most precious resources at one tenth the cost – without giving up taste."[47]

CHAPTER 11
Water: Every Last Drop

When the well is dry, they know the worth of water.

– Benjamin Franklin, *Poor Richard's Almanack*, 1746

Burst water main (Richard Webb, CC BY-SA 2.0)

No Magic

On a cloudless summer afternoon in 2014, UCLA students heading to class were met with the terrifying sound of rushing water. Just before 3:30 p.m., a ninety-year-old water pipe ruptured, creating a thirty-foot geyser that was disgorging thirty-five thousand gallons per minute onto Sunset Boulevard. Firefighters arrived at the scene within minutes and used inflatable boats to save at least five stranded people. The school's storied athletic facility, Pauley Pavilion, was flooded, and parts of campus were unrecognizable. Hundreds of cars were abandoned in underground parking lots as water cascaded down stairs, and some students resorted to getting around on body boards. Emergency responders spent hours looking for the right valves to shut off.

While they did, about ten million gallons of water were lost during the worst drought in the city's history.[1]

Jim McDaniel of the Los Angeles Department of Water and Power later explained that the city is on a three-hundred-year replacement cycle for water main lines, and that there's "no magic" technology to determine when new lines are needed. "Every city that has aging infrastructure has issues like this and we're no exception," he said.[2]

But halfway around the world in Israel, a man named Amir Peleg had already designed such a software system. Called TaKaDu, it employs algorithms and statistical analysis to identify problems like leaks and burst pipes in real time, using data to revolutionize the efficiency and maintenance of water utility infrastructure.

Passing the Water Buck

More than two billion people currently lack access to safe drinking water, and by 2025, at least half the world's population is expected to be living in water-stressed areas.[3] The entire Middle East is headed toward massive water shortages, which in some places will likely lead to disaster of biblical proportions. The United Nations predicts that Egypt will approach a state of "absolute water crisis" in just a few years;[4] Jordan is set to run out of potable water in a matter of decades, and Iranian government officials project that in fewer than twenty-five years, over half the country's population will need to be relocated as water refugees.[5] In Iraq, engineers warn that the Mosul Dam could collapse at any minute, killing 1.5 million people.

According to the World Resources Institute, a global nonprofit that focuses on sustainable development, the crisis is the result of a confluence of issues, from climate change and its effects on a region's aridity to water demand, depleted groundwater, poor water infrastructure, lack of healthy ecosystems, water waste management, and the rising price of water.[6]

Many will be surprised to learn that the trend also holds true for the United States. According to the US Government Accountability Office, over the next ten years, forty states will have at least one region with a water shortage due to the lack of fresh water in lakes, rivers, reservoirs, and aquifers. And in just four years, at least a third of US households will lack potable water.[7] America's water and wastewater bills have increased by more than 30 percent in the last ten years, rising faster than inflation,[8] in large part because rising energy and transportation costs have made repairing and renewing pipes much more expensive. And as the price of water increases, millions of Americans will be unable to pay their water bills.[9]

The United States has approximately 1.6 million miles of water and sewer pipes that are, on average, forty-five years old – with many installed more than a century ago, and at least ten million made of lead that contaminates our water.[10] There are now more than seven hundred water main breaks in the United States every day.[11]

Americans are generally unaware that most of their water utility companies either lose money or barely break even. Between government subsidies and household water bills, water providers collect just enough revenue to conduct their business and handle ongoing problems. According to a recent study by Michigan State's Elizabeth Mack, utility companies are now spending approximately 80 percent of their revenue to maintain infrastructure that was built primarily in the 1930s and 1940s.[12] Mack estimates that updating aging infrastructure will cost over $1 trillion over the next twenty-five years, and that water prices will increase to four times their current levels.

Around the world, there are approximately 250,000 water utility authorities locked in the very same battle with leaks and burst pipes. They often don't discover the problem for days or weeks – if they do at all – or until the leak causes a rupture, impacting homes and businesses and electrical and telecommunications equipment underground, compounding the cost of water even more. Water authorities use a variety of methods to detect leaks, including fiber-optic cables, radar, and physical inspection crews that use listening sticks and acoustic loggers. But these efforts are generally futile, and the highest costs are actually associated with round-the-clock staffing to ensure continuity of service.

"Ninety-nine times out of a hundred, water authorities have traditionally relied on their customers to tell them there is a problem," says Tony Kelly, former CEO of the Yara Valley Water authority in Melbourne, Australia. "And ultimately, it is the consumer that pays the price for this kind of inefficiency."[13]

When water does not reach its customers, it is referred to as non-revenue water, or NRW. Experts believe that 25 to 30 percent of the world's water supply – which could otherwise be used to drink, shower, and irrigate – is NRW lost to distribution, costing about $14 billion annually.[14] The status quo, according to Kelly, isn't just uneconomical – it is unacceptable.

The Mega Problem

In 2008, Israel's Amir Peleg decided to do something about it. A self-described serial entrepreneur with a passion for data analytics, Peleg had already launched and sold three successful companies by the age of forty-two, including Elbit Vision Systems, which specialized in quality-control technology for fabric manufacturing; Cash-U, which focused on the mobile gaming industry; and YaData, a behavior-based digital marketing firm that was acquired by Microsoft. As Israel's drought problems worsened, the Hebrew University of Jerusalem graduate had grown increasingly interested in clean tech. "Israel is scarce of water so we are taught to appreciate it," Peleg says. "I didn't find many companies dealing with innovative water technologies."[15]

Peleg didn't know much about the industry, so he began reading voraciously on the subject and following global corporations investing in the field. One of the companies he did find looking into IT solutions for water utilities was IBM. "If a company like IBM believes in this market," Peleg thought, "there must be something there."[16] He cold-called Peter Williams, then the chief technology officer of IBM's Big Green Innovations, which was set up to tackle environmental problems. "We got along right from the start," Williams recalls. "He is your typical hard-charging driven character and wanted to get things done."[17]

Peleg also formed a relationship with Oded Distel, then the director of the Israel NewTech program at the Ministry of Economy and Industry. "At the time, Peleg only had a vague notion of how he wanted to revolutionize the water industry," Distel says. "I knew I wanted to help him achieve his vision and help guide him to become the new poster boy of saving one of the most important resources on the planet."[18]

Peleg had identified what he saw as a "mega problem" in a very global market.[19] "Water authorities are collecting data, but they aren't doing anything with it," he realized.[20] These entities have sensors on their pipes that measure water flow, pressure, quality, and many other important pieces of data, yet they were still losing so much of their treated water. Over time, he knew that water authorities would only increase the number of sensors they used, making data acquisition faster, cheaper, and more reliable. "The minute I understood a problem existed, that data is collected but not used, and that I could find people to work on the problem, I felt I had the makings of a new company," he says.[21]

In 2009, Peleg hired a few scientists and developed the software they needed, calling the new company TaKaDu. But the first problem they encountered was getting real data to test their algorithms.

Most water authorities they approached were deeply skeptical that data could be properly analyzed to yield actionable results.

Thanks to a phone call from Oded Distel, one company in Jerusalem decided to give them a chance. Distel set up a meeting with Aharon Rosenberg, chief technology officer of Hagihon, Israel's largest water utility, which services around one million people with 750 miles of pipes – on the promise that his colleague's company had a series of tools that could potentially change the way the water authority operated.

"How much will it cost me?" Rosenberg asked Peleg at their first meeting.

"Nothing," replied Peleg. "All I need from you is a CD-ROM with your data from the last year or two."[22] Peleg told him he would use unique algorithms and statistical tools to detect his leaks.

"Let's do it," said Rosenberg, burning the CD for him on the spot.[23]

High-Tech Plumbing

What Peleg's system discovered was astounding. Hagihon was losing a significant amount of water to people tapping into their network and stealing water. And TaKaDu pinpointed the exact location where the thieves were stealing it. His team was also able to identify the exact times and the general location of major burst pipes.

Eventually, more water companies got on board. "These utilities essentially said, 'If you can solve this problem, we're in,'" says Peleg. "'Here's our past data.'"[24]

TaKaDu's data analytics soon discovered that the UK's largest water authority, Thames Water, was losing 25 to 40 percent of its water to leaking pipes before it reached any of its fifteen million customers. Thanks to Peleg's system, they were now able to locate broken pipes in half the time. With the UK facing water shortages that the head of its Environment Agency has called the "jaws of death," the ability to curb the problem is critical.[25]

In Melbourne, the Yarra Valley Water utility, which serves over 700,000 customers with six thousand miles of pipes, was aware of the fact that they were losing about 13 percent of their water to leaky pipes. The managing director, Tony Kelly, was dubious about TaKaDu's ability to make any significant impact, but Peleg convinced him to give the software a chance in 2011. Yarra's pilot program with TaKaDu was able to detect large leaks two weeks faster than it was able to without it.

Over the next few years, Peleg's company started getting more paid clients, including Chile's Aguas de Antofagasta, a utility company that serves 100,000 customers in one of the earth's driest areas.

"We are very proud to be early adopters of the TaKaDu tools," says Marco Kutulas Peet, general manager of Aguas de Antofagasta, which became the first utility in Latin America to use the technology.[26] The Chilean utility increased the efficiency of its repair crews by 50 percent and doubled the amount of water saved with repairs.

TaKaDu software analyzes data collected by sensors located in a variety of places, including pipes, valves, and pumping stations. The challenge has always been what to do with all this information. If they've analyzed the data at all, many water companies have attempted to do so manually or through static algorithms. "This is a lot of information for people to stare at," says Peleg, "and [it] is very labor intensive."[27]

Peleg's system ingests data every fifteen minutes, stores it in the cloud, analyzes it, and compares it to historical data. It is able to detect any unusual activity and immediately classify what is happening, like the crucial difference between a leak, a burst, and a faulty meter. It has also evolved to become a full-blown operational platform that can detect and manage any incidents in a utility's network, including data problems, meter issues, and water quality control. It knows, for example, if an uptick in water usage is due to a national holiday, or if one part of the system is receiving less water because a crew is working on pipes and turned off certain valves. With a map-based user interface, water authorities using TaKaDu can see exactly where the potential issues are and deploy a fix. It also works as an early warning system, predicting adverse events and pinpointing parts of the physical infrastructure that need updating. In effect, Peleg says, TaKaDu has become "the eyes and ears" of water utility companies around the world. "I see myself as a high-tech plumber," he says.[28]

"Utilizing big data has yet to be universally adopted in the water industry," says Keith Hays, managing director of Bluefield Research, an independent water advisory firm. "What is inspiring about TaKaDu is that it is helping water authorities around the world get their act together in order to move from the twentieth century into the twenty-first."[29]

In the last decade, Peleg has secured water authorities in thirteen countries, including Australia, Brazil, Chile, Colombia, Finland, Holland, Israel, Peru, Romania, Spain, the United States, and Vietnam. The utilities using TaKaDu have reported a 30 to 40 percent drop in water loss. The company has since been named a "Technology Pioneer" by the World Economic Forum, "Company of the Year" for Europe and Israel by Bloomberg, and one of the top one hundred companies in the world by Global Cleantech.

"TaKaDu is playing a significant role around the world in helping countries curb the loss of water," says George Theo, CEO of Unitywater in Queensland, Australia.[30]

Christopher Gasson, publisher of Global Water Intelligence, agrees. "Digital systems like TaKaDu are completely changing how we find and stop leaks," he says. "They are making the invisible visible."[31] TaKaDu's reach is helping solve a local issue that when taken in the aggregate represents a massive global challenge.

Thanks to TaKaDu, water utilities can now be the first to detect the problem and proactively initiate repairs, greatly minimizing customer and community impacts. "Water isn't just water," says Seth

M. Siegel, water expert and author of *Let There Be Water*. "In the case of Israel, it's also an inspiring example of how vision and leadership can change a nation and transform the world."[32]

That vision was on full display in Mountain View, California, in 2014 when Governor Jerry Brown and Israeli prime minister Benjamin Netanyahu met to sign a monumental agreement that would transfer Israeli water technology to the Golden State to help mitigate its water crisis. At the time, 74 percent of the state was dealing with extreme drought. Israel, though 60 percent desert, had just announced that it had achieved water independence through smart planning and innovative thinking. No longer reliant on the weather – or its neighbors – for its water needs, Israel became a water superpower by charging users the real cost of water, desalinizing sea water, reusing treated sewage for agriculture, implementing drip irrigation techniques, and mandating that authorities actually spend 100 percent of all water and sewage fees on water and maintaining water infrastructure. And, of course, by using Peleg's software, which warns authorities about leaks, cutting waste by as much as 40 percent.

"California, I hear, has a big water problem," said Netanyahu after the signing. "We in Israel don't have a water problem. We use technology to solve it."[33]

CHAPTER 12

Governance: The Digital Republic

I should have called the Estonians when we were setting up our health care website.

– US President Barak Obama

Toomas Hendrik Ilves, President of Estonia, March 2016 (Chatham House, CC BY 2.0)

127

Leapfrogging: Analog to Digital

It was evening when Estonia declared independence from Mother Russia on August 20, 1991. Soviet tanks rolled through the country-side in an attempt to quell the movement. Paratroopers were on their way to the capital, Tallinn, to cut off the newly formed country's TV tower, which provided a critical means of communication with the population. Civilians and members of the Estonian Defense League, a paramilitary force, rushed to protect various strategic buildings, including the parliament and public broadcasting facilities. The Soviet military action failed, and within a few weeks, Boris Yeltsin's government recognized Estonian independence.[1]

Out from under the shadow of the Iron Curtain, the country's policymakers now vigorously debated how to supercharge the future of their citizens. After fifty years of Soviet occupation, much of the country's public infrastructure dated back to the 1930s, and fewer than half the country's homes had physical phone lines. As a first step, Estonia's leadership knew they had to find a seamless way to communicate with the outside world. They still had a rotary telephone exchange. Before World War II, Estonia's GDP per capita was roughly the same size as Finland's, but in the decades since, Estonians could only watch as their northern neighbors lapped them. Finland was implementing a digital phone network in Helsinki and as a beau geste offered its old 1970s analog telephone exchange to Tallinn. It would have covered all of Estonia's needs at no cost. But free isn't always free.

"I yelled and screamed and fought tooth and nail," recalls Estonia's then-ambassador to the United States and later president Toomas Hendrik Ilves. "We would be stuck with legacy technology."[2]

In a move that would set the stage for Estonia's remarkable reinvention in the decades that followed, then prime minister Maart Laar ultimately declined, knowing that his country's path to success would be tied to rapid technological advancement.[3] Despite the expense, Estonia decided to go with a digital phone exchange similar to Finland's.

With a small population – 1.3 million, about half the size of Silicon Valley – and a landmass roughly the size of Switzerland, the tiny satellite of the Soviet Union hadn't developed an international reputation for anything much beyond its lush forests, high literacy rates, and garlic bread. But in 1993, with the release of the original internet browser, Mosaic, Toomas Hendrik Ilves had two epiphanies: "Everyone," he intuitively felt, "was on a level playing field."[4] The world was now flat, and Estonia could compete at a global level. Ilves also read Jeremy Rifkin's *End of Work*, a book that described how automation put twelve hundred people out of work in a Kentucky steel mill and replaced them with just a hundred employees. Computerization, Rifkin believed, would significantly change the type of work humans did in the future.

Ilves understood that economic success no longer required an economy of scale. If his country played its cards right, the future president thought, Estonia could compete with the superpowers – or at the very least, much larger countries – and reinvent itself as "E-Stonia," a term he later coined.[5]

"From Kentucky's perspective, this was of course terrible," recalls Ilves. "But for Estonia, it was intriguing, because our fundamental existential angst is tied to our smallness."[6]

Ilves was a US citizen until he renounced his citizenship to become the Estonian ambassador to the United States,[7] and growing up in New Jersey, he learned how to code in high school. This deeply influenced his perspective on the role of schools and how to mold young minds. Two years after reading Rifkin's book, Ilves got together with the Estonian minister of education, and together they drew up a plan to computerize the country's school system. "We need to really computerize in every possible way," said Ilves, "to massively increase our functional size."[8]

By 1998, 100 percent of Estonian schools were online.[9] This kicked off a trend in Estonia to look for IT solutions where other countries couldn't or wouldn't because they were locked into legacy technology. "We leapfrogged developed countries that were still depreciating their huge investments in mainframes and couldn't adopt the new technologies as easily as we could," says Estonian IT visionary Linnar Viik.[10] Two years later, the government passed a law mandating internet access as a basic human right, propelling a series of events that fundamentally changed Estonian society.

In 2000, citizens could file their tax returns digitally for the first time. "We also had the additional sweetener that if you filled out your tax return online, you got your money back in a week," says Ilves. "If you did it on paper, it might take maybe three months."[11] Today, 99 percent of Estonians file their returns electronically.[12]

Free wi-fi soon became commonplace, and Estonia installed a widespread fiber-optic cable that reportedly gives citizens the fastest internet connection speeds in the world.[13] The government gave 10 percent of the adult population free computer training, and internet use increased from 29 percent of the population in 2000 to 91 percent in 2016.

Most people would be shocked to learn that Estonia is now the most advanced digital society in the world: the first country to permit online voting; to ensure all tax preparation and payments can be carried out seamlessly in minutes online; to guarantee health records are accessible from anywhere, anytime; to make starting a company as easy as clicking a button; and to teach every child how to code – starting at five years old. Everything from authenticated signatures to paying for parking, school fees, homework, government services, and tax preparation is connected on one digitally linked platform in the cloud using public internet.

"Politically and economically," says Viljar Lubi, deputy secretary general for economic development in the Ministry of Economic Affairs, "Estonia's goal is to become another rich, boring Nordic country."[14]

X Marks the Spot

In Estonia, the most important piece of infrastructure isn't a bridge or a highway – it's a digital network called X-Road. The dynamic platform allows information to be safely stored and exchanged online. Developed by the country's Information System Authority in conjunction with Cybernetica, an Estonian tech company, it resides on local individual servers with end-to-end encryption. Doctors, banks, and schools, for example, each might hold an individual's relevant data. "When a user requests a piece of information," explains journalist Nathan Heller, "it is delivered like a boat crossing a canal via locks."[15]

To get online services, citizens insert their integrated national ID card into a computer, then go through a two-layer authentication process. In most parts of the world, this is now accepted as the gold standard. At the time Estonia adopted these security protocols – long before Google did – it was revolutionary.[16] The country was also a pioneer of the digital signature, which allows citizens to sign legal documents and authenticate themselves to others in both the physical and digital worlds. The government has since integrated all kinds of public and private services into X-Road, from banking and medical records to phone bills, along with thousands of other services. And when its citizens voted in national elections using the system in 2005, Estonia became the first country in the world to do so. Today, nearly half of the population votes online.[17]

If a doctor prescribes medication, he puts it into a user's electronic record. A user then goes to the pharmacy, inserts the ID card, and authenticates it with a personal code, and the pharmacist provides the medication. Medical records are now securely available twenty-four seven to both medical practitioners and patients. A patient who wants a second opinion authorizes a second doctor (or as many as desired) to look at the records and make a determination. Ilves says that Estonia has now "broken a two thousand year Hippocratic tradition in which the doctor is the priest and the patient is the supplicant."[18]

Estonian citizens have their entire lives on the system. Personal profiles include email addresses, phone numbers, educational degrees, current and previous employment, insurance in-force, tax payments due, real-estate ownership, and even pet ownership. But Estonia has also put in place a "once-only" principle, which mandates that the government not ask citizens for data already held by a national public body. Authorities seeking data must first attempt to acquire it from their in-government agency, and if necessary, get permission to do so from citizens. In Estonia, citizens own their data, not the government or private institutions.

"Information technology is the basis for how the country organizes itself," says Robert Krimmer, a professor of e-governance at Tallinn University of Technology, "and its fundamental outlook strives for a hassle-free interaction for its citizens with the State apparatus."[19]

Estonia's approach to data represents a radical departure from both the Chinese and US models. In China, citizens' data is centralized and owned by the government; in the United States, corporations such as Facebook or Google own it. Estonian citizens own their own data, and therefore can chart their own future.

The annual cost of the system is relatively cheap, especially when compared to other e-government systems; Estonia's costs 50–60 million euros annually (the entire government budget is $8 billion), versus Russia's at $90 million and Kazakhstan's at $150 million, neither of which is as good as X-Road.

X-Road reportedly saves Estonia about 2 percent of annual GDP in salaries and other expenses, which it can reinvest elsewhere. "This is roughly the amount Estonia pays to be a member of NATO and in return gets protection," says former president Ilves. "I often joke that Estonia gets its national security for free."[20]

"Estonia is fifty or sixty years ahead of what is going on in Silicon

Valley," says Ilves, "where the private sector is revolutionized and is constantly reinventing itself, but in the public sector, not much has changed. It's time for the public sector around the world to shift from a Nokia to an iPhone mindset."[21]

From Russia with Love

Of course, the move to a completely digital public sector is not without its security risks. Estonia has confronted this reality on more than a few occasions, most profoundly in 2007. It was an eerily quiet night when the country came under attack. As leading newspapers, banks, and government communications went down, Estonia's minister of defense, Jaak Aaviksoo, sent his aide outside to see if there were enemy jets overhead or warships on the shoreline. But this was an invisible enemy – assaulting hundreds of targets simultaneously. Fifty-eight websites went offline on the first day.

Rogue computer networks, known as botnets, were attacking. "This affected the majority of the Estonian population," says Aaviksoo. "This was the first time that a botnet threatened the national security of an *entire* nation."[22] Some analysts have gone so far as to call the incident Web War I.

The minister had trained his mind to think about how to counter missiles, bombs, and traditional military raids. But cyberattacks? He didn't have any relevant experience to draw on. Aaviksoo debated whether to invoke Article 5, which would obligate NATO to join Estonia in a counterattack. But in this war, it was almost impossible to determine who was leading the assault.

The attackers knew exactly what they were doing, evading filters and forcing servers to crash. Computer geeks tried to figure out where the onslaught was coming from – the largest numbers appeared to be coming out of Egypt, followed by Vietnam and Peru. But it was clear that whoever was attacking was just tunneling through these countries as proxies. As websites across Estonia were swamped by foreign visitors, the available bandwidth hit zero. Banks, newspapers, and government agencies were forced to shut down all international web requests. With a click, thousands of sites went dark, and as far as the world was concerned, Estonia had digitally disappeared.

The onslaught lasted three weeks, with over 120 servers affected. Evidence suggests – but could never prove beyond a shadow of a doubt – that Russia was the culprit.

During the attacks, the Estonian government was transparent with its citizens, which built up a tremendous amount of goodwill. And in the aftermath, policymakers took action, doubling down on cybersecurity and the policy of decentralization. Each database is now compartmentalized and therefore distinct from any other server. While this means less efficiency in the short term, it is infinitely more secure in the long term. Since each database or system has a dedicated secure server, the entire system isn't compromised in the event of a breach. "Hackers would need to instantly and successfully hack at least 150 databases," says Marten Kaevats, Estonia's national digital adviser, "to steal someone's identity and do something meaningful with it. That is close to impossible."[23]

Cyberattacks continue to be the norm in Estonia – the country faced more than ten thousand incidents in 2017 alone – and will be for the foreseeable future.[24] In order to deal with the very real possibility of a serious breach, the government has installed a radically new fail-safe system: the world's first digital embassy, housed in a high-security data center in Betzdorf, Luxembourg. In the event of a crisis, Estonians can continue to digitally authenticate themselves, and all public-private services continue to run seamlessly. "It is no longer possible to move back to a paper era," says Siim Sikkut, Estonia's current chief information officer. "The Luxembourg site stores copies of the most critical and confidential data."[25]

Estonia's digital embassy, which has the same protection and immunity afforded to traditional embassies, maintains and preserves ten priority databases, including the treasury information system, pensions insurance, business, land and population registers, and the identity documents database. All this ensures that the country can keep all systems operational under almost any scenario. There are currently plans to put in place a total of six data embassies. "Cut one head off," says Taavi Kotka, the country's previous information officer, "and like Hydra, three more will grow back."[26]

Given the sensitivity of the data, security concerns are addressed on an ongoing basis. "End-to-end verifiability is the holy grail," says Tarvi Martens, the National Electoral Committee's head of e-voting.[27]

In terms of personal data, Estonia has also put in place a policy of complete transparency. Citizens can actually view a log of who has accessed their information, and a user who believes data has been misused or viewed by anyone illegitimately can file a complaint with the country's data ombudsman, resulting in almost real-time remediation. Every time an official of any kind looks at the secure data of an individual online, whether it's a banker, police officer, or government agency, it is recorded. A civil servant must justify the intrusion – looking at someone's personal data without cause is a criminal offense.

"You have to trust the government a little," says Ilves. "Whom do you trust more – putting your credit card number online with a three-digit CVV code? Or is the government sort of the guarantor of your identity?"[28]

Some have likened the system to "Little Brother." Estonia's former chief information officer, Taavi Kotka, has a simple answer for that. "There is no government that knows more about you than Google or Facebook," he says.[29] Estonia has created what he calls a "Lockean contract," where the government cannot access data without a user's knowledge, but citizens no longer have anonymity either.[30] The Estonian government has consistently made the case that the twenty-first-century networked society is a justifiable transparency bargain. Computers can't be bribed, and that means less corruption. "Our goal," says Ilves, "is to make it impossible to do bad things."[31]

Borderless Country

In 2013, then chief information officer Kotka was given a challenge: expand the population of Estonia for economic gain. "Countries are like enterprises," he says. "They want to increase the wealth of their own people."[32] The program he started the following year, known as e-citizenship, had four thousand registrants within the first eighteen hours.[33]

"If everything is digital, and location-independent," says Kotka, "you can run a borderless country."[34]

By handing over €100, a photograph, and submitting fingerprints at one of thirty-eight Estonian embassies around the world, anyone can now become an e-resident of Estonia. In order to access the country's national system, newly minted residents are given an identity card, a cryptographic key, and a pin code. E-residency does not provide a path to citizenship or allow for legal residency, nor can it be used as a travel document. What it does do is provide an individual with a supranational digital identity issued by a nation-state. E-residency changes fundamentally how we think about citizenship, the role of government, and the services it offers, but at its most practical, it's a powerful business tool.

Estonian e-residency provides an ID card that allows its user to authenticate their identity online, digitally sign documents, register a company, conduct online bank transactions, and order prescriptions from anywhere, anytime. Registering a business through the program is particularly useful for internet entrepreneurs in emerging markets and for startups in countries with burdensome financial limitations.

Both Estonian citizens and e-residents can perform nearly every public and private sector transaction in digital form. "The adoption of non-resident ID cards," says Kotka, "is an additional argument in favor of investing in Estonia."[35]

The thinking here is clear: the hope is that e-resident status will attract foreigners of all kinds to Estonia, including investors, digital nomads, specialists, and international policymakers. Because of the country's advanced banking system, the government expects it will attract entrepreneurs and additional revenue.

In 2018, President Kersti Kaljulaid handed Pope Francis his own digital ID card, making His Holiness the 37,647th digital e-citizen of the tiny Baltic country. Japanese prime minister Shinzō Abe, German chancellor Angela Merkel, Luxembourgish prime minister Xavier Bettel, Microsoft founder Bill Gates, Asia's ultra-wealthy Mukesh Ambani, and TV personality Trevor Noah have all become e-residents, giving them access to the country's e-infrastructure and services so they can establish and manage their finances and businesses inside the EU from anywhere.[36]

Because men make up the vast majority of applicants, the United Nations has been encouraging female entrepreneurs from India to apply as well, to great effect.[37] As of 2020, there are more than seventy thousand e-residents from over 165 countries.[38] The program has been so wildly successful that the e-residency rate now exceeds the national birth rate. "We tried to make more babies," says Siim Sikkut, Estonia's chief information officer, "but it's not that easy."[39]

By 2025, Estonia aims to enroll ten million e-residents. "We had to set a goal that resonates," says Taavi Kotka. "Large enough for the society to believe in."[40]

If they get anywhere close to that target, it would be a financial windfall for the country. For every euro that Estonia has invested in developing the e-residency program, it brings in at least 43 euros to the economy, according to the head of the country's e-residency project, Kaspar Korjus. "I envision a time when Estonians will not actually have to pay taxes," Korjus says. "Instead we will offer telemedicine, online education, and pensions to people all over the world who will pay a minor fee which will cover all of our government's expenses. That is when we will achieve E-residency 2.0."[41]

To Infinity and Beyond

In 2015, Estonia took a bold step in making its X-Road technology open source and available to any individual, organization, or country to use as they please. The source code for the program has been published under an MIT license (a nonrestrictive software license developed by the Massachusetts Institute of Technology) and is available free. "This is the beginning of the erosion of the classic nation state hegemony," observes John Clippinger, a digital identity researcher at the Massachusetts Institute of Technology. "It's going to get whittled away from the margins."[42]

Both Finland and Iceland have begun to implement a partial version of X-Road as they begin their long journey toward digital societies. To date, countries such as Canada, Rwanda, New Zealand, Singapore, and Uruguay have made significant progress toward digitizing their e-government public services infrastructure. Many more countries have expressed interest by sending delegations to Tallinn to better understand the Estonian model.

"We are riding the crest of a very powerful wave," says Aaron Maniam, deputy secretary of Singapore's Ministry of Communications and Information, "that in the coming few years will revolutionize how citizens interface with government and their fellow countrymen. This type of experience is unparalleled in human history."[43]

Estonia's position as the global leader in e-government has not gone unnoticed. "You're so much further than we are,"[44] admitted German chancellor Angela Merkel at the European Digital Summit. Even President Obama joked that he "should have called the Estonians" when he was setting up his healthcare website.[45]

Estonian president Kersti Kaljulaid, who identifies herself as the "president to a digital society," sees a world in which international borders will become increasingly irrelevant. "Our citizens will be global soon," she says. "We have to fly like bees from flower to flower to gather those taxes from citizens working in the morning in France, in the evening in the UK, living half a year in Estonia, and then going to Australia."[46]

If she has her way, what is happening in this tiny corner of the Baltics will by no means end there. "We have to embrace digital society with our minds and our souls, without fear," Kaljulaid says. "It is the future."[47]

CHAPTER 13

Security: Google's X-Man

The one thing that unites all human beings, regardless of age, gender, religion, economic status, or ethnic background, is that, deep down inside, we all believe that we are above-average drivers.

— Dave Barry, *Dave Barry Turns Fifty*

Sebastian Thrun speaks onstage during TechCrunch Disrupt SF 2017 (TechCrunch, CC BY 2.0)

The First Self-Driving Cars

Sebastian Thrun was standing in the middle of the Mojave Desert waiting for Stanley. It was a hot, dry day in October 2005, and along with about a thousand other people who had gathered in the grandstands for the $2 million Grand Challenge race held by the Defense Advanced Research Projects Agency (DARPA), Thrun was staring intently out at the horizon when the loudspeaker crackled. "I see a dust trail in the vicinity!" boomed the announcer. "I have a visual on bot number three! Ladies and gentlemen, here comes Stanley!"[1]

Stanford University's self-driving car, a modified Volkswagen Touareg, was about five hundred feet from the finish line when it stopped. Thrun and his racing team held their breath, along with the rest of the crowd. And then Stanley lurched back to life and crossed the finish line, becoming the first autonomous vehicle ever to complete what had started to seem like an unachievable mission set by DARPA.

"The impossible has been achieved," declared Sebastian Thrun, Stanford's Artificial Intelligence Lab director.[2] He and his team had proved that machines could drive safely and speedily over rugged terrain without human assistance. Roughly seven hours after the 132-mile race began, the packed grandstand erupted.

In the months leading up to the event, Stanford graduate students spent countless hours programming Stanley with algorithms that would allow it to self-learn the unforgiving desert contours of DARPA's track. The bot was connected to sensors and customized software that made it smarter with each new ride. That technology, when extrapolated and shared across a connected network as envisioned in autonomous rideshare models, is now known within the automated vehicle industry as fleet learning, which allows cars to improve exponentially with each mile driven. Fifteen cars had entered the previous year's Grand Challenge, but not a single one completed the course. Most crashed, flipped, or rolled within minutes – and the one that traveled the furthest only made it eight miles before bursting into flames. After an eighteen-month development cycle, Stanley was now able to find the most efficient paths, overcome obstacles, and stay on course to navigate a treacherous desert journey the distance of New York to Wilmington – entirely on its own.

It was an astonishing feat that was not lost on Google cofounder Larry Page, who was watching incognito in the stands in a hat and sunglasses. That day, he set his sights on Sebastian Thrun, eventually luring him away from Stanford to Google. Thrun would go on to found and run the company's secretive think-tank research lab, Google x. Its first project? Self-driving cars.

Mr. Roboto

Born in Solingen, Germany, in 1967, Thrun was obsessed with building things since childhood. He spent hours with Legos, putting together trains, cars, and complex structures. And when he turned eleven, he got his first TI-57 programmable calculator, which allowed him to write programs up to fifty steps. "I got very enthusiastic about seeing just what you could do with that," recalls Thrun. "Could you program a game, could you program complex geometry, could you solve financial equations?"[3] Between the ages of twelve and fourteen, he spent every afternoon proving the answer was yes, documenting each successful program he created in a booklet. By sixteen, he was programming his own video games on a NorthStar Horizon computer.[4]

But it was only after the tragic traffic death of his best friend at the age of eighteen that Thrun realized what he really wanted to do with his preternatural talents. Traveling on an icy road, the vehicle's driver had lost control and collided head-on with a truck. "He didn't pay attention for a fraction of a second and that was it,"[5] says Thrun. He knew he couldn't bring his friend back, but he could do something for all the people who die needlessly in car crashes. "I decided I would dedicate my life to saving one million people every year."[6]

Thrun enrolled at the University of Hildesheim and later the University of Bonn for his college and graduate studies. He became interested in the brain and human intelligence and took classes in philosophy, medicine, and psychology, but found what he truly enjoyed was bringing those subjects together holistically through computer science and artificial intelligence. "You could actually build something from the ground up that would then manifest intelligence," says Thrun. "That fascinated me."[7]

Thrun eventually found his way to robotics, which he felt offered the best way to study intelligence. In 1994, at age twenty-seven, he programmed his first robot, called RHINO, which was able to clean kitchens. The state-of-the art functionality was unheard of at the time. He won second place in a US robotics competition. Three years later, he created a robotic tour guide for museums. Visitors to the Deutsches Museum in Bonn and the Smithsonian's National Museum of American History were greeted by Minerva, an autonomous guide that made all its own decisions. It found museum guests by itself, interacted with them, directed them to specific exhibits, and even explained what they were seeing. "It had a face, it could smile, it could frown," says Thrun. "And it was great fun."[8]

One night, he was programming Minerva for the next day when a human guide came by and started speaking to the robot. She looked her up and down, Thrun recalls, and said, "You are not going to replace me."[9]

As an adjunct professor at Carnegie Mellon in Pittsburgh, Thrun took on a variety of projects, including robots that could tend to the elderly and map out abandoned coalmines, as well as autonomous helicopters that could map terrain. In 2003, he moved to Stanford, where he ultimately took over as the director of its Artificial Intelligence Lab and won DARPA's Grand Challenge. When Thrun left Stanford to work as a full-time manager at Google in 2007, he thought it would only be a sabbatical. For his first three years, he developed Street View, a feature of the site's map program that has now systematically photographed more than ten million miles of the world's streets and houses.

By 2010, Thrun was appointed to run Google x, a research lab and innovation center with, as Thrun put it, the "authority to just do crazy things."[10] It's where they work on the moon shot problems, and the self-driving car was first on the agenda. But at the time, Thrun wasn't convinced it was even possible. And at one of the project's early meetings with Google founders Larry Page and Sergei Brin, he let them know as much.

"OK, Sebastian," Page challenged him. "Prove to me it's not possible."

The three sat down and carved out a thousand miles of California streets "that are really insane to drive," recalls Thrun. They included downtown San Francisco and the famously steep twists of Lombard Street, along with Highway 1 from the Bay Area to Los Angeles.[11]

"If you drive those well and completely autonomously," Page and Brin told him, "you'll make a bonus." Thrun insisted it couldn't be done, but Google's founders were adamant. "It can be done," they said. "Just do it."[12]

And that's just what Thrun did. Working in secret, he and a team of engineers took the technology developed for the DARPA race and applied it to the challenge laid down by Page and Brin. "We had a separate building that no one knew about," recalls Thrun. "At least for a year and a half, no one in Google had a clue we existed."[13]

By October 2010, with the help of fellow engineers such as Anthony Levandowski, who would later go on to run Uber's driverless car operation, and Chris Urmson, who founded Aurora, Thrun and his team had once again achieved the impossible. "We have developed technology for cars that can drive themselves," he announced in a statement on Google's blog. The company had officially succeeded in getting their self-driving cars from Google's

Mountain View campus to its office in Santa Monica – down Lombard Street and over the Golden Gate Bridge. In all, their cars had logged over 140,000 miles without a single accident.[14]

"We think this is a first for robotics research," wrote Thrun.[15]

In 2012, the Nevada Department of Motor Vehicles became the first state entity to "license" a driverless car, Google's modified Toyota Prius, after it took officials for a successful cruise down the Las Vegas Strip. California, Florida, and Michigan passed laws permitting autonomous vehicles a year later. After a series of subsequent prototypes, the project became officially known as Waymo, short for "A new way forward in mobility."[16]

In 2013, Google constructed testing grounds for its self-driving cars two hours south of San Francisco in Atwater, California. Originally an Air Force base where bomber pilots trained for war, the secretive ninety-one-acre compound known as the Castle, which is surrounded by an eight-foot perimeter fence, is now used by Google to perfect its self-driving car. Engineers, test drivers, and designers choreograph a universe of driving scenarios, structured tests, and drills that its cars must repeat until they get them right every time. The obstacle course includes curbs, complicated highway merges, busy intersections, roundabouts, driveways, stop signs, traffic lights, and even a railroad crossing. Cars grapple with bikers, malicious potholes, flying debris, orange cones – and reportedly even people leaping out of portable toilets.

The testing at the Castle compliments the billions of miles Waymo's vehicles "drive" in simulators and the millions of actual miles they have now driven on America's roads, in more than twenty-five separate cities. By 2018, the technology was far enough along for Google to launch its self-driving taxi service Waymo One, which allows users in the pilot city of Phoenix, Arizona, to hail driverless rides with their phones. In 2019, Waymo One became the first autonomous taxi service in the world to operate without any safety drivers in the car.

Thrun, who himself drives a Tesla, believes we have already arrived at a point where autonomous vehicles can actually drive better than the best humans.[17] He jokes that one person in particular – his wife – agrees with him: "When you are in the self-driving car," she chides him, "can you please let the car take over?"[18]

Joy Ride

Automobile accidents currently rank as the eighth leading cause of death worldwide, with nearly 1.3 million fatalities each year and an additional twenty to fifty million victims injured or disabled. An estimated 94 percent of those crashes are caused as a result of human decisions, including drunk driving, distractedness, and drowsiness.

"When you put these figures into context, the human tragedy couldn't be more clear," says Eric Danko, director of federal affairs for Cruise, a leading self-driving vehicle company. "We're literally talking about more than a hundred people dying every day on US roads, the equivalent of two 747s falling from the sky every week. AVs hold enormous potential to save lives."[19]

Thrun and others believe that cars will soon become almost entirely immune to fatal collisions by eliminating human intervention. Drunk driving will be all but eradicated. And the shift will represent a revolution for the many millions of people who are blind, have neurological diseases such as Alzheimer's or Parkinson's, or any other physical condition that impairs driving. They'll also give people who are too young or too old to drive a tremendous amount of freedom. And then there's the potential to profoundly reduce traffic – not to mention the hours of productive time we'll all have back when we're not wasting so much of it driving.

"AVs will fundamentally alter transport systems," says Kara Kockelman, professor of transportation engineering at the University of Texas at Austin. "They not only have the potential to avert deadly crashes, but they can also provide mobility to the elderly and disabled, increase road capacity, save fuel, and lower harmful emissions."[20]

But perhaps most fundamentally of all, Thrun also envisions a future society where we don't have a need for private car ownership – and the tremendous environmental impact that will bring beyond just reduced emissions. Cars would come to consumers on demand, meaning we wouldn't need our own garages or driveways, and workplaces wouldn't need as many parking spots.[21] Cities currently allocate approximately a third of their usable land for parking. Thrun and other industry experts hope to reinvent the curb for green spaces and pedestrian use.

"I'm really looking forward to a time when generations after us look back at us," Thrun says, "and say how ridiculous it was that humans were driving cars."[22]

Perfect: The Enemy of Good

Like all other revolutionary innovations, self-driving cars will force society to grapple with technical and moral questions, particularly when it comes to safety. Can autonomous vehicles ever be 100 percent safe? And do they actually need to be? In the United States, human-driven cars cause one death for every hundred million miles driven.[23] In a Rand Corporation study titled "The Enemy of Good," researchers concluded that deploying cars that are just 10 percent safer than the average human driver would save more lives over the long term than waiting until they are almost perfect. In other words, more lives could be lost while we wait for the unflawed autonomous vehicle.[24]

"In a perfect world, autonomous vehicles should be at least as good as human-driven conventional ones," says the director of Princeton's transportation program, Alain Kornhauser, "but for the foreseeable future, we cannot produce that because when humans pay attention, we are really good. The problem is we're rarely ever fully focused, so over the long haul, we're better off relying on technology that doesn't need sleep, argue with its spouse, play with a cellphone, or have one too many drinks."[25]

For now, the biggest obstacle in getting self-driving cars safely on the road appears to be human. According to *Axios*, from 2014 to 2018, people were responsible for eighty-one of the eighty-eight accidents involving AVs in the State of California. Of the sixty-two accidents that took place while the car was in complete autonomous mode, only one was caused by computer error.[26]

One accident in particular captivated the world precisely because it was technical, not human, error that caused it – leading many to question the wisdom of self-driving cars. In March 2018, an Uber autonomous vehicle killed a pedestrian for the first time in history. The accident took place at night in Tempe, Arizona, just as forty-nine-year-old Elaine Herzberg was crossing the road with her bicycle outside of the sanctioned crosswalk.

According to the police report, the self-driving Uber's safety employee behind the wheel was not watching the road in the moments leading up to the crash, but rather watching Hulu. In September 2020, the driver was charged with negligent homicide. In the aftermath of the accident, Uber temporarily suspended autonomous road testing in Tempe, Pittsburg, San Francisco, and Toronto. "It was not an indictment of the industry," says Uber senior safety program analyst Chan Lieu, "but it was a wakeup call that showed we needed to dial it up to eleven to ensure complete safety."[27]

While Google and Thrun have done amazing things to further the safety of autonomous vehicles, they are far from alone in the space. Beyond Waymo and Uber's Advanced Technologies Group, almost every automaker in the world is working feverishly to create the ultimate self-driving machine – and carve out a piece of what is expected to be an $8 trillion industry. There's the billion-dollar GM acquisition Cruise and the billion-dollar Ford acquisition Argo AI, as well as many more smaller competitors like Aurora, which was started by former Google and Tesla chiefs. And then there's Tesla itself, which – unlike Waymo and other companies developing autonomous vehicles – doesn't rely on an internal test fleet to collect data.

By 2020, there were 730,000 Teslas on the road that logged over three billion miles using its autopilot capabilities.[28] "More than any other car manufacturer, Tesla is racking up autopilot miles to ultimately ensure road safety," says Scott Hardman of the Institute of Transportation Studies. "This is the long tail of black swans that will train automated vehicles to deal with extremely rare events."[29]

In recent years, Waymo announced that its 360 degree LiDAR (light detection and ranging) system can now accurately provide a bird's-eye view of cars, cyclists, and pedestrians surrounding its vehicles. The technology enables Waymo cars to navigate the complexities of chaotic urban streets and spot hazards such as highway debris from hundreds of meters away. It makes Stanley's 2005 amble through the empty desert look like a baby's first steps.

When my youngest son, Yaniv, first saw one of these giant LiDAR cylinders spinning around on top of an autonomous vehicle near the US Capitol building, he pointed at it in excited confusion. I explained what the funny-looking thing did and why it meant that humans wouldn't be driving for much longer. "No way, Baba," he said. "You mean when I'm big, the car will drive itself?!"

Phantoms at the Wheel

Inventors have been dreaming of autonomous vehicles since shortly after the birth of the first motorcar around 1885. Forty years later, in 1925, Francis Houdina innovated a radio-controlled car that drove through the streets of New York City without a human physically steering. According to the *New York Times*, the vehicle was able to start its engine, shift gears, and sound its horn, "as if a phantom hand were at the wheel." And in the 1990s, Dean Pomerleau created the first bare-bones self-driving vehicle that was able to use raw images from the road to steer in real time. Pomerleau and Todd Jochem, both Carnegie Mellon researchers, drove their minivan 2,797 miles from Pittsburgh to San Diego in what they called "No Hands Across America," by only having to control speed and breaking.

But even then, the idea of being driven around by a series of zeros and ones still seemed insane. Two decades later, thanks to Thrun and scores of others in the industry, summoning robot taxis from wireless devices in our pockets is an actual reality. General Motors CEO Mary Barra predicts that the automotive industry will change more in the next five to ten years than it has in the last fifty. "I believe only 1 percent of interesting things have been invented yet," says Thrun.[30] By the end of this decade, fully autonomous vehicles are expected to be available at a car dealership near you, ready to drive themselves off the lot.

"You can't just sit back and say, no, it's not going to happen," says former GM vice president Lawrence Burns, whose book, *Autonomy*, explores the potential for driverless cars to completely reshape our world. "You can't hide from the amount of technology coming. We have passed the tipping point, it's inevitable."[31]

Humanity 2.0

The future is brighter than we think.

– Ray Kurzweil, CeBIT keynote

"Kilometer 104," the conductor barked over the loudspeaker. The train stopped, and my guide and I stepped into the darkness. Outside, there was no real station. Just a dirt road and a sign that read, "Welcome to the Inka Trail." I had come to Peru to see Machu Picchu, one of the Seven Wonders of the World.

As Andean condors hissed above us, my guide and I set off on our journey up the mountains, equipped with only what we could carry in our backpacks: snacks, water, bug spray, and coca leaf candy for altitude sickness.

Soon, the sun began peaking over the horizon, and I could see what the darkness had hidden – lush green gorges and ancient stone temples, majestic valleys, and llamas grazing in the grass. As we climbed high into the Andes, I took in the panoramic views, but by the time we reached the ten-thousand-foot summit, I was lightheaded. More than once, I had to stop and take a deep breath.

After hours of hiking, we reached the majestic Inti Punku, or the Sun Gate, which marks one of the main entrances to the ancient city. I tried to imagine the place before it was abandoned in the sixteenth century, before the mighty Incan empire fell to the Spanish conquistadors. I wondered: Was the collapse of this civilization inevitable? Was the collapse of *every* civilization inevitable?

In the relatively short arch of recorded human history, few advanced societies have lasted more than a few hundred years, and just a handful more than a thousand. The Incans came and went in just three hundred years. Could technology and innovation have saved them?

Archeological evidence suggests that most of the world's great civilizations, from ancient Rome to the Mayans, fell due to familiar forces such as population movement, disease, famine, climate, and war. As I stared at the Urubamba River thousands of feet below, I thought about the challenges we will face in the future, and how they'll dwarf anything that's come before.

For the most part, we only have ourselves to blame for most of the Earth-sized problems we now face. From food scarcity to water insecurity, pollution to global warming, we have been hastening the planet's destruction at an alarming rate. And if we don't change our behavior, we may drive ourselves to extinction. But we are also at a unique inflection point, because for the first time in our history, technology has given us the ability to change our destiny. We can consciously choose to turn the tide, to break the patterns that have undone us in the past. And for our civilization to survive – and even thrive – will require a generation that's not only inspired by the question of what's next, but hears it as a clarion call to action.

The visionaries I've had the privilege of writing about have already demonstrated that our future *can* be better – and has the potential to be more wonderful than anything we've yet experienced as a species.

Underneath it all, there's also a compelling economic argument for progress. Until the Industrial Revolution, the world was always a winner-takes-all kind of place. The majority of people worked on farms, and for thousands of years, nothing much changed: a neighbor's loss was your gain, so conquering, plundering, and stealing generally worked. The result was extreme economic inequality. But in the age of high tech, the more people become educated, the more they can produce. The more they can produce, the more money they make, and the more money they make, the more they are able to pay to find solutions to longstanding problems, whether they be cures for diseases or more efficient ways to travel. Theoretically, this creates a virtuous cycle of increased innovation, profit, and abundance – and not just for the people at the top; there's an economic incentive to reduce inequality. "In a positive-sum world," says economist Max Roser, "the more people are well-off, the better your own life is."[1]

The innovations and entrepreneurs presented in this book are taking Roser's theoretical idea and making it a reality. We all have the power to identify, solve, and implement long-lasting environmental and societal change for the benefit of humanity. "From government officials and corporations to do-it-yourself innovators and techno-philanthropists, we can all do our part to improve the world around us," says Gidi Grinstein, founder of Tikkun Olam Makers, a global network of communities creating solutions for people with disabilities.[2]

"It's not your way or my way," wrote *Seven Habits of Highly Effective People* author Frank Covey, "it's a better way."[3] But the path forward requires taking Covey's famous "win-win" solutions one step further. The innovators here have adopted a win-win-win outlook: good for me, good for you, and good for humanity. As John Mackey, the founder of Whole Foods, explains, "Every problem we have is a failure of imagination. Everything is solvable, it just requires innovation and thinking about win-win-win solutions for the world's greatest challenges."[4]

The future belongs to those who choose hope – and those who leverage technology to positively impact what's next for humanity. It's the answer to my son's question: a reality that can be better, brighter, and more life affirming than anything we've seen before. That's what's next, if we will it.

Acknowledgments

I have been blessed with a rich circle of friends and colleagues who have broadened my vision of what humanity can and must achieve in the decades ahead to identify the grand global challenges humanity will face and to find the creative solutions necessary to solve them. Our ability to positively impact the lives of billions of people has never been more imperative, nor more possible. I interviewed nearly 150 people for this book (often more than once), including innovators, scientists, geneticists, doctors, astronauts, economists, venture capitalists, sustainability experts, engineers, teachers, food and water specialists, CEOs, NGO executives, university professors, lawyers, and social impact makers, among others. With every conversation, I could literally feel my entire body's DNA stretching. Each of these individuals was committed to making the world a better place and embodied the great privilege and obligation to tackle the greatest challenges of the twenty-first century.

My children – Eiden, Oren, and Yaniv – were the ultimate champions of this book. I would often share with them stories from my interviews. They in turn would grill me about what my interviewees said, what questions I asked, or about their own vision of the future. The boys would often come up with their own prospective solutions for solving these challenges. They are the greatest gift the universe has given me, and I am grateful for them every day.

Aviv and Einat Ezra not only served as great cheerleaders, but as a constant source of love, friendship, and support as I weathered highs and lows. Our meetings in Washington, DC, Chicago, and Israel made all the difference in the world as major changes presented themselves.

Jonathan Kessler, the CEO of Heart of a Nation, served as a stalwart sounding board, ally, friend, colleague, and mentor. As the world hunkered down for the coronavirus pandemic, we would meet often virtually on Zoom and on his building's roof deck off Dupont Circle. A force of nature, he would constantly push me hard to be a nuanced thinker and find compassion for those around me.

I am deeply grateful to Yaakov Katz, the editor in chief of the *Jerusalem Post*, who would check in on me regularly to assess my progress on the manuscript and my state of sanity. Our meetings in Jerusalem at various cafés in Baqa and on park benches throughout Capitol Hill were a source of inspiration, joy, and humor.

I had the great fortune to work with two brilliant editors, Ross Schneiderman and Adam Laukhuf, both of whom worked tirelessly to ensure this book's stories were told in the most compelling fashion possible and read well. Working with them both was among the most gratifying parts of writing *Next*.

My sincerest thanks to Ilan Berman, senior vice president of the American Foreign Policy Council, where I serve as a senior fellow. Ilan both read the manuscript and served as my travel partner to some of the world's most interesting countries. When we weren't looking into our crystal ball trying to discern what it would take to bring about a brighter future for humankind, we would head out on ATVs, sit cross-legged on the floor for dinner, and ask tough questions of some of the world's most important policymakers.

Michael Potter and Carol Goldstein served as amazing guides on my exploration to the world of Singularity University and to the space community. They opened their rolodexes and their hearts as they went to bat securing for me interviews with some of the world's most forward-thinking luminaries. Between our meetings in New

York, DC, and Austin, they read portions of the manuscript and made invaluable corrections.

I had an ongoing dialogue with my good friend and colleague Gidi Grinstein, founder of Reut Institute, that always forced me to look at the social impact side of the innovators I interviewed. Daniel Kraft, the founder of Exponential Medicine and Singularity University's Chair of Medicine, was both a gentleman and a scholar – I greatly appreciate his generosity with his time and contacts. During our walks to the National Mall, Eric Danko introduced me with his no-nonsense attitude to the world of autonomous and electric vehicles. Sema Sgaier, on our walks to Roosevelt Island, broadened my vision on pandemics, science, and human psychology. And Stratos Costalas, on countless phone calls and dinners in New York and Washington, DC, always made sure I was progressing and in good spirits.

My friends and colleagues in YPO, and in particular my chapter mates at Mosaic, the staff at M2MX, and Alina Eskinazi went above and beyond in connecting me to my interviewees, but also served as sources of support during the entire writing process. I also thank Ken Kwartler, who shepherded me once again through the copyright process at the Library of Congress (as it so happens, as Washington, DC, experienced unprecedented historical events).

Once again, Georgetown law professor Brad Snyder took me under his wing and pushed me regularly to get out another book. Our meetings often took place as we watched our kids run around the neighborhood playgrounds or in his backyard sipping coffee and noshing on goodies. I am grateful for his gift of friendship, sense of humor, and cheerful personality. My business partner, Larry Glick, remains one of my closest friends, mentors, and cheerleaders. I am grateful to the universe every day for bringing our paths together.

I am beyond grateful to Ilan Greenfield, the owner of Gefen Publishing House. Ilan has become a good friend, colleague, and member of the extended family. Between book adventures in New

York, DC, and around Israel, I could not have asked for a more creative publisher. And Kezia Raffel Pride's tremendous editing skills and eye for detail were a pleasure to work with. I am also extremely grateful to Lisa Mendelow, who designed the beautiful cover for *Next*.

As I shuttled back and forth to Israel for the writing process, I was grateful for the support of my mother, Marlene Schieber, and my truly exceptional sister Simone Pinsky and her tribe. Shlomit Shusan always kept the door open to her home and to her lovely bustan garden. Irit Lerner offered unwavering support, as did Avi Lichter, who continues to serve as a close friend, colleague, and family member. And my sincerest appreciation to the extended Gordon family for their ongoing support and love.

As I look back and think about all the amazing people featured in this book, alongside all the human beings working on making the world a better place, I know more than ever that our biggest mistake in life is not dreaming, but rather not dreaming big enough. Humanity's best days are ahead.

Avi Jorisch
Washington, DC
September 2022

Endnotes

Preface – The Future Is Now

1. David Brock, "How Gordon Moore Made 'Moore's Law,'" *Wired*, April 16, 2015, https://www.wired.com/2015/04/how-gordon-moore-made -moores-law/.

2. Thomas Friedman, "Moore's Law Turns 50," *New York Times*, May 13, 2015, https://www.nytimes.com/2015/05/13/opinion/thomas-friedman -moores-law-turns-50.html. Moore witnessed exponential growth in his own career. In 1968, he and Robert Noyce founded NM Electronics, which eventually became the Intel Corporation, the world's second largest semi-conductor chip manufacturer and supplier of processors for computer systems including Apple, Lenovo, Hewlett-Packard, and Dell, along with many other devices that focus on communication and computing.

3. Ray Kurzweil, "The Law of Accelerating Returns," Kurzweilai.net, March 7, 2001, https://www.kurzweilai.net/the-law-of-accelerating-returns.

4. "The Future Is Better Than You Think: Predictions on AI and Develop-ment from Ray Kurzweil," *ITUNews*, May 29, 2019, https://news.itu.int /the-future-is-better-than-you-think-predictions-on-ai-and-development -from-ray-kurzweil/.

5. Monica Hunter-Hart, "8 Staggering Predictions from Ray Kurzweil," *Inverse*, May 29, 2017, https://www.inverse.com/article/30913-8-staggering -predictions-ray-kurzweil.

6. Christianna Reedy, "Ray Kurzweil Claims Singularity Will Happen by 2045," *Futurism*, May 10, 2017, https://futurism.com/kurzweil-claims-that -the-singularity-will-happen-by-2045.

7. Nick Bostrom, "Existential Risks: Analyzing Human Extinction Scenar-

ios and Related Hazards," *Journal of Evolution and Technology* 9, no. 1 (2002), www.nickbostrom.com/existential/risks.html.

8. Edward Geist and Andrew J. Lohn, "How Might Artificial Intelligence Affect the Risk of Nuclear War?" Rand Corporation, 2018, www.rand.org /pubs/perspectives/PE296.html.

9. Catherine Clifford, "Elon Musk: 'Mark My Words – A.I. Is Far More Dangerous than Nukes,'" CNBC, March 14, 2018, www.cnbc.com/2018/03/13 /elon-musk-at-sxsw-a-i-is-more-dangerous-than-nuclear-weapons.html.

10. Elon Musk (@elonmusk), "Competition for AI superiority at national level most likely cause of WW3 imo," Twitter, September 4, 2017, 12:33 p.m., https://twitter.com/elonmusk/status/904638455761612800.

11. Marc Goodman, "A Vision of Crimes in the Future," TEDGlobal 2012, June 2012, www.ted.com/talks/marc_goodman_a_vision_of_crimes _in_the_future?language=en.

12. Fiona Harvey, "Humanity under Threat from Perfect Storm of Crises – Study," *The Guardian*, February 6, 2020, https://www.theguardian.com /environment/2020/feb/06/humanity-under-threat-perfect-storm-crises -study-environment?fbclid=IwAR3r0RN91V7VtZY8vHsEQv3ScicNTSR JCr8hyay4u_Sm24J6DnB7lmsoyxQ.

13. Larry Elliott, "Climate Crisis Fills Top 5 Places of World Economic Forum's Risk Report," *The Guardian*, January 15, 2020, https://www .theguardian.com/business/2020/jan/15/climate-crisis-environment -top-five-places-world-economic-forum-risks-report.

14. John F. Kennedy, "Text of President John Kennedy's Rice Stadium Moon Speech," NASA, September 12, 1962, https://er.jsc.nasa.gov/seh /ricetalk.htm.

15. Greg Ip, "The Moonshot Mind-Set Once Came from the Government. No Longer," *Wall Street Journal*, July 14, 2019, www.wsj.com/articles /the-moonshot-mind-set-once-came-from-the-government-no-longer -11563152820. See also Casey Dreier, "Reconstructing the Cost of the 1 Giant Leap," *The Planetary Society*, June 16, 2019, https://www.planetary .org/blogs/casey-dreier/2019/reconstructing-the-price-of-apollo.html.

16. Astro Teller and Megan Smith, "What Is Your X? Amplifying Technology Moonshots," Google Official Blog, February 6, 2012, https://googleblog .blogspot.com/2012/02/whats-your-x-amplifying-technology.html.

17. Cited in John Bell, "To the Moon: Google X's Astro Teller Encourages Creatives to Think Big," *The Guardian*, June 20, 2013, www.theguardian

.com/media-network/media-network-blog/2013/jun/20/google-x-astro
-teller-creatives.

18. "Singularity University Addresses the World's Greatest Challenges at SU Global Summit," Singularity University, August 9, 2016, https://su.org /press-room/press-releases/singularity-university-addresses-the-worlds -greatest-challenges-at-su-global-summit/.

19. Afshin Molavi, author's phone interview, March 16, 2021.

20. Jun Sato, author's phone interview, May 4, 2020.

21. Pagan Kennedy, "William Gibson's Future Is Now," *New York Times*, January 13, 2012, https://www.nytimes.com/2012/01/15/books/review /distrust-that-particular-flavor-by-william-gibson-book-review.html.

Chapter 1 – Space: Print Me Up, Scotty!

1. Jason Dunn, author's phone interview, July 20, 2020; NASA's Ames Research Center, "Jason Dunn – The Future of Making Things in Space," January 31, 2017, www.youtube.com/watch?list=PLfnpkfDmrBqYgX1O3 kRQnc5Sjzz_LMwD0&time_continue=3313&v=ZXYCKoTclCc.

2. Olivia Solon, "'It's about Expanding Earth': Could We Build Cities in Space?" *The Guardian*, April 21, 2018, https://www.theguardian.com /science/2018/apr/21/expanding-earth-could-we-build-cities-in-space.

3. Zachary T. Sampson, "First 3-D Printing in Space Had Bay Area Start," *Tampa Bay Times*, December 8, 2014, https://www.tampabay.com/archive /2014/12/08/first-3-d-printing-in-space-had-bay-area-start/.

4. Solon, "'It's about Expanding Earth.'"

5. Jason Dunn, author's phone interview, July 20, 2020.

6. Jason Dunn, author's phone interview, July 20, 2020. See also Solon, "'It's about Expanding Earth.'"

7. Aaron Kemmer, author's phone interview, July 3, 2020.

8. "ISS National Laboratory," NASA, https://www.nasa.gov/mission _pages/station/research/nlab/index.html.

9. Aaron Kemmer, author's phone interview, July 3, 2020.

10. Jason Dunn, author's phone interview, July 20, 2020. See also Solon, "'It's about Expanding Earth.'"

11. Jason Dunn, author's phone interview, July 20, 2020.

12. Aaron Kemmer, author's phone interview, July 3, 2020.

13. Aaron Kemmer, author's phone interview, July 3, 2020.

14. Yvonne Cagle, author's phone interview, July 21, 2020.

15. Jason Dunn, author's phone interview, July 20, 2020. See also Sampson, "First 3-D Printing in Space."

16. Jason Dunn, author's phone interview, July 20, 2020. See also Solon, "'It's about Expanding Earth.'"

17. Bernard Kutter, author's phone interview, May 20, 2020.

18. Ramin Khadem, author's phone interview, April 27, 2020.

19. Brian Weeden, author's phone interview, April 30, 2020.

20. Yonatan Winetraub, author's phone interview, April 24, 2020.

21. Dave Mosher, "Congress and Trump are Running out of Time to Fix a $100-Billion Investment in the Sky, NASA Auditor Says," *Business Insider*, May 18, 2018, www.businessinsider.com/space-station-trump-plan -problems-astronaut-risk-2018-5.

22. Jackie Wattles, "NASA Says Moon Rocket Could Cost as Much as $1.6 Billion Per Launch," CNN, December 9, 2019, www.cnn.com/2019/12/09 /tech/nasa-sls-price-cost-artemis-moon-rocket-scn/index.html.

23. NASA's Ames Research Center, "Jason Dunn – The Future of Making Things in Space," January 31, 2017, 25:00, www.youtube.com/watch?list= PLfnpkfDmrBqYgX1O3kRQnc5Sjzz_LMwD0&time_continue=3313& v=ZXYCK0TclCc.

24. Chris Stott, author's phone interview, April 21, 2020.

25. Andrew Wade, "Made in Space: New Production Frontiers," *The Engineer*, February 8, 2016, https://www.theengineer.co.uk/made-in-space -new-production-frontiers/.

26. Michael Potter, author's phone interview, April 17, 2020.

27. Carol Goldstein, author's phone interview, April 19, 2020.

28. Rachel Layne, "Space Case: Why Reaching for the Stars Could Soon Be a $1 Trillion Industry," CBS News, July 16, 2019, https://www.cbsnews .com/news/space-is-a-more-than-400-billion-market-and-getting-bigger/.

29. Peter Garretson, author's phone interview, May 12, 2020.

30. "Made in Space, Inc. to Demonstrate Manufacture of Exotic Optical Fiber in Space," PR.com, July 20, 2016, https://www.pr.com/press-release /680087.

31. Andy Patrizio, "IDC: Expect 175 Zettabytes of Data Worldwide by 2025," NetworkWorld, December 3, 2018, www.networkworld.com/article /3325397/idc-expect-175-zettabytes-of-data-worldwide-by-2025.html.

32. Andrew Rush, CEO, Made in Space, testimony to Senate Commerce, Science and Transportation Subcommittee on Space, Science, and Compet-

itiveness Hearing, "Reopening the American Frontier: Reducing Regulatory Barriers and Expanding American Free Enterprise in Space," April 26, 2017, https://www.commerce.senate.gov/2017/4/reopening-the-american -frontier-reducing-regulatory-barriers-and-expanding-american-free -enterprise-in-space. See also "Made in Space, Inc. to Demonstrate Manufacture of Exotic Optical Fiber in Space."

33. Mike Wall, "In-Space Manufacturing Is about to Get a Big Test," Space .com, December 11, 2017, https://www.space.com/39039-made-in-space -off-earth-manufacturing-test.html.

34. Stephen Eisele, author's phone interview, April 28, 2020.

35. William Kramer, author's phone interview, April 28, 2020.

36. Aaron Kemmer, author's phone interview, July 3, 2020.

37. Christian Sallaberger, author's phone interview, May 7, 2020.

Chapter 2 – Learning: The Internet Academy

1. Clive Thompson, "How Khan Academy Is Changing the Rules of Education," *Wired*, July 15, 2011, www.wired.com/2011/07/ff_khan/. See also www.linkedin.com/in/khanacademy/. See also Bryant Urstadt, "Salman Khan: The Messiah of Math," *Bloomberg Businessweek*, May 19, 2011, www .bloomberg.com/news/articles/2011-05-19/salman-khan-the-messiah-of -math.

2. Claudia Dreifus, "It All Started with a 12-Year-Old Cousin," *New York Times*, January 28, 2014, http://www.nytimes.com/2014/01/28/science /salman-khan-turned-family-tutoring-into-khan-academy.html.

3. Michael Noer, "One Man, 1 Computer, 10 Million Students: How Khan Academy Is Reinventing Education," Forbes, November 19, 2012, www .forbes.com/sites/michaelnoer/2012/11/02/one-man-one-computer -10-million-students-how-khan-academy-is-reinventing-education/ #7e17495444e0.

4. Sarah Benson, "Salman Khan," Sutori, www.sutori.com/story/salman -khan--Lvux5bFpvn8zTBS222BUgLRN.

5. Helena de Bertodano, "Khan Academy: The Man Who Wants to Teach the World," *The Guardian*, September 28, 2018, www.telegraph.co.uk /education/educationnews/9568850/Khan-Academy-The-man-who -wants-to-teach-the-world.html. See also Nikhil Menon, "How Sal Khan Is Exorcising the Math Spectre from the Minds of Millions of Students Worldwide," *The Economic Times*, August 10, 2012, https://economictimes

.indiatimes.com/how-sal-khan-is-exorcising-the-math-spectre-from-the
-minds-of-millions-of-students-worldwide/articleshow/15425169.cms.

6. Salman Khan, *The 1 World School House* (New York: Twelve, 2012), 152–55.

7. Somini Sengupta, "Online Learning, Personalized," *New York Times*, December 4, 2011, https://www.nytimes.com/2011/12/05/technology /khan-academy-blends-its-youtube-approach-with-classrooms.html. See also "Grace King High School," *U.S. News and World Report*, www.usnews .com/education/best-high-schools/louisiana/districts/jefferson-parish -public-school-system/grace-king-high-school-8639.

8. "Sal Khan's Academy Lights the Way," *Financial Express* (Bangladesh), December 26, 2010.

9. Par Parekh, "The Math of Khan: Salman Khan: Founder of the Kahn Academy," Bidoun, www.bidoun.org/articles/the-math-of-khan.

10. Menon, "How Sal Khan Is Exorcising the Math Spectre."

11. Thompson, "How Khan Academy Is Changing the Rules of Education."

12. Bruce Love, "Sal Khan: An Educational Entrepreneur," CampdenFB, May 7, 2015, https://www.campdenfb.com/article/sal-khan-educational -entrepreneur.

13. Guy Raz, "Sal Khan: Can Technology Help Create a Global Classroom," *NPR TED Radio Hour*, August 11, 2017.

14. Dreifus, "It All Started with a 12-Year-Old Cousin."

15. Dreifus, "It All Started with a 12-Year-Old Cousin." See also Raz, "Sal Khan."

16. Khan, *The 1 World School House*, 25.

17. "How Khan Academy Is Changing Education with Videos Made in a Closet," Mixergy, June 28, 2010, https://mixergy.com/interviews/salman -khan-academy-interview/.

18. Dreifus, "It All Started with a 12-Year Old Cousin."

19. Thompson, "How Khan Academy Is Changing the Rules of Education."

20. Khan, *The 1 World School House*, 26–27.

21. "Next Knowledge Factbook 2010," Kellogg Northwestern, 2010, www.kellogg.northwestern.edu/faculty/jones-ben/htm /NextKnowledgeFactbook2010.pdf.

22. Noer, "One Man, 1 Computer, 10 Million Students."

23. Kasra Koushan, "Sal Khan on Creating a Better Future," The Signal, July 20, 2017, https://thesign.al/sal-khan/.

24. Sowmya Nandakumar, "Salman Khan: World's Most Influential Online

Educator," *Indo-American News*, May 17, 2012, page 6, https://issuu.com /indoamericannews/docs/may18_pages_1-36.

25. Khan, *The 1 World School House*, 219–21.

26. Nicole Stott, author's phone interview, May 11, 2020.

27. Aleta Margolis, author's phone conversation, May 26, 2020.

28. Robert Murphy, author's telephone interview, May 27, 2020.

29. Noer, "One Man, 1 Computer, 10 Million Students."

30. Surojit Gupta, " Salman's India Dream: Coaching 450m in 10 years," *Times of India*, December 5, 2015, https://timesofindia.indiatimes.com /india/salmans-india-dream-coaching-450m-in-10-years/articleshow /50036337.cms.

31. De Bertodano, "Khan Academy."

32. Khan, *The 1 World School House*, 155–56.

33. Noer, "One Man, 1 Computer, 10 Million Students." See also Menon, "How Sal Khan Is Exorcising the Math Spectre." See also de Bertodano, "Khan Academy." See also David A. Kaplan, "Bill Gates' Favorite Teacher," *Fortune*, August 24, 2010, https://archive.fortune.com/2010/08/23 /technology/sal_khan_academy.fortune/index.htm. See also Jeffrey R. Young, "College 2.0: A Self-Appointed Teacher Runs a One-Man 'Academy' on YouTube," *Chronicle of Higher Education*, June 6, 2010, www.chronicle .com/article/College-20-A-Self-Appointed/65793.

34. Khan, *The 1 World School House*, 157.

35. Thompson, "How Khan Academy Is Changing the Rules of Education."

36. Khan Academy, "Bill Gates Talks about the Khan Academy at Aspen Ideas Festival 2010," July 19, 2010, www.youtube.com/watch?v= 6Ao7Pj71TUA. See also Chidanand Rajghatta, "Modi to Meet Salman Khan, the Educator not the Movie Star," *Times of India*, September 28, 2015, https://timesofindia.indiatimes.com/india/modi-to-meet-salman-khan -the-educator-not-the-movie-star/articleshow/49113900.cms.

37. De Bertodano, "Khan Academy."

38. Rajghatta, "Modi to Meet Salman Khan." See also Gupta, "Khan Academy CEO Salman Khan's India Dream." See also "Businessman Carlos Slim Will Invest More Than 317 US Dollar Millions in Education," European Press Agency (EPA), January 19, 2013. See also "Tata Trusts to Support Khan Academy for Free Online Education," *Hindustan Times*, December 7, 2015, www.hindustantimes.com/education/tata-trusts-to-support-khan

-academy-for-free-online-education/story-kpQuo1Ph4QGi9HDBrT3SVP
.html.

39. "Sal Khan on Why Khan Academy Is a Non-Profit," *Overheard with Evan Smith*, season 5, episode 18, aired April 20, 2015, www.youtube.com /watch?v=LI7UOuX9Qjs.

40. Gupta, "Khan Academy CEO Salman Khan's India Dream." See also Alex Wagner, "Can Sal Khan Reform Education in America?" *Huffington Post*, June 4, 2011, www.huffingtonpost.com/2011/04/04/the-khan-academy -and-educ_n_844390.html.

41. Thompson, "How Khan Academy Is Changing the Rules of Education."

42. Gupta, "Khan Academy CEO Salman Khan's India Dream." See also Arie Passwaters, "President's Lecture Series to Present Educational Innovator Salman Khan," Rice University Office of Public Affairs, September 24, 2018, https://news.rice.edu/2018/09/24/presidents-lecture-series-to-present -educational-innovator-salman-khan/.

43. "What Languages Is Khan Academy Available In," Khan Academy, May 1, 2020, https://support.khanacademy.org/hc/en-us/articles/226457308 -Is-Khan-Academy-available-in-other-languages-.

44. Supriya Tripathi, author's phone interview, May 23, 2020.

45. David Arnold, author's phone interview, May 28, 2020.

46. Kaplan, "Bill Gates' Favorite Teacher."

47. Gary Stager, author's phone interview, May 22, 2020. See also Thompson, "How Khan Academy Is Changing the Rules of Education."

48. Karim Ani, author's phone interview, May 19, 2020.

49. Sylvia Martinez, author's phone interview, May 19, 2020. See also Thompson, "How Khan Academy Is Changing the Rules of Education."

50. Valerie Strauss, "Khan Academy: The Revolution that Isn't," *Washington Post*, July 23, 2012, www.washingtonpost.com/blogs/answer-sheet/post /khan-academy-the-hype-and-the-reality/2012/07/23/gJQAuw4J3W _blog.html?utm_term=.36e13b742375.

51. Thompson, "How Khan Academy Is Changing the Rules of Education."

52. Dana Goldstein, "Research Shows Students Falling Months Behind during Virus Disruptions," *New York Times*, June 5, 2020, www.nytimes .com/2020/06/05/us/coronavirus-education-lost-learning.html.

53. "Khan Academy Launches Free LSAT Prep for All," Law School Admission Council, June 1, 2018, https://www.lsac.org/about/news/khan -academy-launches-free-lsat-test-prep-all.

54. Kent D. Lollis, "Living, Working, and Achieving While Black," Law School Admission Council, June 16, 2020, www.lsac.org/blog/living -working-and-achieving-while-black.

55. Nadia Rahman, LinkedIn profile, retrieved May 23, 2020, www.linkedin .com/in/nadia-rahman-62203182/.

56. Helen Walters, "Two Giants of Online Learning Discuss the Future of Education," Ideas.Ted.com, January 28, 2014, https://ideas.ted.com /in-conversation-salman-khan-sebastian-thrun-talk-online-education/.

Chapter 3 – Shelter: Let There Be Light

1. Netta Achituv, "The Israeli Who Is Bringing Electricity, Agriculture and Medicine Cheaply to the Poorest Countries in the World" [in Hebrew], *The Marker*, July 6, 2016, https://www.themarker.com/themarker-women /MAGAZINE-1.2998657.

2. Sivan Yaari, author's interview, Innovation: Africa Office, Herzliya, August 8, 2019.

3. Sivan Yaari, "Africa: Is Good Good Enough?" TEDx Tel Aviv University, February 15, 2016, https://www.youtube.com/watch?v=tfgAexR5Z2w.

4. Ian Zelaya, "Lighting a Continent," *Washington Jewish Week*, November 13, 2013, http://washingtonjewishweek.com/7152/lighting-a-continent /news/world-news/. See also "New Perspectives: Influencing Circum-stances through Human Connection– Spotlight: Sivan Yaari '02," *Altitude*, Winter 2020, https://www.alumni.pace.edu/s/1655/bp20/interior.aspx ?sid=1655&gid=2&pgid=2383.

5. Sivan Yaari, author's interview, Innovation: Africa Office, Herzliya, August 8, 2019.

6. Shlomit Lan, "Positive Energy" [in Hebrew], *Globes*, May 17, 2010, https://www.globes.co.il/news/article.aspx?did=1000560436.

7. "Philip LaRocco: Adjunct Professor of International and Public Affairs," Columbia University School of International and Public Affairs, https:// sipa.columbia.edu/faculty-research/faculty-directory/philip-larocco.

8. Phil LaRocco, author's phone interview, March 25, 2020.

9. Yaari, "Africa: Is Good Good Enough?"

10. Sivan Yaari, author's interview, Innovation: Africa Office, Herzliya, August 8, 2019.

11. Phil LaRocco, author's phone interview, March 25, 2020.

12. Yaari, "Africa: Is Good Good Enough?"

13. Yaari, "Africa: Is Good Good Enough?"

14. Sivan Yaari, author's interview, Innovation: Africa Office, Herzliya, August 8, 2019.

15. Stephen Oryszczuk, "Africa Gains from Israel's Solar System," *Jewish News*, April 12, 2018, https://jewishnews.timesofisrael.com/africa-gains -from-israels-solar-system/.

16. Yaari, "Africa: Is Good Good Enough?"

17. Yaari, "Africa: Is Good Good Enough?"

18. Rebeca Kuropatwa, "Helping 1 Village at a Time," *Jewish Independent*, June 16, 2017, https://www.jewishindependent.ca/tag/sivan-yaari/.

19. Gil Haskel, author's phone interview, March 10, 2020.

20. Sivan Yaari, author's interview, Innovation: Africa Office, Herzliya, August 8, 2019.

21. Natie Kirsh, author's phone interview, March 25, 2020.

22. Stephen Koseff, author's phone interview, March 19, 2020.

23. David Arison, author's phone interview, March 30, 2020.

24. Sivan Yaari, author's interview, Innovation: Africa Office, Herzliya, August 8, 2019.

25. Clive Cookson, "Africa to Propel World's Population towards 10bn by 2050," *Financial Times*, June 17, 2019, https://www.ft.com/content /868e20d0-90ec-11e9-b7ea-60e35ef678d2.

26. Sivan Yaari, author's interview, Innovation: Africa Office, Herzliya, August 8, 2019.

Chapter 4 – Environment: Water World

1. Henk Ovink, author's phone interview, April 1, 2020. See also Russell Shorto, "How to Think Like the Dutch in a Post-Sandy World," *New York Times Magazine*, April 9, 2014, https://www.nytimes.com/2014/04/13 /magazine/how-to-think-like-the-dutch-in-a-post-sandy-world.html.

2. David Wolman, "Before the Levees Break: A Plan to Save the Nether- lands," *Wired*, December 22, 2008, https://www.wired.com/2008/12/ff -dutch-delta/.

3. Denise Lu and Christopher Flavelle, "Rising Seas Will Erase More Cities by 2050, New Research Shows," *New York Times*, October 29, 2019, https://www.nytimes.com/interactive/2019/10/29/climate/coastal-cities -underwater.html.

4. Stefan Rahmstorf, author's phone interview, March 26, 2020.

5. "Dutch Flood Expertise Is Big Export Business," *Telegram & Gazette*, November 13, 2017.

6. Henk Ovink, author's phone interview, April 1, 2020. See also Shorto, "How to Think Like the Dutch in a Post-Sandy World."

7. Arun Gupta, "Disaster Capitalism Hits New York," *In These Times*, February 2013, https://inthesetimes.com/article/14430/disaster_capitalism_hits_new_york.

8. Jos Dijkman, author's phone interview, April 11, 2020.

9. Alexandra Wynne, "Special Report: Plugging the Floods Will Mean Going Dutch," *New Civil Engineer*, June 3, 2014, https://www.newcivilengineer.com/archive/special-report-plugging-the-floods-will-mean-going-dutch-03-06-2014/.

10. Mike Corder, "Water Wizards: Dutch Flood Expertise Is Big Export Business," Associated Press, November 12, 2017, https://apnews.com/article/1bc1f137cb134fdca67afdff08c242bc.

11. "Seven Wonders of the Modern World as Named by ASCE," Herff College of Engineering, University of Memphis, http://www.ce.memphis.edu/1101/interesting_stuff/7wonders.html.

12. Bas Jonkman, author's phone interview, April 14, 2020.

13. Marinke Steenhuis, author's phone interview, April 14, 2020.

14. Wynne, "Special Report: Plugging the Floods Will Mean Going Dutch."

15. David Waggonner, author's phone interview, April 13, 2020.

16. Marlise Simons, "Dutch Floods Came in the Back Door," *New York Times*, February 5, 1995, https://www.nytimes.com/1995/02/05/world/dutch-floods-came-in-the-back-door.html.

17. Tracy Metz, author's phone interview, April 6, 2020.

18. Will Storr, "Flooded Britain: How Can Holland Help?" *Daily Telegraph* (UK), April 26, 2014, https://www.telegraph.co.uk/culture/art/architecture/10769974/Flooded-Britain-how-can-Holland-help.html.

19. Henk Ovink, author's phone interview, April 1, 2020.

Chapter 5 – Hygiene: There Will Be Blood

1. Arunachalam Muruganantham, author's phone interview, February 21, 2020. See also "From Rags to Riches," *The Nation* (Nigeria), September 20, 2014, https://thenationonlineng.net/from-rags-to-riches/. See also Stephanie Nolen, "The Absorbing Tale of 1 Man's Quest for Better Feminine Hygiene," *Globe and Mail* (Canada), October 4, 2012.

2. Arunachalam Muruganantham, author's phone interview, February 21, 2020. See also Arunachalam Muruganantham, "How I Started a Sanitary Napkin Revolution," TED@Bangalore, May 2012, www.ted.com/talks/arunachalam_muruganantham_how_i_started_a_sanitary_napkin_revolution?language=en#t-70857.

3. Arunachalam Muruganantham, author's phone interview, February 21, 2020. See also Muruganantham, "How I Started a Sanitary Napkin Revolution."

4. Kristie Lu Stout, " India's 'Pad Man' Becomes Bollywood Blockbuster," CNN, February 8, 2018, http://edition.cnn.com/TRANSCRIPTS/1802/08/nwsm.01.html.

5. Arunachalam Muruganantham, author's phone interview, February 21, 2020; April 20, 2021.

6. Arunachalam Muruganantham, author's phone interview, February 21, 2020; April 20, 2021. See also "India's 'Menstruation Man' Reinvents Sanitary Pads," *Pakistan Today*, May 15, 2016, https://archive.pakistantoday.com.pk/2016/05/15/indias-menstruation-man-reinvents-sanitary-pads/. See also Nolen, "The Absorbing Tale."

7. Arunachalam Muruganantham, author's phone interview, February 21, 2020.

8. Vishal Gondal, author's phone interview, April 8, 2020.

9. Arunachalam Muruganantham, author's phone interview, February 21, 2020; April 20, 2021. See also Manjusha Radhakrishnan, "Meet the Real 'Pad Man' Arunachalam Muruganatham," *Gulf News*, February 7, 2018.

10. Arunachalam Muruganantham, author's phone interview, February 21, 2020; April 20, 2021.

11. Arunachalam Muruganantham, author's phone interview, February 21, 2020.

12. Arunachalam Muruganantham, author's phone interview, February 21, 2020.

13. Arunachalam Muruganantham, author's phone interview, February 21, 2020.

14. S. R. Ramesh, author's phone interview, March 28, 2020.

15. Sashi Anand, author's phone interview, March 30, 2020.

16. Arunachalam Muruganantham, author's phone interview, February 21, 2020.

17. Arunachalam Muruganantham, author's phone interview, February 21, 2020.

18. Arunachalam Muruganantham, author's phone interview, February 21, 2020.

19. Arunachalam Muruganantham, author's phone interview, February 21, 2020. See also "Who Is Arunachalam Muruganantham?" *Financial Express* (Bangladesh), February 8, 2018, www.financialexpress.com/entertainment /who-is-arunachalam-muruganantham-the-real-padman-who-was-the -inspiration-for-akshay-kumar-movie/1059638/.

20. Arunachalam Muruganantham, author's phone interview, February 21, 2020; April 20, 2021.

21. Arunachalam Muruganantham, author's phone interview, April 20, 2021. Yudhijit Bhattacharjee, "Launch Pad," *New York Times*, November 10, 2016, https://www.nytimes.com/interactive/2016/11/13/magazine/design-issue -sanitary-pads-india.html.

22. "Environment-Friendly Sanitary Pads: Work in Progress," *Free Press Journal* (India), December 6, 2018, https://www.freepressjournal.in/cmcm /environment-friendly-sanitary-pads-work-in-progress. See also Priyanka Golikeri, "An Enterprise Aimed at Boosting Women's Health," DNA, June 9, 2011, https://www.dnaindia.com/business/report-an-enterprise-aimed -at-boosting-women-s-health-1552766. See also Abigail Jones, "The Silence That Still Surrounds Periods," *The Independent* (UK), April 25, 2016, https:// www.independent.co.uk/life-style/health-and-families/silence-around -menstruation-a7000051.html.

23. "National Family Health Survey (NFHS-4)," *India Fact Sheet, Ministry of Health and Family Welfare*, 2015-2016, http://rchiips.org/NFHS/pdf /NFHS4/India.pdf.

24. Arunachalam Muruganantham, author's phone interview, February 21, 2020. *Pakistan Today*, "India's 'Menstruation Man' Reinvents Sanitary Pads." See also Radhakrishnan, "Meet the Real 'Pad Man.'" See also Adeline Dorcas, "Pad Man Makes Nationwide Campaign for Use of Sanitary Napkins," *Medindia*, May 11, 2018, https://www.medindia.net/news/healthwatch /pad-man-makes-nationwide-campaign-for-use-of-sanitary-napkins -179368-1.htm. See also Jones, "The Silence that Still Surrounds Periods."

25. Radhakrishnan, "Meet the Real 'Pad Man.'"

26. Babu Yogeswaran, author's phone interview, March 26, 2020.

27. Arunachalam Muruganantham, author's phone interview, February 21, 2020

28. Arunachalam Muruganantham, author's phone interview, February 21, 2020

29. Arunachalam Muruganantham, author's phone interview, February 21, 2020. See also Betsy Teutsch, "How Sanitary Pads Can Help Women Improve their Health and Education," *The Atlantic*, April 22, 2014, https://www.theatlantic.com/business/archive/2014/04/sanitary-napkin-business/360297/.

30. Arunachalam Muruganantham, author's phone interview, February 21, 2020. See also Gilson, "India's Menstruation Man."

31. Arunachalam Muruganantham, author's phone interview, February 21, 2020

32. Arunachalam Muruganantham, author's phone interview, February 21, 2020. See also Brian Wang, "Cheap Sanitary Pads Are Better Than Apple iPads for Poor Women in India by Improving Lives, Improving Health and Providing Thousands of Jobs," *Next Big Future*, March 5, 2014, https://www.nextbigfuture.com/2014/03/cheap-sanitary-pads-are-better-than.html. See also Gilson, "India's Menstruation Man."

33. Arunachalam Muruganantham, author's phone interview, February 21, 2020. See also Gilson, "India's Menstruation Man." See also "This Man Is a Sanitary Pad Revolutionary. Watch Him Take On the Age-Old Taboo" [in Hindi], *Daily Bhaskar*, March 3, 2016, https://daily.bhaskar.com/news/TOP-sanitary-pad-revolutionary-arunachalam-muruganantham-menstruation-man-5265202-PHO.html. See also Wang, "Cheap Sanitary Pads Are Better Than Apple iPads."

34. Arunachalam Muruganantham, author's phone interview, February 21, 2020.

35. Venkatesh Mahadevan, author's phone interview, April 2, 2020.

36. Dr. Sujithra Beena, author's phone interview, March 28, 2020.

37. Dr. Rengaraj Venkatesh, author's phone interview, March 18, 2020.

38. Arunachalam Muruganantham, author's phone interview, February 21, 2020; April 20, 2021.

Chapter 6 – Medicine: Playing God – Genetic Editing

1. "The First Trial of 'Gene Editing Baby' Sentenced He Jiankui and 3 Other Defendants to Be Held Criminally Responsible" [in Chinese], *Xin-*

huanet, December 30, 2019, http://www.xinhuanet.com/legal/2019-12/30 /c_1125403802.htm.

2. "He Jiankui Defends 'World's First Gene-Edited Babies,'" BBC, November 28, 2018, https://www.bbc.com/news/world-asia-china-46368731. See also Edward Lanphier, Fyodor Urnov, Sarah Ehlen Haecker, et al., "Don't Edit the Human Germ Line," *Nature*, March 12, 2015, www.nature.com /news/don-t-edit-the-human-germ-line-1.17111.

3. Akshat Rathi and Echo Huang, "More Than 100 Chinese Scientists Have Condemned the CRISPR Baby Experiment as 'Crazy,'" *Quartz*, November 26, 2018, https://qz.com/1474530/chinese-scientists-condemn-crispr -baby-experiment-as-crazy/. See also Jon Cohen, "The Untold Story of the 'Circle of Trust' behind the World's First Gene-Edited Babies," *Science*, August 1, 2019, www.sciencemag.org/news/2019/08/untold-story-circle -trust-behind-world-s-first-gene-edited-babies.

4. Alexandra Harney and Kate Kelland, "China Orders Investigation after Scientist Claims First Gene-Edited Babies," Reuters, November 26, 2018, https://www.reuters.com/article/us-health-china-babies-genes/china -orders-investigation-after-scientist-claims-first-gene-edited-babies -idUSKCN1NV19T.

5. Carl Zimmer, "From Fearsome Predator to Man's Best Friend," *New York Times*, May 16, 2013, www.nytimes.com/2013/05/16/science/dogs-from -fearsome-predator-to-mans-best-friend.html.

6. "The Evolution of Corn," Genetics Learning Center, University of Utah, July 2015, http://learn.genetics.utah.edu/content/selection/corn/. See also Hatice Bilgic, Erdogan Hakki, Anamika Pandey, Mohd Kamran Khan, and Mahinur Akkaya, "Ancient DNA from 8400 Year-Old Çatalhöyük Wheat: Implications for the Origin of Neolithic Agriculture," *PloS 1* 11, no. 3 (2016), https://www.ncbi.nlm.nih.gov/pmc/articles/PMC4801371/.

7. Rodolphe Barrangou, author's interview, October 12, 2020.

8. Prashant Nair, "QnAs with Rodolphe Barrangou," PNAS, July 11, 2017, www.pnas.org/content/114/28/7183. In 2011, Dupont purchased Danisco for USD $6.3 billion and began enhancing all of its yogurts and cheeses. This food giant owns a significant portion of the global dairy market, and so a significant number of people have consumed products that were manufactured using CRISPR cultures.

9. Martin Jinek, Krzysztof Chrlinski, et al., "A Programmable Dual-RNA-

Guided DNA Endonuclease in Adaptive Bacterial Immunity," *Science,* August 17, 2012, https://science.sciencemag.org/content/337/6096/816.

10. *Human Nature,* directed by Adam Bolt, Greenwich Entertainment, March 13, 2020.

11. *Human Nature,* directed by Adam Bolt, Greenwich Entertainment, March 13, 2020. See also Le Cong, F. Ann Ran, David Cox, Shuailiang Lin, et al., "Multiplex Genome Engineering Using CRISPR/Cas Systems," *Nature,* February 15, 2013, http://science.sciencemag.org/content/339/6121/819.long.

12. Mark Shwartz, "Target, Delete, Repair," *Stanford Medicine,* Winter 2018, https://stanmed.stanford.edu/2018winter/CRISPR-for-gene-editing-is-revolutionary-but-it-comes-with-risks.html.

13. *Human Nature,* directed by Adam Bolt, Greenwich Entertainment, March 13, 2020.

14. Megan Molteni, "The Wired Guide to CRISPR," *Wired,* March 12, 2019, https://www.wired.com/story/wired-guide-to-crispr/.

15. Shwartz, "Target, Delete, Repair."

16. Daniel Kraft, author's phone interview, February 19, 2020. See also Stephan Spencer, "Exponential Medicine in a COVID-19 World with Dr. Daniel Kraft," *Get Yourself Optimized,* no. 246, May 7, 2020, www.getyourselfoptimized.com/exponential-medicine-in-a-covid-19-world-with-dr-daniel-kraft/.

17. Rodolphe Barrangou, author's phone interview, June 16, 2020.

18. Timothy Winegard, "People v Mosquitos: What to Do about Our Biggest Killer," *The Guardian,* September 20, 2019, https://www.theguardian.com/environment/2019/sep/20/man-v-mosquito-biggest-killer-malaria-crispr.

19. World Health Organization, "Mosquito Sterilization Offers New Opportunity to Control Chikungunya, Dengue, and Zika," November 14, 2019, https://www.who.int/news-room/detail/14-11-2019-mosquito-sterilization-offers-new-opportunity-to-control-chikungunya-dengue-and-zika.

20. Anthony James, author's phone interview, June 12, 2020.

21. Jennifer Khan, "The Gene Drive Dilemma: We Can Alter Entire Species, but Should We?" *New York Times,* January 8, 2020, https://www.nytimes.com/2020/01/08/magazine/gene-drive-mosquitoes.html.

22. Alta Charo, author's phone interview, September 1, 2020. Khan, "The Gene Drive Dilemma."

23. Shwartz, "Target, Delete, Repair."

24. @BloombergQuickTake, "Co-Inventor of CRISPR says she's 'horrified,'" *Twitter*, November 28, 2018, https://twitter.com/QuickTake/status /1067772480511766528.

25. Eric Lander, Françoise Baylis, Feng Zhang, Emmanuelle Charpentier, Paul Berg, et al., "Adopt a Moratorium on Heritable Genome Editing," *Nature*, March 13, 2019, https://www.nature.com/articles/d41586-019 -00726-5.

26. Tshaka Cunningham, author's phone interview, October 8, 2020.

27. Megan Molteni, "The World Health Organization Says No More Gene-Edited Babies," *Wired*, July 30, 2019, www.wired.com/story/the -world-health-organization-says-no-more-gene-edited-babies/.

28. Sui-Lee Wee, "Chinese Scientist Who Genetically Edited Babies Gets 3 Years in Prison," *New York Times*, December 30, 2019, https://www.nytimes .com/2019/12/30/business/china-scientist-genetic-baby-prison.html.

29. Ken Dilanian, "China Has Done Human Testing to Create Biologically Enhanced Super Soldiers, Says Top U.S. Official," NBC News, December 4, 2020, https://www.nbcnews.com/politics/national-security/china -has-done-human-testing-create-biologically-enhanced-super-soldiers -n1249914. See also "China Conducts Biological Test on Its Army to Create Super-Soldiers, Says Top US Official," *Business Today* (India), December 9, 2020, https://www.businesstoday.in/current/world/china-conducts -biological-test-on-its-army-to-create-super-soldiers-says-top-us-official /story/424341.html. See also Antonio Regalado, "First Gene-Edited Dogs Reported in China," MIT *Technology Review*, October 19, 2015, https://www .geneticsandsociety.org/article/first-gene-edited-dogs-reported-china.

30. Ruptly, "Russia: Putin Warns a GM Human Could Be 'Worse Than Nuclear Bomb,'" October 21, 2017, www.youtube.com/watch?v= E6pD96RRIUQ.

31. *Human Nature*, directed by Adam Bolt, Greenwich Entertainment, March 13, 2020.

32. Claudia Geib, "Genetic Engineering Can Treat Rare Diseases, but Could Also Give Wealthy Children a Biological Advantage," *Futurism*, August 9, 2017, https://futurism.com/neoscope/expert-argues-that-gene -editing-will-widen-economic-class-gap.

33. *Human Nature*, directed by Adam Bolt, Greenwich Entertainment, March 13, 2020.

34. Daniel MacArthur (@dgmacarthur), "Prediction: my grandchildren will be embryo-screened, germline-edited," Twitter, November 30, 2015, 4:31 p.m., https://twitter.com/dgmacarthur/status/671335629687406592?lang=en.

35. *Human Nature*, directed by Adam Bolt, Greenwich Entertainment, March 13, 2020.

36. Jenny Straiton, "Genetically Modified Humans: The X-Men of Scientific Research," *BioTechniques* 66, no. 6 (June 2019), https://www.future-science.com/doi/pdf/10.2144/btn-2019-0056.

Chapter 7 – Disaster Resilience: The Ring of Fire

1. Shigeru Ban, "Emergency Shelters Made from Paper," TEDxTokyo, August 13, 2013, https://www.ted.com/talks/shigeru_ban_emergency_shelters_made_from_paper/details.

2. Ban, "Emergency Shelters Made from Paper."

3. Ban, "Emergency Shelters Made from Paper."

4. Mark Schreiber, "Hell on Earth in '23," *Japan Times*, August 26, 2001, www.japantimes.co.jp/community/2001/08/26/general/hell-on-earth-in-23/#.Xkww7S2ZORu.

5. Yuichi Ono, author's phone interview, April 16, 2020.

6. David Pilling, "Lessons Learnt from Kobe Quake," *Financial Times*, May 11, 2011, https://www.ft.com/content/5290f95e-4bc4-11e0-9705-00144feab49a.

7. Ban, "Emergency Shelters Made from Paper."

8. Rajib Shaw, author's phone interview, April 20, 2020.

9. Jun Sato, author's phone interview, May 4, 2020.

10. John W. van de Lindt, author's phone interview, April 23, 2020.

11. "Tokyo, the Earthquake-Proof City," *We Build Value*, June 27, 2018, www.webuildvalue.com/en/reportage/tokyo-the-earthquake-proof-city.html.

12. Toro Takeuchi, author's phone interview, April 17, 2020.

13. Sigrid Adriaenssens, author's phone interview, April 16, 2020.

14. Joyce Meri, author's phone interview, April 7, 2020.

15. Satoru Nishikawa, author's phone interview, April 6, 2020.

16. "Disaster Prevention Information," *Disaster Preparedness Tokyo*, 2019,

https://www.bousai.metro.tokyo.lg.jp/book/pdf/en/01_Simulation_of _a_Major_Earthquake.pdf.

17. Takeshi Komino, author's phone interview, April 13, 2020.

18. "Disaster Prevention Information," *Disaster Preparedness Tokyo*, 2019.

19. "Manga Comic: 'Tokyo "X" Day,'" *Disaster Preparedness Tokyo*, 2019, https://www.bousai.metro.tokyo.lg.jp/book/pdf/en/comic.pdf.

20. Mikio Ishiwatari, author's interview, April 19, 2020.

21. "Safe Cities Index 2019," *The Economist*, https://safecities.economist .com/safe-cities-index-2019/.

22. Cameron Allan Mckean, "Tokyo's Disaster Parks," *The Guardian*, August 19, 2014, www.theguardian.com/cities/2014/aug/19/tokyo-disaster-parks -hi-tech-survival-bunkers-hidden-green-spaces-earthquake.

23. Thu Ngo Nha, "A Glimpse of Japan's Deadly Earthquakes," ArcGIS StoryMaps, August 18, 2019, https://storymaps.arcgis.com/stories/da0a cfccaece4fc481353b1a01589259.

24. *We Build Value*, "Tokyo, the Earthquake-Proof City."

25. "Earthquake-Proof Tokyo Named Safest City in the World," *Architecture*, April 11, 2019, www.architecturelab.net/earthquake-safest-city-in-the -world/.

26. Evan Reis, author's phone interview, April 23, 2020.

27. Rajib Shaw, author's phone interview, April 20, 2020.

28. "Osaka Quake Exposes Japan's Aging Infrastructure," *Nikkei Asian Review*, June 19, 2018, https://asia.nikkei.com/Economy/Osaka-quake -exposes-Japan-s-aging-infrastructure.

29. Amy Davidson Sorkin, "Japan: Earthquake, Water, Fire," *New Yorker*, March 11, 2011, https://www.newyorker.com/news/amy-davidson/japan -earthquake-water-fire.

30. Nikil Saval, "Shigeru Ban," *New York Times*, October 18, 2019, www .nytimes.com/interactive/2019/10/15/t-magazine/shigeru-ban.html.

Chapter 8 – Energy: The Electric Slide

1. Marc Tarpenning, author's phone interview, November 17, 2020. See also Stanford Center for Professional Development, "Stanford Seminar: Electric Vehicles and Startups," January 5, 2017, https://www.youtube.com/watch ?v=s47Cy8OUNcM.

2. Stanford Center for Professional Development, "Stanford Seminar: Electric Vehicles and Startups."

3. Martin Eberhard, author's phone interview, November 23, 2020. See also Stanford Center for Professional Development, "Stanford Seminar: Electric Vehicles and Startups." See also Drake Baer, "The Making of Tesla: Invention, Betrayal, and the Birth of the Roadster," *Business Insider*, November 11, 2014, www.businessinsider.com/tesla-the-origin-story-2014-10.

4. Martin Eberhard, author's phone interview, November 23, 2020. See also Baer, "The Making of Tesla."

5. Stanford Center for Professional Development, "Stanford Seminar: Electric Vehicles and Startups."

6. Baer, "The Making of Tesla."

7. Martin Eberhard, author's phone interview, November 23, 2020. See also Baer, "The Making of Tesla."

8. Marc Tarpenning, author's phone interview, November 17, 2020. See also Marc Tarpenning and Shernaz Daver, "The Story of Building Tesla," Startup Grind, June 3, 2018, https://www.youtube.com/watch?v=pGf1tyPXBpA.

9. Martin Eberhard, author's phone interview, November 23, 2020. See also Stanford Center for Professional Development, "Stanford Seminar: Electric Vehicles and Startups."

10. Chris Nuttall, "Tale of a Supercharged Start-Up Entrepreneurship," *Financial Times*, April 12, 2007, https://www.ft.com/content/ab94e730 -e83c-11db-b2c3-000b5df10621.

11. Baer, "The Making of Tesla."

12. Baer, "The Making of Tesla."

13. Baer, "The Making of Tesla."

14. Seth Weintraub, author's phone interview, May 12, 2020.

15. Marc Tarpenning, author's phone interview, November 17, 2020. See also Baer, "The Making of Tesla."

16. Marc Tarpenning, author's phone interview, November 17, 2020. See also Baer, "The Making of Tesla."

17. Baer, "The Making of Tesla."

18. Martin Eberhard, author's phone interview, November 23, 2020. See also Nuttall, "Tale of a Supercharged Start-Up Entrepreneurship."

19. Marc Tarpenning, author's phone interview, November 17, 2020. See also John Reed, "Elon Musk's Groundbreaking Electric Car," *Financial Times*, July 24, 2009, https://www.ft.com/content/e117987e-74eb-11de-9ed5-00144feabdc0. See also Tarpenning and Daver, "The Story of Building Tesla."

20. Marc Tarpenning, author's phone interview, November 17, 2020. See

also MIT Club of Northern California, "Pioneers in Clean Technology – Marc Tarpenning – Tesla Motors," March 6, 2014, https://www.youtube .com/watch?v=EDCYoAQmmAA.

21. Martin Eberhard, author's phone interview, November 23, 2020. See also Baer, "The Making of Tesla."

22. Martin Eberhard, author's phone interview, November 23, 2020.

23. Michael Shnayerson, "Quiet Thunder," *Vanity Fair*, May 2007, https://www.vanityfair.com/news/2007/05/tesla200705.

24. Mike Musgrove, "An Electric Car with Juice," *Washington Post*, July 22, 2006, http://www.washingtonpost.com/wp-dyn/content/article/2006 /07/21/AR2006072101515.html.

25. Baer, "The Making of Tesla."

26. Claire Cain Miller, "Musk Unplugged: Tesla CEO Discusses Car Troubles," *New York Times*, October 24, 2008, https://bits.blogs.nytimes.com /2008/10/24/musk-unplugged-tesla-ceo-discusses-car-troubles/.

27. Martin Eberhard, author's phone interview, November 23, 2020.

28. Marc Tarpenning, author's phone interview, November 17, 2020. See also Tarpenning and Daver, "The Story of Building Tesla."

29. Scott Pelley, "U.S., China, Russia, Elon Musk: Entrepreneur's 'Insane' Vision Becomes Reality," CBS News, May 22, 2012, https://www.cbsnews .com/news/us-china-russia-elon-musk-entrepreneurs-insane-vision -becomes-reality/.

30. "About Tesla," https://www.tesla.com/about.

31. Lawrence Burns, author's phone interview, April 27, 2020.

32. "The Global Electric Vehicle Market in 2020: Statistics & Forecasts," Virta, https://www.virta.global/global-electric-vehicle-market. See also Fred Lambert, "Tesla Produces Its 1 Millionth Electric Car," *Electrek*, March 9, 2020, https://electrek.co/2020/03/09/tesla-produces-1000000th -electric-car/.

33. "Shell Quest Carbon Capture and Storage Project Reaches Milestone of 4M Tonnes," *Canada Press*, May 23, 2019, https://www.cbc.ca/news/canada /calgary/carbon-storage-cnrl-shell-quest-1.5146857. See also Tesla, "Impact Report," https://www.tesla.com/ns_videos/tesla-impact-report-2019.pdf.

34. Marc Tarpenning, author's phone interview, November 17, 2020.

35. Julia Carrie Wong, "Elon Musk Unveils Tesla Electric Truck – and a Surprise New Sports Car," *The Guardian*, November 17, 2017, https://www

.theguardian.com/technology/2017/nov/17/elon-musk-tesla-electric-truck
-sports-car-surprise.

36. Daniel Sperling, author's phone interview, May 11, 2020.

37. Roland Hwang, author's phone interview, May 15, 2020.

38. Mark Kane, "Close to 1.18 Million Plug-In Electric Cars Were Sold in China in 2019," *InsideEVs*, January 22, 2020, https://insideevs.com/news/394229/plugin-electric-car-sales-china-2019/.

39. Yunshi Wang, author's phone interview, May 12, 2020. Peter Marsters, "Electric Cars: The Drive for a Sustainable Solution in China," *Wilson Center*, August 2009, https://www.wilsoncenter.org/publication/electric-cars-the-drive-for-sustainable-solution-china.

40. David Nikel, "Electric Cars: Why Little Norway Leads the World In EV Usage," Forbes, June 18, 2019, https://www.forbes.com/sites/davidnikel/2019/06/18/electric-cars-why-little-norway-leads-the-world-in-ev-usage/.

41. Robbie Diamond, author's phone interview, April 17, 2020.

42. Martin Eberhard, author's phone interview, November 23, 2020. See also "Martin Eberhard Calls Tesla His 'Baby', Talks about Being Ousted from Company's Board," *Economic Times*, March 1, 2019, https://economictimes.indiatimes.com/magazines/panache/martin-eberhard-calls-tesla-his-baby-talks-about-being-ousted-from-companys-board/articleshow/68211761.cms.

43. Marc Tarpenning, author's phone interview, November 17, 2020.

44. Elon Musk (@ElonMuskNewsOrg), "If you get up in the morning...," Twitter, January 2, 2017, 3:30 a.m., https://twitter.com/elonmusknewsorg/status/815731862601666560?lang=en.

Chapter 9 – Prosperity: The King of Microfinance

1. "Bangladesh Continues to Reduce Poverty but at a Slower Pace," World Bank, October 24, 2017, www.worldbank.org/en/news/feature/2017/10/24/bangladesh-continues-to-reduce-poverty-but-at-slower-pace. See also Randeep Ramesh, "Giving a Hand Up, Not a Handout," *The Guardian*, December 27, 2006, https://www.theguardian.com/business/2006/dec/27/money.

2. Julia Kagen, "Microfinance," *Investopedia*, April 21, 2020, www.investopedia.com/terms/m/microfinance.asp.

3. "Muhammad Yunus – Nobel Lecture," Nobel Prize, December 10, 2006,

www.nobelprize.org/prizes/peace/2006/yunus/26090-muhammad
-yunus-nobel-lecture-2006-2/.

4. "Yunus, Grameen Bank win Nobel Peace Prize for Loans to the Poor," *Salt Lake Tribune*, October 13, 2006, https://archive.sltrib.com/article.php ?id=4486938&itype=NGPSID.

5. Muhammad Yunus, *Banker to the Poor: Micro-Lending and the Battle against World Poverty* (New York: PublicAffairs, 1999), vii.

6. Yunus, *Banker to the Poor*, viii.

7. Yunus, *Banker to the Poor*, viii.

8. Yunus, *Banker to the Poor*, ix.

9. Yunus, *Banker to the Poor*, 47.

10. Yunus, *Banker to the Poor*, 48.

11. Yunus, *Banker to the Poor*, 48.

12. Yunus, *Banker to the Poor*, 48.

13. Yunus, *Banker to the Poor*, 50. See also Doug Mellgren, "Bangladeshi Economist Wins Nobel Peace Prize," *Seattle Times*, October 13, 2006, https://www.seattletimes.com/nation-world/bangladeshi-economist-wins-nobel -peace-prize/.

14. Yunus, *Banker to the Poor*, 52.

15. "United Nations Dignitaries Hail Nobel Peace Prize Winners in Special Tribute to Muhammad Yunus, Grameen Bank," United Nations, November 17, 2006, https://www.un.org/press/en/2006/dev2610.doc.htm.

16. Yunus, *Banker to the Poor*, 55.

17. Yunus, *Banker to the Poor*, ix.

18. Yunus, *Banker to the Poor*, ix.

19. Muhammad Yunus, "Grameen Bank at a Glance," Yunus Centre, March 12, 2008, https://www.muhammadyunus.org/post/370/grameen-bank -at-a-glance.

20. Anand Giridharadas and Keith Bradsher, "Microloan Pioneer and His Bank Win Nobel Peace Prize," *New York Times*, October 13, 2006, https://www.nytimes.com/2006/10/13/business/14nobelcnd.html.

21. Andrew Foster, author's phone interview, May 18, 2020.

22. Yunus, *Banker to the Poor*, 64.

23. Yunus, "Grameen Bank at a Glance."

24. Yunus, "Grameen Bank at a Glance."

25. Christian Ahlin, author's phone interview, May 29, 2020.

26. M. Nurul Alam and Dr. Mike Getubig, "Guidelines for Establishing and

Operating Grameen-Style Microcredit Programs," Grameen Foundation, 2010, https://grameenfoundation.org/documents/GrameenGuidelines .pdf.

27. World Data Lab, "World Poverty Clock," September 17, 2020, https:// worldpoverty.io.

28. Max Roser and Esteban Ortiz-Ospina, "Global Extreme Poverty," Our World in Data, 2013, https://ourworldindata.org/extreme-poverty.

29. "CGAP Launches Global Microfinance Survey to Inform COVID-19 Response," Consultative Group to Assist the Poor, June 1, 2020, www.cgap .org/news/cgap-launches-global-microfinance-survey-inform-covid-19 -response.

30. Shahidur R. Khandker, author's phone interview, June 1, 2020. See also Shahidur R. Khandker, M. A. Baqui Khalily, and Hussain A. Samad, *Beyond Ending Poverty: The Dynamics of Microfinance in Bangladesh*, World Bank Group, 2016, http://documents.worldbank.org/curated/en /366431468508832455/pdf/106672-PUB.pdf.

31. Mark Pitt, author's phone interview, May 16, 2020.

32. Bruce Wydick, author's phone interview, May 14, 2020.

33. Cynthia Kinnan, author's phone interview, May 21, 2020.

34. Jonathan Morduch, author's phone interview, May 27, 2020. See also Jonathan Morduch, "The Role of Subsidies in Microfinance: Evidence from the Grameen Bank," *Journal of Development Economics* 60 (1999): 229–48, https://s18798.pcdn.co/jmorduch/wp-content/uploads/sites/5267/2016 /12/Morduch-Grameen-Subsidies-JDE-1999.pdf.

35. Tim Ogden, author's phone interview, May 26, 2020.

36. "Is Grameen Bank Different from Convential Banks," Grameen Bank, March 12, 2011, https://www.grameen-info.org/is-grameen-bank-different -from-conventional-banks/.

37. Britt F. Hagstrom, "The Man behind the Nobel Prize," *Daily Star*, December 10, 2006, https://archive.thedailystar.net/suppliments/2006 /december/bangladeshstandingtall/index.htm.

38. Syed Zain al-Mahmood, "Muhammad Yunus and Bangladesh Government Battle over Grameen," *The Guardian*, November 21, 2012, https://www .theguardian.com/global-development/2012/nov/21/muhammad-yunus -bangladesh-grameen-bank.

Chapter 10 – Food: Green Meat

1. Frederico Alisson-Silva, Kunio Kawanishi, and Ajit Varki, "Human Risk of Diseases Associated with Red Meat Intake: Analysis of Current Theories and Proposed Role for Metabolic Incorporation of a Non-Human Sialic Acid," *Molecular Aspects of Medicine* 51 (October 2016): 16–30, https://www.ncbi.nlm.nih.gov/pmc/articles/PMC5035214/.

2. National Institutes of Health, "Eating Red Meat Daily Triples Heart Disease-Related Chemical," *NIH Research Matters*, January 15, 2019.

3. Mosa Meat, "Why We Need to Change How We Make Meat," July 5, 2018, https://www.youtube.com/watch?v=oSl9yZuPrdo.

4. Scott May, author's phone interview, June 8, 2020.

5. Stephen J. Bronner, "With $72 Million in Funding, the Entrepreneur behind Beyond Meat Pursues Innovation over Profit," *Entrepreneur*, January 22, 2018, https://www.entrepreneur.com/article/307715.

6. Colin Finkle, "Beyond Meat Brand Profile," Brand Marketing Blog, July 21, 2019, https://brandmarketingblog.com/articles/good-branding/beyond-meat-brand-profile/.

7. Anna Starostinetskaya, "Beyond Meat Is about to Go Public; Founder Ethan Brown Speaks about the Evolution of Meat," VegNews, April 4, 2019, https://vegnews.com/2019/4/beyond-meat-is-about-to-go-public-founder-ethan-brown-speaks-about-the-evolution-of-meat. See also Alice Park, "Why We Don't Need Animals to Keep Enjoying Meat," *Time*, June 6, 2019, https://time.com/5601980/beyond-meat-ceo-ethan-brown-interview/.

8. Laurence Darmiento, "Ethan Brown Went Vegan but Missed Fast Food. So He Started a Revolution," *Los Angeles Times*, January 20, 2020, https://www.latimes.com/business/story/2020-01-08/beyond-meat-founder-ethan-brown.

9. Darmiento, "Ethan Brown Went Vegan but Missed Fast Food."

10. Shira Zakai, author's phone interview, January 27, 2020.

11. "Peter G. Brown," Faculty of Agricultural and Environmental Sciences, McGill University, www.mcgill.ca/nrs/academic-0/brown.

12. Tom Foster, "Friends Thought Beyond Meat's Founder Was Crazy. His Billion-Dollar IPO Proved Them Wrong," *Inc.* August 2019, https://www.inc.com/magazine/201908/tom-foster/ethan-brown-beyond-meat-alternative-protein-plant-burger-ipo-public-whole-foods.html.

13. Bronner, "With $72 Million in Funding."

14. "Livestock and Climate Change," World Watch, November/December 2009, https://awellfedworld.org/wp-content/uploads/Livestock-Climate -Change-Anhang-Goodland.pdf.

15. Foster, "Friends Thought Beyond Meat's Founder Was Crazy."

16. Darmiento, "Ethan Brown Went Vegan but Missed Fast Food."

17. Foster, "Friends Thought Beyond Meat's Founder Was Crazy."

18. "Meat: The Future Series; Alternative Proteins," World Economic Forum White Paper, 2019, http://www3.weforum.org/docs/WEF_White _Paper_Alternative_Proteins.pdf. See also "Carbon Footprint Factsheet," University of Michigan, Center for Sustainable Systems, Pub. No. CSS09-05, 2020, http://css.umich.edu/factsheets/carbon-footprint-factsheet. See Hannah Ritchie, "You Want to Reduce the Carbon Footprint of Your Food? Focus on What You Eat, Not Whether Your Food Is Local," Our World in Data, January 24, 2020, https://ourworldindata.org/food-choice -vs-eating-local.

19. Zach Hrynowski, "What Percentage of Americans are Vegetarian?" Gallup, September 27, 2019, https://news.gallup.com/poll/267074/percentage -americans-vegetarian.aspx.

20. Bronner, "With $72 Million in Funding."

21. Darmiento, "Ethan Brown Went Vegan but Missed Fast Food."

22. "Live Episode! Beyond Meat: Ethan Brown," NPR Radio, February 16, 2017, www.npr.org/2017/02/16/515420148/live-episode-beyond-meat -ethan-brown.

23. Fu-Hung Hsieh, author's written correspondence, May 30, 2020.

24. Mark Barna, "Bock Soy," Mizzou, November 7, 2012, https://mizzoumag .missouri.edu/2012/11/bock-soy/index.html.

25. Bronner, "With $72 Million in Funding."

26. Darmiento, "Ethan Brown Went Vegan but Missed Fast Food."

27. Foster, "Friends Thought Beyond Meat's Founder Was Crazy."

28. Darmiento, "Ethan Brown Went Vegan but Missed Fast Food."

29. Darmiento, "Ethan Brown Went Vegan but Missed Fast Food."

30. Darmiento, "Ethan Brown Went Vegan but Missed Fast Food."

31. Darmiento, "Ethan Brown Went Vegan but Missed Fast Food."

32. Darmiento, "Ethan Brown Went Vegan but Missed Fast Food."

33. Bill Gates, "Future of Food," GatesNotes, March 18, 2013, www.gatesnotes .com/About-Bill-Gates/Future-of-Food.

34. Bronner, "With $72 Million in Funding."

35. Darmiento, "Ethan Brown Went Vegan but Missed Fast Food."

36. Ali Bouzari, author's phone interview, May 28, 2020.

37. Martin C. Heller and Gregory A. Keoleian, "Beyond Meat's Beyond Burger Life Cycle Assessment: A Detailed Comparison between a Plant-Based and an Animal-Based Protein Source," Center for Sustainable Systems Report, University of Michigan, September 14, 2018, http://css.umich .edu/publication/beyond-meats-beyond-burger-life-cycle-assessment -detailed-comparison-between-plant-based.

38. Marthe Fourcade and Corinne Gretler, "McDonald's Picks Beyond for Canada Trial, U.S. Prize Remains," Bloomberg, September 26, 2019, www .bloomberg.com/news/articles/2019-09-26/mcdonald-s-to-test-veggie -burger-from-beyond-meat-in-canada.

39. Michelle King, "Dunkin' and Beyond Meat Accelerate Nationwide Launch of Beyond Sausage Sandwich," Dunkin' News Release, October 21, 2019, https://news.dunkindonuts.com/news/releases-20191021.

40. Paul R. La Monica, "Impossible Whoppers Are a Huge Hit at Burger King, Fueling Its Best Quarter in 4 Years," CNN Business, October 28, 2019, www.cnn.com/2019/10/28/investing/restaurant-brands-earnings-burger -king-popeyes/index.html. See also "Sweet Earth Debuts New Plant-Based Culinary Innovations, Awesome Burger & Awesome Grounds," Cision PRNewswire, September 25, 2019, www.prnewswire.com/news-releases /sweet-earth-debuts-new-plant-based-culinary-innovations-awesome -burger--awesome-grounds-300924874.html.

41. Bronner, "With $72 Million in Funding."

42. Nir Goldstein, author's phone interview, June 25, 2020.

43. Rusty Schwartz, author's phone interview, June 2, 2020.

44. "Ad: Fake Meat Grows in Factories, Not on Vines," Center for Consumer Freedom, August 13, 2019, www.consumerfreedom.com/2019/08 /ad-fake-meat-grows-in-factories-not-on-vines/.

45. Darmiento, "Ethan Brown Went Vegan but Missed Fast Food."

46. Darmiento, "Ethan Brown Went Vegan but Missed Fast Food."

47. Brett Hurt, author's phone interview, June 4, 2020.

Chapter 11 – Water: Every Last Drop

1. Associated Press, "A Broken Water Pipe Floods UCLA," *New York Post*, July 29, 2014, https://nypost.com/2014/07/29/a-broken-water-pipe-is -flooding-ucla/.

2. Associated Press, "A Broken Water Pipe Floods UCLA."

3. Simona Shemer, "On World Water Day, a Look at the Innovative Tech That Makes Israel a Water Superpower," No Camels, March 22, 2018, http://nocamels.com/2018/03/on-world-water-day-a-look-at-the-innovative-tech-that-makes-israel-a-water-superpower/. See also World Health Organization, "Drinking Water," June 14, 2009, http://www.who.int/news-room/fact-sheets/detail/drinking-water.

4. Mada Masr, "'We Woke Up in a Desert' – The Water Crisis Taking Hold across Egypt," *The Guardian*, August 4, 2015, www.theguardian.com/world/2015/aug/04/egypt-water-crisis-intensifies-scarcity.

5. Arash Karami, "Iran Official Warns Water Crisis Could Lead to Mass Migration," *Al-Monitor*, April 28, 2015, www.al-monitor.com/pulse/originals/2015/04/iran-water-crisis-mass-migration.html.

6. Leah Schleifer, "7 Reasons We're Facing a Global Water Crisis," World Resources Institute, August 24, 2017, https://www.wri.org/blog/2017/08/7-reasons-were-facing-global-water-crisis.

7. US Government Accountability Office, "Supply Concerns Continue, and Uncertainties Complicate Planning," May 20, 2014, www.gao.gov/products/GAO-14-430.

8. Rachel Layne, "Water Costs Are Rising across the US – Here's Why," CBS, August 27, 2019, https://www.cbsnews.com/news/water-bills-rising-cost-of-water-creating-big-utility-bills-for-americans/.

9. Sarah Frostenson, "America Has a Water Crisis No 1 Is Talking About," *Vox*, March 22, 2018, www.vox.com/science-and-health/2017/5/9/15183330/america-water-crisis-affordability-millions.

10. Hiroko Tabuchi, "$300 Billon War beneath the Street: Fighting to Replace America's Water Pipes," *New York Times*, November 10, 2017, https://www.nytimes.com/2017/11/10/climate/water-pipes-plastic-lead.html.

11. Allison Kosik, "Experts: U.S. Water Infrastructure in Trouble," CNN, January 21, 2011, http://edition.cnn.com/2011/US/01/20/water.main.infrastructure/.

12. Elizabeth Mac, "A Burgeoning Crisis? A Nationwide Assessment of the Geography of Water Affordability in the United States," *PloS 1* 12, no. 4 (January 11, 2017), https://journals.plos.org/plosone/article?id=10.1371/journal.pone.0169488.

13. Tony Kelly, author's phone interview, April 1, 2020.

14. Bill Kingdom, Roland Liemberger, and Philippe Marin, "The Challenge

of Reducing Non-Revenue Water (NRW) in Developing Countries – How the Private Sector Can Help: A Look at Performance-Based Service Contracting," World Bank, *Water Supply and Sanitation Sector Board Discussion Paper Series*, no. 8, December 2006, https://openknowledge.worldbank .org/handle/10986/17238.

15. Elie Ofek and Matthew Preble, "Takadu," Harvard Business School Case 514-011, July 2013 (revised August 2017).

16. Ofek and Preble, "Takadu."

17. Peter Williams, author's phone interview, March 11, 2020.

18. Oded Distel, author's phone interview, March 12, 2020.

19. Amir Peleg, author's interview, Washington, DC, April 2, 2019.

20. Amir Peleg, author's interview, Washington, DC, April 2, 2019.

21. Ofek and Preble, "Takadu."

22. Amir Peleg, author's interview, Washington, DC, April 2, 2019.

23. Amir Peleg, author's interview, Washington, DC, April 2, 2019.

24. Ofek and Preble, "Takadu."

25. Damian Carrington, "England Could Run Short of Water within 25 years," *The Guardian*, March 18, 2019, https://www.theguardian.com /environment/2019/mar/18/england-to-run-short-of-water-within-25 -years-environment-agency.

26. Elise Ackerman, "Israeli Startup Mines Data to Solve Global Water Crisis," *Forbes*, December 31, 2013, https://www.forbes.com/sites /eliseackerman/2013/12/31/israeli-startup-mines-data-to-solve-global -water-crisis/?sh=4ff87d7d2f46.

27. Ofek and Preble, "Takadu."

28. Ofek and Preble, "Takadu."

29. Keith Hays, author's phone interview, April 4, 2020.

30. George Theo, author's phone interview, March 30, 2020.

31. Christopher Gasson, author's phone interview, March 30, 2020.

32. Seth M. Siegel, author's correspondence, October 29, 2016.

33. Jonathan Ferziger, "Netanyahu Offers to Help Brown Manage California Drought," Bloomberg, March 5, 2014, www.bloomberg.com/news/articles /2014-03-05/netanyahu-offers-to-help-brown-manage-california-drought.

Chapter 12 – Governance: The Digital Republic

1. "Estonia Celebrates the Day of Restoration of Independence," Estonian World, August 20, 2017, https://estonianworld.com/life/estonia-celebrates -the-day-of-restoration-of-independence/.

2. Toomas Hendrik Ilves, author's phone interview, March 27, 2020. See also Ripon Society, "The Estonian Example – Q&A with Toomas Hendrick Ilves," *The Ripon Forum* 47, no. 1 (Winter 2013), https://www.riponsociety .org/article/the-estonian-example-qa-with-toomas-hendrik-ilves/.

3. Wen Hoe, "E-Stonia: 1 Small Country's Digital Government Is Having a Big Impact," Harvard Government Innovators Network, June 7, 2017, https://www.innovations.harvard.edu/blog/estonia-one-small-country -digital-government-having-big-impact-x-road. See also e-Governance Academy, "Toomas Hendrik Ilves – Estonia as a Think Tank of e-Government. The eGA/GISI Initative," May 16, 2013, https://www.youtube.com /watch?v=BBcUORzU3CA.

4. A.A.K., "How Estonia Became a Leader in Technology," *The Economist*, July 31, 2013, https://www.economist.com/the-economist-explains/2013 /07/30/how-did-estonia-become-a-leader-in-technology.

5. Toomas Hendrik Ilves, "e-Estonia and the New Europe," Välisministee- rium, October 25, 2005, https://vm.ee/et/node/42610.

6. Toomas Hendrik Ilves, author's phone interview, March 27, 2020. See also Ripon Society, "The Estonian Example." See also Hoe, "E-Stonia." See also See also e-Governance Academy, "Toomas Hendrik Ilves."

7. Toomas Hendrik Ilves, author's phone interview, March 27, 2020. See also Jamie Kitman, "President Ilves: The Man Who Made E-Stonia," *The Guardian*, November 3, 2011, www.theguardian.com/world/2011/nov/03 /president-ilves-made-estonia.

8. Toomas Hendrik Ilves, author's phone interview, March 27, 2020. See also Tim Mansel, "How Estonia Became E-Stonia," BBC, May 16, 2013, www .bbc.com/news/business-22317297.

9. e-Governance Academy, "Toomas Hendrik Ilves." See also Hoe, "E-Sto- nia."

10. Linnar Viik, author's phone interview, August 20, 2019.

11. Ripon Society, "The Estonian Example." See also e-Governance Acad- emy, "Toomas Hendrik Ilves."

12. Toomas Hendrik Ilves, author's phone interview, March 27, 2020. See also Ott Ummelas, "World's Most High-Tech Voting System to Get Hacking

Defenses," Bloomberg, July 18, 2017, https://www.bloomberg.com/news/articles/2017-07-17/world-s-most-high-tech-voting-system-to-get-new-hacking-defenses.

13. Nina Kolyako, "Estonia Ranked First Worldwide in Terms of Broadband Internet Speeds," *Baltic Course*, January 27, 2012, http://www.baltic-course.com/eng/good_for_business/?doc=52217.

14. Viljar Lubi, author's phone interview, April 4, 2020.

15. Nathan Heller, "Estonia, The Digital Republic," *New Yorker*, December 11, 2017, https://www.newyorker.com/magazine/2017/12/18/estonia-the-digital-republic.

16. Ripon Society, "The Estonian Example."

17. "Statistics about Internet Voting in Estonia," Valimised, www.valimised.ee/en/archive/statistics-about-internet-voting-estonia.

18. Ripon Society, "The Estonian Example."

19. Dr. Robert Krimmer, author's phone interview, April 8, 2020.

20. Toomas Hendrik Ilves, author's phone interview, March 27, 2020.

21. Toomas Hendrik Ilves, author's phone interview, March 27, 2020. See also Georgeta Gheorghe, "Estonia's Toomas Hendrik Ilves Talks Digitalisation, from X-Road to Digital Embassies and E-Residency," *Business Review*, August 11, 2017, http://business-review.eu/featured/estonias-toomas-hendrik-ilves-talks-digitalisation-between-x-road-digital-embassies-e-resdiency-152141.

22. Joshua Davis, "Hackers Take Down the Most Wired Country in Europe," *Wired*, August 21, 2007, https://www.wired.com/2007/08/ff-estonia/.

23. Marten Kaevats, author's phone interview, April 6, 2020.

24. Elizabeth Schultze, "How a Tiny Country Bordering Russia Became 1 of the Most Tech-Savvy Societies in the World," CNBC, February 8, 2019, https://www.cnbc.com/2019/02/08/how-estonia-became-a-digital-society.html.

25. "Estonia to Open World's First Data Embassy in Luxembourg," e-estonia, June 2017, https://e-estonia.com/estonia-to-open-the-worlds-first-data-embassy-in-luxembourg/.

26. Taavi Kotka, author's phone interview, August 1, 2019.

27. Tarvi Martens, author's phone interview, July 30, 2019.

28. Ripon Society, "The Estonian Example."

29. Taavi Kotka, author's phone interview, August 1, 2019.

30. Andrew Keen, "E-Stonia: The Country Using Tech to Rebrand Itself

as Anti-Russia," *The Guardian*, April 21, 2016. https://www.theguardian
.com/world/2016/apr/21/e-stonia-country-using-technology-to-rebrand
-itself-as-the-anti-russia.

31. Toomas Hendrik Ilves, author's phone interview, March 27, 2020. See
also Keen, "E-Stonia."

32. Taavi Kotka, author's phone interview, August 1, 2019.

33. "Ministry Hopes Great Success for Estonian e-Residency Service," LETA
(Latvian Information Agency), October 7, 2014.

34. Taavi Kotka, author's phone interview, August 1, 2019.

35. Taavi Kotka, author's phone interview, August 1, 2019.

36. Xolo, "10 Notable People Who Are E-Residents of Estonia," October
11, 2016, https://blog.leapin.eu/10-notable-people-who-are-e-residents-of
-estonia-c3b7dcd3c7d6. See also Kaspar Korjus, "Welcome to Our Digital
Nation, Bill Gates," *Medium*, October 18, 2018, https://medium.com/e-
residency-blog/welcome-to-our-digital-nation-bill-gates-a8c33edd79a8.

37. Héller, "Estonia, The Digital Republic."

38. Danica Kirka, "No More Paperwork: Estonia Edges toward Digital
Government," Associated Press, December 26, 2018, https://apnews.com
/article/da5e0dd3bf364bbda436fc16690f842c.

39. Heller, "Estonia, the Digital Republic."

40. Taavi Kotka, author's phone interview, August 1, 2019.

41. Kaspar Korjus, author's phone interview, April 29, 2020.

42. Hal Hodson, "E-Citizens Unite," *NewScientist* 224, no. 2991 (October
18, 2014): 24.

43. Aaron Maniam, author's phone interview, April 15, 2020.

44. Kersti Kaljulaid, "Tallinn Digital Summit – Opening Address by
Estonia's President Kersti Kaljulaid," September 29, 2017, https://www
.youtube.com/watch?v=h1I4LGaP6Io.

45. CNN, "Estonia: Obama on Obamacare Website," July 21, 2016, www
.youtube.com/watch?v=v6vF_ARdlBA.

46. Kaljulaid, "Tallinn Digital Summit."

47. Kersti Kaljulaid, author's interview, Washington, DC, March 3, 2020.

Chapter 13 – Security: Google's X-Man

1. Bjorn Carey and Elizabeth Svoboda, "Live Reports from the 2005 Darpa
Grand Challenge," *Popular Science*, October 8, 2005, https://www.popsci
.com/scitech/article/2005-10/live-reports-2005-darpa-grand-challenge/.

2. CNBC International TV, "Sebastian Thrun, Founder of Udacity," *The Brave Ones*, May 15, 2017, https://www.youtube.com/watch?v=DtO3pcNnEuA.

3. Gideon Rose, "Google's Original X-Man: A Conversation with Sebastian Thrun," *Foreign Affairs*, November/December 2013, www.foreignaffairs.com/interviews/2013-10-15/googles-original-x-man.

4. CNBC International TV, "Sebastian Thrun, Founder of Udacity."

5. Rohan Abraham, "A Personal Loss, a $2-mm Win and a Soaring Ambition Led Sebastian Thrun on the Road to Innovation," *Economic Times*, April 2, 2019, https://economictimes.indiatimes.com/magazines/panache/a-personal-loss-a-2-mn-win-a-soaring-ambition-led-sebastian-thrun-on-the-road-to-innovation/articleshow/68680571.cms.

6. Sebastian Thrun, "Leave the Driving to the Car, and Reap Benefits in Safety and Mobility," *New York Times*, December 5, 2011, https://www.nytimes.com/2011/12/06/science/sebastian-thrun-self-driving-cars-can-save-lives-and-parking-spaces.html. See also Sebastian Thrun, "Google's Driverless Car," Ted2011, March 2011, https://www.ted.com/talks/sebastian_thrun_google_s_driverless_car?referrer=playlist-planes_trains_and_automobiles.

7. Rose, "Google's Original X-Man."

8. Rose, "Google's Original X-Man."

9. Rose, "Google's Original X-Man."

10. CNBC International TV, "Sebastian Thrun, Founder of Udacity."

11. CNBC International TV, "Sebastian Thrun, Founder of Udacity."

12. CNBC International TV, "Sebastian Thrun, Founder of Udacity."

13. Lucy Handley, "The Education of Sebastian Thrun," CNBC, January 1, 2017, https://www.cnbc.com/2017/06/01/sebastian-thrun-udacity-googlex.html.

14. Sebastian Thrun, "What We're Driving At," *Google Official Blog*, October 9, 2010, https://googleblog.blogspot.com/2010/10/what-were-driving-at.html.

15. Thrun, "What We're Driving At."

16. Darrel Etherington and Lora Kolodny, "Google's Self-Driving Car Unit Becomes Waymo," December 13, 2016, https://techcrunch.com/2016/12/13/googles-self-driving-car-unit-spins-out-as-waymo/.

17. Shernaz Daver, author's phone interview, November 16, 2020.

18. Rose, "Google's Original X-Man."

19. Eric Danko, author's phone interview, June 11, 2020.

20. Kara Kockelman, author's phone interview, April 27, 2020.

21. Thrun, "Leave the Driving to the Car."

22. Thrun, "Google's Driverless Car."

23. Insurance Institute for Highway Safety, Highway Loss Data Institute, "Fatality Facts 2018, State by State," https://www.iihs.org/topics/fatality-statistics/detail/state-by-state.

24. Nidhi Kalra and David Groves, "The Enemy of Good: Estimating the Cost of Waiting for Nearly Perfect Autonomous Vehicles," Rand Corporation, 2017, https://www.rand.org/pubs/research_reports/RR2150.html.

25. Alain Kornhauser, author's phone interview, April 29, 2020.

26. Kristin Houser, "Many Self-Driving Car Accidents Have Been Caused by Humans," *Business Insider*, September 5, 2018, https://www.businessinsider.com/self-driving-car-accidents-caused-by-humans-2018-9.

27. Chan Lieu, author's phone interview, April 23, 2020.

28. Johnna Crider, "Over 730,000 Tesla Vehicles with Autopilot 2 & 3 on the Road," *Cleantechnica*, January 5, 2020, https://cleantechnica.com/2020/01/05/over-730000-tesla-vehicles-with-autopilot-2-3-on-the-road/. See also Fred Lambert, "Tesla Drops a Bunch of New Autopilot Data, 3 Billion Miles and More," *Electrek*, April 22, 2020, https://electrek.co/2020/04/22/tesla-autopilot-data-3-billion-miles/.

29. Scott Hardman, author's phone interview, May 7, 2020.

30. Sebastian Thrun and Chris Anderson, "What AI Is – and Isn't," Ted2017, April 2017, https://www.ted.com/talks/sebastian_thrun_and_chris_anderson_what_ai_is_and_isn_t?language=en.

31. Lawrence Burns, author's phone interview, April 27, 2020. See also David Dorsey, "Expert Says Driverless Cars Will Disrupt Transportation Industry within 5 Years," *Fort Myers News-Press*, January 31, 2020, https://www.news-press.com/story/news/local/2020/01/31/driverless-cars-larry-burns-predicts-autonomous-cars-go-mainstream-within-five-years-disrupt-transpo/4625273002/.

Afterword – Humanity 2.0

1. Kurzgesagt – In a Nutshell, "A Selfish Argument for Making the World a Better Place – Egoistic Altruism," March 18, 2018, https://www.youtube.com/watch?v=rvskMHnosqQ&vl=en.

2. Gidi Grinstein, author's phone interview, December 17, 2020.

3. Frank Covey, *The 7 Habits of Highly Effective People* (New York: Free Press, 1989), 207.

4. John Mackey, author's phone interview, June 15, 2020.

Bibliography

Books

Burns, Lawrence. *Autonomy: The Quest to Build the Driverless Car – And How It Will Reshape Our World*. New York: Ecco, 2018.

Covey, Frank. *The Seven Habits of Highly Effective People*. New York: Free Press, 1989.

Diamandis, Peter, and Steven Kotler. *Abundance: The Future Is Better Than You Think*. New York: Free Press, 2012.

———. *Bold: How to Go Big, Bank, and Better the World*. New York: Simon and Schuster, 2015.

———. *The Future Is Faster Than You Think*. New York: Simon and Schuster, 2020.

Goodman, Marc. *Future Crimes: Everything Is Connected, Everyone Is Vulnerable and What We Can Do about It*. New York: Doubleday, 2015.

Khan, Salman. *The One World School House*. New York: Twelve, 2012.

Kurzweil, Ray. *The Age of Spiritual Machines: When Computers Exceed Human Intelligence*. New York: Viking, 1999.

———. *The Singularity Is Near*. New York: Viking, 2005.

Martinez, Sylvia Libow, and Gary S. Stager. *Invent to Learn: Making, Tinkering, and Engineering in the Classroom*. Torrance, CA: Constructing Modern Knowledge Press, 2013.

Siegel, Seth M. *Let There Be Water*. New York: Thomas Dunne Books, 2015.

Winegard, Timothy. *The Mosquito: A Human History of our Deadliest Predator*. London: Allen Lane, 2019.

Yunus, Muhammad. *Banker to the Poor: Micro-Lending and the Battle against World Poverty*. New York: Public Affairs, 1999.

Articles and Lectures

A.A.K. "How Estonia Became a Leader in Technology." *The Economist*, July 31, 2013. https://www.economist.com/the -economist-explains/2013/07/30/how-did-estonia-become -a-leader-in-technology.

Abraham, Rohan. "A Personal Loss, a $2-mm Win and a Soaring Ambition Led Sebastian Thrun on the Road to Innovation." *Economic Times*, April 2, 2019. https://economictimes .indiatimes.com/magazines/panache/a-personal-loss-a-2-mn -win-a-soaring-ambition-led-sebastian-thrun-on-the-road-to -innovation/articleshow/68680571.cms.

Achituv, Netta. "The Israeli Who Is Bringing Electricity, Agriculture and Medicine Cheaply to the Poorest Countries in the World." [In Hebrew.] *The Marker*, July 6, 2016. https://www.themarker .com/themarker-women/MAGAZINE-1.2998657.

Ackerman, Elise. "Israeli Startup Mines Data to Solve Global Water Crisis." *Forbes*, December 31, 2013. https://www.forbes.com/sites /eliseackerman/2013/12/31/israeli-startup-mines-data-to-solve -global-water-crisis/?sh=4ff87d7d2f46.

al-Mahmood, Syed Zain. "Muhammad Yunus and Bangladesh Government Battle over Grameen." *The Guardian*, November 21, 2012. https://www.theguardian.com/global-development /2012/nov/21/muhammad-yunus-bangladesh-grameen-bank.

Alam, M. Nurul, and Dr. Mike Getubig. "Guidelines for Establishing and Operating Grameen-Style Microcredit Programs." Grameen Foundation, 2010. https://grameenfoundation.org/documents /GrameenGuidelines.pdf.

Alisson-Silva, Frederico, Kunio Kawanishi, and Ajit Varki. "Human

Risk of Diseases Associated with Red Meat Intake: Analysis of Current Theories and Proposed Role for Metabolic Incorporation of a Non-Human Sialic Acid." *Molecular Aspects of Medicine* 51 (October 2016). https://www.ncbi.nlm.nih.gov/pmc/articles /PMC5035214/.

Architecture. "Earthquake-Proof Tokyo Named Safest City in the World." April 11, 2019. www.architecturelab.net/earthquake -safest-city-in-the-world/.

Associated Press. "A Broken Water Pipe Floods UCLA." *New York Post*, July 29, 2014. https://nypost.com/2014/07/29/a-broken -water-pipe-is-flooding-ucla/.

Baer, Drake. "The Making of Tesla: Invention, Betrayal, and the Birth of the Roadster." *Business Insider*, November 11, 2014. www .businessinsider.com/tesla-the-origin-story-2014-10.

Ban, Shigeru. "Emergency Shelters Made from Paper." TEDxTokyo, August 13, 2013. https://www.ted.com/talks/shigeru_ban _emergency_shelters_made_from_paper/details.

Barna, Mark. "Bock Soy." *Mizzou*, November 7, 2012. https:// mizzoumag.missouri.edu/2012/11/bock-soy/index.html.

BBC. "He Jiankui Defends 'World's First Gene-Edited Babies.'" November 28, 2018. https://www.bbc.com/news/world-asia -china-46368731.

Bell, John. "To the Moon: Google x's Astro Teller Encourages Creatives to Think Big." *The Guardian*, June 20, 2013. www .theguardian.com/media-network/media-network-blog/2013 /jun/20/google-x-astro-teller-creatives.

Benson, Sarah. "Salman Khan." Sutori. www.sutori.com/story /salman-khan--Lvux5bFpvn8zTBS222BUgLRN.

Bhattacharjee, Yudhijit. "Launch Pad." *New York Times*, November 10, 2016. https://www.nytimes.com/interactive/2016/11/13 /magazine/design-issue-sanitary-pads-india.html.

Bilgic, Hatice, Erdogan Hakki, Anamika Pandey, Mohd Kamran Khan, and Mahinur Akkaya. "Ancient DNA from 8400 Year-Old

Çatalhöyük Wheat: Implications for the Origin of Neolithic Agriculture." *PloS One* 11, no. 3 (2016). https://www.ncbi.nlm.nih.gov/pmc/articles/PMC4801371/.

Bostrom, Nick.. "Existential Risks: Analyzing Human Extinction Scenarios and Related Hazards." *Journal of Evolution and Technology* 9, no. 1 (2002). www.nickbostrom.com/existential/risks.html.

Brock, David. "How Gordon Moore Made 'Moore's Law.'" *Wired*, April 16, 2015. https://www.wired.com/2015/04/how-gordon-moore-made-moores-law/.

Bronner, Stephen J. "With $72 Million in Funding, the Entrepreneur behind Beyond Meat Pursues Innovation over Profit." *Entrepreneur*, January 22, 2018. https://www.entrepreneur.com/article/307715.

Business Today (India). "China Conducts Biological Test on Its Army to Create Super-Soldiers, Says Top US Official." December 9, 2020. https://www.businesstoday.in/current/world/china-conducts-biological-test-on-its-army-to-create-super-soldiers-says-top-us-official/story/424341.html.

Canada Press. "Shell Quest Carbon Capture and Storage Project Reaches Milestone of 4M Tonnes." May 23, 2019. https://www.cbc.ca/news/canada/calgary/carbon-storage-cnrl-shell-quest-1.5146857.

Carey, Bjorn, and Elizabeth Svoboda. "Live Reports from the 2005 Darpa Grand Challenge." *Popular Science*, October 8, 2005. https://www.popsci.com/scitech/article/2005-10/live-reports-2005-darpa-grand-challenge/.

Carrington, Damian. "England Could Run Short of Water within 25 years." *The Guardian*, March 18, 2019. https://www.theguardian.com/environment/2019/mar/18/england-to-run-short-of-water-within-25-years-environment-agency.

Center for Consumer Freedom. "Ad: Fake Meat Grows in Factories,

Not on Vines." August 13, 2019. www.consumerfreedom.com /2019/08/ad-fake-meat-grows-in-factories-not-on-vines/.

Cision PRNewswire. "Sweet Earth Debuts New Plant-Based Culinary Innovations, Awesome Burger & Awesome Grounds." September 25, 2019. www.prnewswire.com/news-releases/sweet -earth-debuts-new-plant-based-culinary-innovations-awesome -burger--awesome-grounds-300924874.html.

Clifford, Catherine. "Elon Musk: 'Mark My Words – A.I. Is Far More Dangerous than Nukes.'" CNBC, March 14, 2018. www.cnbc.com /2018/03/13/elon-musk-at-sxsw-a-i-is-more-dangerous-than -nuclear-weapons.html.

CNBC International TV. "Sebastian Thrun, Founder of Udacity." *The Brave Ones*, May 15, 2017. https://www.youtube.com/watch?v= DtO3pcNnEuA.

CNN. "Estonia: Obama on Obamacare Website." July 21, 2016. www .youtube.com/watch?v=v6vF_ARdlBA.

Cohen, Jon. "The Untold Story of the 'Circle of Trust' behind the World's First Gene-Edited Babies." *Science*, August 1, 2019. www.sciencemag.org/news/2019/08/untold-story-circle-trust -behind-world-s-first-gene-edited-babies.

Cong, Le, F. Ann Ran, David Cox, Shuailiang Lin, et al. "Multiplex Genome Engineering Using CRISPR/Cas Systems. *Nature*, February 15, 2013. http://science.sciencemag.org/content/339 /6121/819.long.

Consultative Group to Assist the Poor. "CGAP Launches Global Microfinance Survey to Inform COVID-19 Response." June 1, 2020. www.cgap.org/news/cgap-launches-global-microfinance -survey-inform-covid-19-response.

Cookson, Clive. "Africa to Propel World's Population towards 10bn by 2050." *Financial Times*, June 17, 2019. https://www.ft.com /content/868e20d0-90ec-11e9-b7ea-60e35ef678d2.

Corder, Mike. "Water Wizards: Dutch Flood Expertise Is Big Export

Business." Associated Press, November 12, 2017. https://apnews
.com/article/1bc1f137cb134fdca67afdff08c242bc.

Crider, Johnna. "Over 730,000 Tesla Vehicles with Autopilot 2 & 3 on
the Road." *Cleantechnica*, January 5, 2020. https://cleantechnica
.com/2020/01/05/over-730000-tesla-vehicles-with-autopilot-2-3
-on-the-road/.

Daily Bhaskar. "This Man Is a Sanitary Pad Revolutionary. Watch Him
Take On the Age-Old Taboo" [in Hindi]. March 3, 2016. https://
daily.bhaskar.com/news/TOP-sanitary-pad-revolutionary
-arunachalam-muruganantham-menstruation-man-5265202
-PHO.html.

Darmiento, Laurence. "Ethan Brown Went Vegan but Missed Fast
Food. So He Started a Revolution." *Los Angeles Times*, January
20, 2020. https://www.latimes.com/business/story/2020-01-08
/beyond-meat-founder-ethan-brown.

Davis, Joshua. "Hackers Take Down the Most Wired Country in
Europe." *Wired*, August 21, 2007. https://www.wired.com/2007
/08/ff-estonia/.

de Bertodano, Helena. "Khan Academy: The Man Who Wants
to Teach the World." *The Guardian*, September 28, 2018. www
.telegraph.co.uk/education/educationnews/9568850/Khan
-Academy-The-man-who-wants-to-teach-the-world.html.

Dilanian, Ken. "China Has Done Human Testing to Create
Biologically Enhanced Super Soldiers, Says Top U.S. Official."
NBC News, December 4, 2020. https://www.nbcnews.com
/politics/national-security/china-has-done-human-testing
-create-biologically-enhanced-super-soldiers-n1249914.

Disaster Preparedness Tokyo. "Disaster Prevention Information."
2019. https://www.bousai.metro.tokyo.lg.jp/book/pdf/en/01
_Simulation_of_a_Major_Earthquake.pdf.

————. "Manga Comic: 'Tokyo "X" Day.'" 2019. https://www
.bousai.metro.tokyo.lg.jp/book/pdf/en/comic.pdf.

Dorcas, Adeline. "Pad Man Makes Nationwide Campaign for Use

of Sanitary Napkins." *Medindia,* May 11, 2018. https://www
.medindia.net/news/healthwatch/pad-man-makes-nationwide
-campaign-for-use-of-sanitary-napkins-179368-1.htm.

Dorsey, David. "Expert Says Driverless Cars Will Disrupt Transportation Industry within 5 Years." *Fort Myers News-Press,* January 31, 2020. https://www.news-press.com/story /news/local/2020/01/31/driverless-cars-larry-burns-predicts -autonomous-cars-go-mainstream-within-five-years-disrupt -transpo/4625273002/.

Dreifus, Claudia. "It All Started with a 12-Year-Old Cousin." *New York Times,* January 28, 2014. http://www.nytimes.com/2014/01 /28/science/salman-khan-turned-family-tutoring-into-khan -academy.html.

e-estonia. "Estonia to Open World's First Data Embassy in Luxembourg." June 2017. https://e-estonia.com/estonia-to-open -the-worlds-first-data-embassy-in-luxembourg/.

Economic Times. "Martin Eberhard Calls Tesla His 'Baby', Talks about Being Ousted from Company's Board." March 1, 2019, https:// economictimes.indiatimes.com/magazines/panache/martin -eberhard-calls-tesla-his-baby-talks-about-being-ousted-from -companys-board/articleshow/68211761.cms.

Economist. "Safe Cities Index 2019." https://safecities.economist .com/safe-cities-index-2019/.

e-Governance Academy. "Toomas Hendrik Ilves – Estonia as a Think Tank of e-Government. The eGA/GISI Initative." May 16, 2013. https://www.youtube.com/watch?v=BBcUORzU3CA.

Elliott, Larry. "Climate Crisis Fills Top Five Places of World Economic Forum's Risk Report." *The Guardian,* January 15, 2020. https://www.theguardian.com/business/2020/jan/15/climate -crisis-environment-top-five-places-world-economic-forum -risks-report.

Estonian World. "Estonia Celebrates the Day of Restoration of

Independence." August 20, 2017. https://estonianworld.com/life
/estonia-celebrates-the-day-of-restoration-of-independence/.

Etherington, Darrel, and Lora Kolodny. "Google's Self-Driving Car
Unit Becomes Waymo." December 13, 2016. https://techcrunch
.com/2016/12/13/googles-self-driving-car-unit-spins-out-as
-waymo/.

European Press Agency (EPA). "Businessman Carlos Slim Will
Invest More Than 317 US Dollar Millions in Education." January
19, 2013.

Ferziger, Jonathan. "Netanyahu Offers to Help Brown Manage
California Drought." Bloomberg, March 5, 2014. www.bloomberg
.com/news/articles/2014-03-05/netanyahu-offers-to-help
-brown-manage-california-drought.

Financial Express (Bangladesh). "Sal Khan's Academy Lights the
Way." December 26, 2010.

———. "Who Is Arunachalam Muruganantham?" February
8, 2018. www.financialexpress.com/entertainment/who-is
-arunachalam-muruganantham-the-real-padman-who-was-the
-inspiration-for-akshay-kumar-movie/1059638/.

Finkle, Colin. "Beyond Meat Brand Profile." Brand Marketing Blog,
July 21, 2019. https://brandmarketingblog.com/articles/good
-branding/beyond-meat-brand-profile/.

Foster, Tom. "Friends Thought Beyond Meat's Founder Was Crazy.
His Billion-Dollar IPO Proved Them Wrong." *Inc.* August 2019.
https://www.inc.com/magazine/201908/tom-foster/ethan
-brown-beyond-meat-alternative-protein-plant-burger-ipo
-public-whole-foods.html.

Fourcade, Marthe, and Corinne Gretler. "McDonald's Picks
Beyond for Canada Trial, U.S. Prize Remains." Bloomberg,
September 26, 2019. www.bloomberg.com/news/articles/2019
-09-26/mcdonald-s-to-test-veggie-burger-from-beyond-meat
-in-canada.

Free Press Journal (India). "Environment-Friendly Sanitary

Pads: Work in Progress." December 6, 2018. https://www
.freepressjournal.in/cmcm/environment-friendly-sanitary-pads
-work-in-progress.

Friedman, Thomas. "Moore's Law Turns 50." *New York Times*, May
13, 2015. https://www.nytimes.com/2015/05/13/opinion/thomas
-friedman-moores-law-turns-50.html.

"From Rags to Riches." *The Nation* (Nigeria), September 20, 2014.
https://thenationonlineng.net/from-rags-to-riches/.

Frostenson, Sarah. "America Has a Water Crisis No One Is Talking
About." *Vox*, March 22, 2018. www.vox.com/science-and-health
/2017/5/9/15183330/america-water-crisis-affordability-millions.

Gates, Bill. "Future of Food." *GatesNotes*, March 18, 2013. www
.gatesnotes.com/About-Bill-Gates/Future-of-Food.

Geib, Claudia. "Genetic Engineering Can Treat Rare Diseases, but
Could Also Give Wealthy Children a Biological Advantage."
Futurism, August 9, 2017. https://futurism.com/neoscope/expert
-argues-that-gene-editing-will-widen-economic-class-gap.

Geist, Edward, and Andrew J. Lohn. "How Might Artificial
Intelligence Affect the Risk of Nuclear War?" Rand Corporation,
2018. www.rand.org/pubs/perspectives/PE296.html.

Gheorghe, Georgeta. "Estonia's Toomas Hendrik Ilves Talks
Digitalisation, from X-Road to Digital Embassies and
E-Residency." *Business Review*, August 11, 2017. http://business
-review.eu/featured/estonias-toomas-hendrik-ilves-talks
-digitalisation-between-x-road-digital-embassies-e-resdiency
-152141.

Gilson, Dirk. "India's Menstruation Man." *Aljazeera*. https://
interactive.aljazeera.com/aje/shorts/india-menstruation-man/.

Giridharadas, Anand, and Keith Bradsher. "Microloan Pioneer and
His Bank Win Nobel Peace Prize." *New York Times*, October
13, 2006. https://www.nytimes.com/2006/10/13/business
/14nobelcnd.html.

Goldstein, Dana. "Research Shows Students Falling Months Behind

during Virus Disruptions." *New York Times*, June 5, 2020. www
.nytimes.com/2020/06/05/us/coronavirus-education-lost
-learning.html.

Golikeri, Priyanka. "An Enterprise Aimed at Boosting Women's
Health." DNA, June 9, 2011. https://www.dnaindia.com/business
/report-an-enterprise-aimed-at-boosting-women-s-health
-1552766.

Goodman, Marc. "A Vision of Crimes in the Future." TEDGlobal
2012, June 2012. www.ted.com/talks/marc_goodman_a_vision
_of_crimes_in_the_future?language=en.

Gupta, Arun. "Disaster Capitalism Hits New York." *In These Times*,
February 2013. https://inthesetimes.com/article/14430/disaster
_capitalism_hits_new_york.

Gupta, Surojit. " Salman's India Dream: Coaching 450m in 10 years,"
Times of India, December 5, 2015, https://timesofindia.indiatimes
.com/india/salmans-india-dream-coaching-450m-in-10-years
/articleshow/50036337.cms.

Hagstrom, Britt F. "The Man behind the Nobel Prize." *Daily
Star*, December 10, 2006. https://archive.thedailystar.net
/suppliments/2006/december/bangladeshstandingtall/index
.htm

Handley, Lucy. "The Education of Sebastian Thrun." CNBC, January
1, 2017. https://www.cnbc.com/2017/06/01/sebastian-thrun
-udacity-googlex.html.

Harney, Alexandra, and Kate Kelland. "China Orders Investigation
after Scientist Claims First Gene-Edited Babies." Reuters,
November 26, 2018. https://www.reuters.com/article/us-health
-china-babies-genes/china-orders-investigation-after-scientist
-claims-first-gene-edited-babies-idUSKCN1NV19T.

Harvey, Fiona. "Humanity under Threat from Perfect Storm of
Crises – Study." *The Guardian*, February 6, 2020. https://www
.theguardian.com/environment/2020/feb/06/humanity
-under-threat-perfect-storm-crises-study-environment?fbclid

=IwAR3roRN91V7VtZY8vHsEQv3ScicNTSRJCr8hyay4u
_Sm24J6DnB7lmsoyxQ.

Heller, Martin C., and Gregory A. Keoleian. "Beyond Meat's Beyond
Burger Life Cycle Assessment: A Detailed Comparison between
a Plant-Based and an Animal-Based Protein Source." Center for
Sustainable Systems Report, University of Michigan, September
14, 2018. http://css.umich.edu/publication/beyond-meats
-beyond-burger-life-cycle-assessment-detailed-comparison
-between-plant-based.

Heller, Nathan. "Estonia, The Digital Republic." *New Yorker*,
December 11, 2017. https://www.newyorker.com/magazine
/2017/12/18/estonia-the-digital-republic.

Hindustan Times. "Tata Trusts to Support Khan Academy for Free
Online Education." December 7, 2015. www.hindustantimes
.com/education/tata-trusts-to-support-khan-academy-for-free
-online-education/story-kpQuo1Ph4QGi9HDBrT3SVP.html.

Hodson, Hal. "E-Citizens Unite." *NewScientist* 224, no. 2991 (October
18, 2014): 24.

Hoe, Wen. "E-Stonia: One Small Country's Digital Government
Is Having a Big Impact." Harvard Government Innovators
Network, June 7, 2017. https://www.innovations.harvard.edu
/blog/estonia-one-small-country-digital-government-having
-big-impact-x-road.

Houser, Kristin. "Many Self-Driving Car Accidents Have Been
Caused by Humans." *Business Insider*, September 5, 2018. https://
www.businessinsider.com/self-driving-car-accidents-caused
-by-humans-2018-9.

Hunter-Hart, Monica. "8 Staggering Predictions from Ray Kurzweil."
Inverse, May 29, 2017. https://www.inverse.com/article/30913
-8-staggering-predictions-ray-kurzweil.

Hrynowski, Zach. "What Percentage of Americans are Vegetarian?"
Gallup, September 27, 2019. https://news.gallup.com/poll
/267074/percentage-americans-vegetarian.aspx.

Ilves, Toomas Hendrik. "e-Estonia and the New Europe." Välisministeerium, October 25, 2005. https://vm.ee/et/node /42610.

Insurance Institute for Highway Safety, Highway Loss Data Institute. "Fatality Facts 2018, State by State." https://www.iihs.org/topics /fatality-statistics/detail/state-by-state.

International Space Hall of Fame at the New Mexico Museum of Space History. "The Father of Astronautics and Rocket Dynamics." https://www.nmspacemuseum.org/inductee /konstantin-e-tsiolkovsky/.

Ip, Greg. "The Moonshot Mind-Set Once Came from the Government. No Longer," *Wall Street Journal*, July 14, 2019. www .wsj.com/articles/the-moonshot-mind-set-once-came-from -the-government-no-longer-11563152820. See also Casey Dreier, "Reconstructing the Cost of the One Giant Leap," *The Planetary Society*, June 16, 2019, https://www.planetary.org/blogs/casey -dreier/2019/reconstructing-the-price-of-apollo.html.

"ISS National Laboratory," NASA, https://www.nasa.gov/mission _pages/station/research/nlab/index.html.

ITUNews. "The Future Is Better Than You Think: Predictions on AI and Development from Ray Kurzweil." May 29, 2019. https:// news.itu.int/the-future-is-better-than-you-think-predictions -on-ai-and-development-from-ray-kurzweil/.

Jinek, Martin, Krzysztof Chrlinski, et al. "A Programmable Dual-RNA-Guided DNA Endonuclease in Adaptive Bacterial Immunity." *Science*, August 17, 2012. https://science.sciencemag.org/content /337/6096/816.

Jones, Abigail. "The Silence That Still Surrounds Periods." *The Independent* (UK), April 25, 2016. https://www.independent .co.uk/life-style/health-and-families/silence-around -menstruation-a7000051.html.

Kagen, Julia. "Microfinance." *Investopedia*, April 21, 2020. www .investopedia.com/terms/m/microfinance.asp.

Kaljulaid, Kersti. "Tallinn Digital Summit – Opening Address by Estonia's President Kersti Kaljulaid." September 29, 2017. https://www.youtube.com/watch?v=h1I4LGaP6Io.

Kalra, Nidhi, and David Groves. "The Enemy of Good: Estimating the Cost of Waiting for Nearly Perfect Autonomous Vehicles." Rand Corporation, 2017. https://www.rand.org/pubs/research_reports/RR2150.html.

Kane, Mark. "Close to 1.18 Million Plug-In Electric Cars Were Sold in China in 2019." *InsideEVs*, January 22, 2020. https://insideevs.com/news/394229/plugin-electric-car-sales-china-2019/.

Kaplan, David A. "Bill Gates' Favorite Teacher." *Fortune*, August 24, 2010. https://archive.fortune.com/2010/08/23/technology/sal_khan_academy.fortune/index.htm.

Karami, Arash. "Iran Official Warns Water Crisis Could Lead to Mass Migration." *Al-Monitor*, April 28, 2015. www.al-monitor.com/pulse/originals/2015/04/iran-water-crisis-mass-migration.html.

Keen, Andrew. "E-Stonia: The Country Using Tech to Rebrand Itself as Anti-Russia." *The Guardian*, April 21, 2016. https://www.theguardian.com/world/2016/apr/21/e-stonia-country-using-technology-to-rebrand-itself-as-the-anti-russia.

Kennedy, Pagan. "William Gibson's Future Is Now." *New York Times*, January 13, 2012. https://www.nytimes.com/2012/01/15/books/review/distrust-that-particular-flavor-by-william-gibson-book-review.html.

Khan, Jennifer. "The Gene Drive Dilemma: We Can Alter Entire Species, but Should We?" *New York Times*, January 8, 2020. https://www.nytimes.com/2020/01/08/magazine/gene-drive-mosquitoes.html.

Khan Academy. "Bill Gates Talks about the Khan Academy at Aspen Ideas Festival 2010." July 19, 2010. www.youtube.com/watch?v=6Ao7Pj71TUA.

Khandker, Shahidur R., M. A. Baqui Khalily, and Hussain A.

Samad. *Beyond Ending Poverty: The Dynamics of Microfinance in Bangladesh*. World Bank Group, 2016. http://documents .worldbank.org/curated/en/366431468508832455/pdf/106672 -PUB.pdf.

King, Michelle. "Dunkin' and Beyond Meat Accelerate Nationwide Launch of Beyond Sausage Sandwich." Dunkin' News Release, October 21, 2019. https://news.dunkindonuts.com/news /releases-20191021.

Kingdom, Bill, Roland Liemberger, and Philippe Marin. "The Challenge of Reducing Non-Revenue Water (NRW) in Developing Countries – How the Private Sector Can Help: A Look at Performance-Based Service Contracting," World Bank, *Water Supply and Sanitation Sector Board Discussion Paper Series*, no. 8, December 2006, https://openknowledge.worldbank.org /handle/10986/17238.

Kirka, Danica. "No More Paperwork: Estonia Edges toward Digital Government." Associated Press, December 26, 2018. https:// apnews.com/article/da5e0dd3bf364bbda436fc16690f842c.

Kitman, Jamie. "President Ilves: The Man Who Made E-Stonia." *The Guardian*, November 3, 2011. www.theguardian.com/world/2011 /nov/03/president-ilves-made-estonia.

Kolyako, Nina. "Estonia Ranked First Worldwide in Terms of Broadband Internet Speeds." *Baltic Course*, January 27, 2012. http://www.baltic-course.com/eng/good_for_business/?doc =52217.

Korjus, Kaspar. "Welcome to Our Digital Nation, Bill Gates." *Medium*, October 18, 2018. https://medium.com/e-residency -blog/welcome-to-our-digital-nation-bill-gates-a8c33edd79a8.

Kosik, Allison. "Experts: U.S. Water Infrastructure in Trouble." CNN, January 21, 2011. http://edition.cnn.com/2011/US/01/20/water .main.infrastructure/.

Koushan, Kasra. "Sal Khan on Creating a Better Future." The Signal, July 20, 2017. https://thesign.al/sal-khan/.

Kuropatwa, Rebeca. "Helping One Village at a Time." *Jewish Independent*, June 16, 2017. https://www.jewishindependent.ca /tag/sivan-yaari/.

Kurzgesagt – In a Nutshell. "A Selfish Argument for Making the World a Better Place – Egoistic Altruism." March 18, 2018. https:// www.youtube.com/watch?v=rvskMHnosqQ&vl=en.

Kurzweil, Ray. "The Law of Accelerating Returns," Kurzweilai .net, March 7, 2001. https://www.kurzweilai.net/the-law-of -accelerating-returns.

La Monica, Paul R. "Impossible Whoppers Are a Huge Hit at Burger King, Fueling Its Best Quarter in Four Years." CNN Business, October 28, 2019. www.cnn.com/2019/10/28/investing /restaurant-brands-earnings-burger-king-popeyes/index.html.

Lambert, Fred. "Tesla Drops a Bunch of New Autopilot Data, 3 Billion Miles and More." *Electrek*, April 22, 2020. https://electrek .co/2020/04/22/tesla-autopilot-data-3-billion-miles/.

———. "Tesla Produces Its 1 Millionth Electric Car." *Electrek*, March 9, 2020. https://electrek.co/2020/03/09/tesla-produces -1000000th-electric-car/.

Lan, Shlomit. "Positive Energy" [in Hebrew]. *Globes*, May 17, 2010. https://www.globes.co.il/news/article.aspx?did=1000560436.

Lander, Eric, Françoise Baylis, Feng Zhang, Emmanuelle Charpentier, Paul Berg, et al. "Adopt a Moratorium on Heritable Genome Editing." *Nature*, March 13, 2019. https://www.nature.com /articles/d41586-019-00726-5.

Lanphier, Edward, Fyodor Urnov, Sarah Ehlen Haecker, et al. "Don't Edit the Human Germ Line." *Nature*, March 12, 2015. www.nature .com/news/don-t-edit-the-human-germ-line-1.17111.

Law School Admission Council. "Khan Academy Launches Free LSAT Prep for All." June 1, 2018. https://www.lsac.org/about /news/khan-academy-launches-free-lsat-test-prep-all.

Layne, Rachel. "Space Case: Why Reaching for the Stars Could Soon Be a $1 Trillion Industry." CBS News, July 16, 2019. https://www

.cbsnews.com/news/space-is-a-more-than-400-billion-market
-and-getting-bigger/.

—————. "Water Costs Are Rising across the US – Here's Why." CBS,
August 27, 2019. https://www.cbsnews.com/news/water-bills
-rising-cost-of-water-creating-big-utility-bills-for-americans/.

LETA (Latvian Information Agency). "Ministry Hopes Great Success
for Estonian e-Residency Service." October 7, 2014.

Lollis, Kent D. "Living, Working, and Achieving While Black." Law
School Admission Council, June 16, 2020. www.lsac.org/blog
/living-working-and-achieving-while-black.

Love, Bruce. "Sal Khan: An Educational Entrepreneur." CampdenFB,
May 7, 2015. https://www.campdenfb.com/article/sal-khan
-educational-entrepreneur.

Lu, Denise, and Christopher Flavelle. "Rising Seas Will Erase More
Cities by 2050, New Research Shows." *New York Times*, October
29, 2019. https://www.nytimes.com/interactive/2019/10/29
/climate/coastal-cities-underwater.html.

Mac, Elizabeth. "A Burgeoning Crisis? A Nationwide Assessment
of the Geography of Water Affordability in the United States."
PloS One 12, no. 4 (January 11, 2017). https://journals.plos.org
/plosone/article?id=10.1371/journal.pone.0169488.

Mansel, Tim. "How Estonia Became E-Stonia." BBC, May 16, 2013.
www.bbc.com/news/business-22317297.

Marsters, Peter. "Electric Cars: The Drive for a Sustainable Solution
in China." *Wilson Center*, August 2009. https://www.wilsoncenter
.org/publication/electric-cars-the-drive-for-sustainable
-solution-china.

Masr, Mada. "'We Woke Up in a Desert' – The Water Crisis
Taking Hold across Egypt." *The Guardian*, August 4, 2015. www
.theguardian.com/world/2015/aug/04/egypt-water-crisis
-intensifies-scarcity.

Mckean, Cameron Allan. "Tokyo's Disaster Parks." *The Guardian*,
August 19, 2014. www.theguardian.com/cities/2014/aug/19

/tokyo-disaster-parks-hi-tech-survival-bunkers-hidden-green
-spaces-earthquake.

Mellgren, Doug. "Bangladeshi Economist Wins Nobel Peace Prize." *Seattle Times,* October 13, 2006. https:// www.seattletimes.com/nation-world/bangladeshi-economist-wins-nobel-peace-prize/.

Menon, Nikhil. "How Sal Khan Is Exorcising the Math Spectre from the Minds of Millions of Students Worldwide." *The Economic Times,* August 10, 2012. https://economictimes.indiatimes.com /how-sal-khan-is-exorcising-the-math-spectre-from-the-minds -of-millions-of-students-worldwide/articleshow/15425169.cms.

Miller, Claire Cain. "Musk Unplugged: Tesla CEO Discusses Car Troubles." *New York Times,* October 24, 2008. https://bits.blogs .nytimes.com/2008/10/24/musk-unplugged-tesla-ceo-discusses -car-troubles/.

MIT Club of Northern California. "Pioneers in Clean Technology – Marc Tarpenning – Tesla Motors." March 6, 2014. https://www .youtube.com/watch?v=EDCYoAQmmAA.

Mixergy. "How Khan Academy Is Changing Education with Videos Made in a Closet." June 28, 2010. https://mixergy.com/interviews /salman-khan-academy-interview/.

MOJO Story. "Twinkle Khanna & the 'Pad-Man' with Barkha Dutt." December 11, 2017. www.youtube.com/watch?v=V4 _MeS6SOwk.

Molteni, Megan. "The Wired Guide to CRISPR." *Wired,* March 12, 2019. https://www.wired.com/story/wired-guide-to-crispr/.

———. "The World Health Organization Says No More Gene-Edited Babies." *Wired,* July 30, 2019. www.wired.com/story/the -world-health-organization-says-no-more-gene-edited-babies/.

Morduch, Jonathan. "The Role of Subsidies in Microfinance: Evidence from the Grameen Bank." *Journal of Development Economics* 60 (1999). https://s18798.pcdn.co/jmorduch

/wp-content/uploads/sites/5267/2016/12/Morduch-Grameen
-Subsidies-JDE-1999.pdf.

Mosa Meat. "Why We Need to Change How We Make Meat." July 5,
2018. https://www.youtube.com/watch?v=oSl9yZuPrdo.

Mosher, Dave. "Congress and Trump are Running out of Time to
Fix a $100-Billion Investment in the Sky, NASA Auditor Says."
Business Insider, May 18, 2018. www.businessinsider.com/space
-station-trump-plan-problems-astronaut-risk-2018-5.

Muruganantham, Arunachalam. "How I Started a Sanitary Napkin
Revolution." TED@Bangalore, May 2012. www.ted.com/talks
/arunachalam_muruganantham_how_i_started_a_sanitary
_napkin_revolution?language=en#t-70857.

Musgrove, Mike. "An Electric Car with Juice." *Washington Post*, July
22, 2006. http://www.washingtonpost.com/wp-dyn/content
/article/2006/07/21/AR2006072101515.html.

Nair, Prashant. "QnAs with Rodolphe Barrangou." PNAS, July 11, 2017.
www.pnas.org/content/114/28/7183.

Nandakumar, Sowmya. "Salman Khan: World's Most Influential
Online Educator." *Indo-American News*, May 17, 2012, page 6.
https://issuu.com/indoamericannews/docs/may18_pages
_1-36.

NASA's Ames Research Center. "Jason Dunn – The Future of Making
Things in Space." January 31, 2017, 25:00. www.youtube.com
/watch?list=PLfnpkfDmrBqYgX1O3kRQnc5Sjzz_LMwDo&
time_continue=3313&v=ZXYCKoTclCc.

"New Perspectives: Influencing Circumstances through Human
Connection – Spotlight: Sivan Ya'ari '02." *Altitude*, Winter 2020,
https://www.alumni.pace.edu/s/1655/bp20/interior.aspx?sid=
1655&gid=2&pgid=2383.

Nha, Thu Ngo. "A Glimpse of Japan's Deadly Earthquakes." ArcGIS
StoryMaps, August 18, 2019. https://storymaps.arcgis.com
/stories/daoacfccaece4fc481353b1a01589259.

Nikel, David. "Electric Cars: Why Little Norway Leads the World

In EV Usage." Forbes, June 18, 2019. https://www.forbes.com /sites/davidnikel/2019/06/18/electric-cars-why-little-norway -leads-the-world-in-ev-usage/.

Nikkei Asian Review. "Osaka Quake Exposes Japan's Aging Infrastructure." June 19, 2018. https://asia.nikkei.com/Economy /Osaka-quake-exposes-Japan-s-aging-infrastructure.

Nobel Prize. "Muhammad Yunus – Nobel Lecture." December 10, 2006. www.nobelprize.org/prizes/peace/2006/yunus/26090 -muhammad-yunus-nobel-lecture-2006-2/.

Noer, Michael. "One Man, One Computer, 10 Million Students: How Khan Academy Is Reinventing Education." Forbes, November 19, 2012. www.forbes.com/sites/michaelnoer/2012/11/02/one -man-one-computer-10-million-students-how-khan-academy -is-reinventing-education/#7e17495444e0.

Nolen, Stephanie. "The Absorbing Tale of One Man's Quest for Better Feminine Hygiene." Globe and Mail (Canada), October 4, 2012.

NPR Radio. "Live Episode! Beyond Meat: Ethan Brown." February 16, 2017. www.npr.org/2017/02/16/515420148/live-episode-beyond -meat-ethan-brown.

Nuttall, Chris. "Tale of a Supercharged Start-Up Entrepreneurship." Financial Times, April 12, 2007. https://www.ft.com/content /ab94e730-e83c-11db-b2c3-000b5df10621.

Ofek, Elie, and Matthew Preble. "Takadu." Harvard Business School Case 514-011, July 2013 (revised August 2017).

Oryszczuk, Stephen. "Africa Gains from Israel's Solar System." Jewish News, April 12, 2018. https://jewishnews.timesofisrael.com /africa-gains-from-israels-solar-system/.

Pakistan Today. "India's 'Menstruation Man' Reinvents Sanitary Pads." May 15, 2016. https://archive.pakistantoday.com.pk/2016 /05/15/indias-menstruation-man-reinvents-sanitary-pads/.

Parekh, Par. "The Math of Khan: Salman Khan: Founder of the Kahn Academy." Bidoun. www.bidoun.org/articles/the-math-of-khan.

Park, Alice. "Why We Don't Need Animals to Keep Enjoying Meat." *Time*, June 6, 2019. https://time.com/5601980/beyond-meat-ceo -ethan-brown-interview/.

Passwaters, Arie. "President's Lecture Series to Present Educational Innovator Salman Khan." Rice University Office of Public Affairs, September 24, 2018. https://news.rice.edu/2018/09/24 /presidents-lecture-series-to-present-educational-innovator -salman-khan/.

Patrizio, Andy. "IDC: Expect 175 Zettabytes of Data Worldwide by 2025." NetworkWorld, December 3, 2018. www.networkworld .com/article/3325397/idc-expect-175-zettabytes-of-data -worldwide-by-2025.html.

Pelley, Scott. "U.S., China, Russia, Elon Musk: Entrepreneur's 'Insane' Vision Becomes Reality." CBS News, May 22, 2012. https://www .cbsnews.com/news/us-china-russia-elon-musk-entrepreneurs -insane-vision-becomes-reality/.

Pilling, David. "Lessons Learnt from Kobe Quake." *Financial Times*, May 11, 2011. https://www.ft.com/content/5290f95e-4bc4-11e0 -9705-00144feab49a.

Radhakrishnan, Manjusha. "Meet the Real 'Pad Man' Arunachalam Muruganatham." *Gulf News*, February 7, 2018.

Rajghatta, Chidanand. "Modi to Meet Salman Khan, the Educator not the Movie Star." *Times of India*, September 28, 2015. https:// timesofindia.indiatimes.com/india/modi-to-meet-salman -khan-the-educator-not-the-movie-star/articleshow/49113900 .cms.

Ramesh, Randeep. "Giving a Hand Up, Not a Handout." *The Guardian*, December 27, 2006. https://www.theguardian.com /business/2006/dec/27/money.

Rathi, Akshat, and Echo Huang. "More Than 100 Chinese Scientists Have Condemned the CRISPR Baby Experiment as 'Crazy.'" *Quartz*, November 26, 2018. https://qz.com/1474530/chinese -scientists-condemn-crispr-baby-experiment-as-crazy/.

Raz, Guy. "Sal Khan: Can Technology Help Create a Global Classroom." *NPR TED Radio Hour*, August 11, 2017.

Reed, John. "Elon Musk's Groundbreaking Electric Car." *Financial Times*, July 24, 2009. https://www.ft.com/content/e117987e -74eb-11de-9ed5-00144feabdc0.

Reedy, Christianna. "Ray Kurzweil Claims Singularity Will Happen by 2045." *Futurism*, May 10, 2017. https://futurism.com/kurzweil -claims-that-the-singularity-will-happen-by-2045.

Regalado, Antonio. "First Gene-Edited Dogs Reported in China." MIT *Technology Review*, October 19, 2015. https://www .geneticsandsociety.org/article/first-gene-edited-dogs-reported -china.

Ripon Society. "The Estonian Example – Q&A with Toomas Hendrick Ilves." *The Ripon Forum* 47, no. 1 (Winter 2013). https:// www.riponsociety.org/article/the-estonian-example-qa-with -toomas-hendrik-ilves/.

Ritchie, Hannah. "You Want to Reduce the Carbon Footprint of Your Food? Focus on What You Eat, Not Whether Your Food Is Local." Our World in Data, January 24, 2020. https:// ourworldindata.org/food-choice-vs-eating-local.

Rose, Gideon. "Google's Original X-Man: A Conversation with Sebastian Thrun." *Foreign Affairs*, November/December 2013. www.foreignaffairs.com/interviews/2013-10-15/googles -original-x-man.

Roser, Max, and Esteban Ortiz-Ospina. "Global Extreme Poverty." Our World in Data, 2013. https://ourworldindata.org/extreme -poverty.

Ruptly. "Russia: Putin Warns a GM Human Could Be 'Worse Than Nuclear Bomb.'" October 21, 2017. www.youtube.com/watch ?v=E6pD96RRIUQ.

Salt Lake Tribune. "Yunus, Grameen Bank win Nobel Peace Prize for Loans to the Poor." October 13, 2006. https://archive.sltrib .com/article.php?id=4486938&itype=NGPSID.

Sampson, Zachary T. "First 3-D Printing in Space Had Bay Area Start." *Tampa Bay Times*, December 8, 2014. https://www.tampabay .com/archive/2014/12/08/first-3-d-printing-in-space-had-bay -area-start/.

Saval, Nikil. "Shigeru Ban." *New York Times*, October 18, 2019. www .nytimes.com/interactive/2019/10/15/t-magazine/shigeru-ban .html.

Schleifer, Leah. "7 Reasons We're Facing a Global Water Crisis." World Resources Institute, August 24, 2017. https://www.wri .org/blog/2017/08/7-reasons-were-facing-global-water-crisis.

Schreiber, Mark. "Hell on Earth in '23." *Japan Times*, August 26, 2001. www.japantimes.co.jp/community/2001/08/26/general/hell -on-earth-in-23/#.Xkww7S2ZORu.

Schultze, Elizabeth. "How a Tiny Country Bordering Russia Became One of the Most Tech-Savvy Societies in the World." CNBC, February 8, 2019. https://www.cnbc.com/2019/02/08/how -estonia-became-a-digital-society.html.

Sengupta, Somini. "Online Learning, Personalized." *New York Times*, December 4, 2011. https://www.nytimes.com/2011/12 /05/technology/khan-academy-blends-its-youtube-approach -with-classrooms.html.

"Seven Wonders of the Modern World as Named by ASCE." Herff College of Engineering, University of Memphis. http://www.ce .memphis.edu/1101/interesting_stuff/7wonders.html.

Shemer, Simona. "On World Water Day, a Look at the Innovative Tech That Makes Israel a Water Superpower." No Camels, March 22, 2018. http://nocamels.com/2018/03/on-world-water -day-a-look-at-the-innovative-tech-that-makes-israel-a-water -superpower/.

Shnayerson, Michael. "Quiet Thunder." *Vanity Fair*, May 2007. https://www.vanityfair.com/news/2007/05/tesla200705.

Shorto, Russell. "How to Think Like the Dutch in a Post-Sandy World." *New York Times Magazine*, April 9, 2014. https://www

.nytimes.com/2014/04/13/magazine/how-to-think-like-the
-dutch-in-a-post-sandy-world.html.

Shwartz, Mark. "Target, Delete, Repair." *Stanford Medicine*, Winter
2018. https://stanmed.stanford.edu/2018winter/CRISPR-for
-gene-editing-is-revolutionary-but-it-comes-with-risks.html.

Simons, Marlise. "Dutch Floods Came in the Back Door." *New York
Times*, February 5, 1995, https://www.nytimes.com/1995/02/05
/world/dutch-floods-came-in-the-back-door.html.

Singularity University. "Singularity University Addresses the
World's Greatest Challenges at SU Global Summit." August
9, 2016. https://su.org/press-room/press-releases/singularity
-university-addresses-the-worlds-greatest-challenges-at-su
-global-summit/.

Smith, Evan. "Sal Khan on Why Khan Academy Is a Non-Profit."
Overheard with Evan Smith. Season 5, episode 18, aired April 20,
2015. www.youtube.com/watch?v=LI7UOuX9Qjs.

Solon, Olivia. "'It's about Expanding Earth': Could We Build
Cities in Space?" *The Guardian*, April 21, 2018. https://www
.theguardian.com/science/2018/apr/21/expanding-earth-could
-we-build-cities-in-space.

Sorkin, Amy Davidson. "Japan: Earthquake, Water, Fire." *New
Yorker*, March 11, 2011. https://www.newyorker.com/news/amy
-davidson/japan-earthquake-water-fire.

Spencer, Stephan. "Exponential Medicine in a COVID-19 World
with Dr. Daniel Kraft." *Get Yourself Optimized*, no. 246, May 7,
2020. www.getyourselfoptimized.com/exponential-medicine
-in-a-covid-19-world-with-dr-daniel-kraft/.

Stanford Center for Professional Development. "Stanford Seminar:
Electric Vehicles and Startups." January 5, 2017. https://www
.youtube.com/watch?v=s47Cy8OUNcM.

Starostinetskaya, Anna. "Beyond Meat Is about to Go Public;
Founder Ethan Brown Speaks about the Evolution of Meat."
VegNews, April 4, 2019. https://vegnews.com/2019/4/beyond

-meat-is-about-to-go-public-founder-ethan-brown-speaks-about
-the-evolution-of-meat.

Storr, Will. "Flooded Britain: How Can Holland Help?" *Daily Telegraph* (UK), April 26, 2014. https://www.telegraph.co.uk /culture/art/architecture/10769974/Flooded-Britain-how-can -Holland-help.html.

Stout, Kristie Lu. "India's 'Pad Man' Becomes Bollywood Blockbuster." CNN, February 8, 2018. http://edition.cnn.com /TRANSCRIPTS/1802/08/nwsm.01.html.

Straiton, Jenny. "Genetically Modified Humans: The X-Men of Scientific Research." *BioTechniques* 66, no. 6 (June 2019). https:// www.future-science.com/doi/pdf/10.2144/btn-2019-0056.

Strauss, Valerie. "Khan Academy: The Revolution that Isn't." *Washington Post*, July 23, 2012. www.washingtonpost.com /blogs/answer-sheet/post/khan-academy-the-hype-and-the -reality/2012/07/23/gJQAuw4J3W_blog.html?utm_term= .36e13b742375.

Tabuchi, Hiroko. "$300 Billon War beneath the Street: Fighting to Replace America's Water Pipes." *New York Times*, November 10, 2017. https://www.nytimes.com/2017/11/10/climate/water -pipes-plastic-lead.html.

Tarpenning, Marc, and Shernaz Daver. "The Story of Building Tesla." Startup Grind, June 3, 2018. https://www.youtube.com/watch ?v=pGfityPXBpA.

Telegram & Gazette. "Dutch Flood Expertise Is Big Export Business." November 13, 2017.

Teller, Astro, and Megan Smith. "What Is Your X? Amplifying Technology Moonshots." Google Official Blog, February 6, 2012. https://googleblog.blogspot.com/2012/02/whats-your -x-amplifying-technology.html.

Tesla. "Impact Report." https://www.tesla.com/ns_videos/tesla -impact-report-2019.pdf.

Teutsch, Betsy. "How Sanitary Pads Can Help Women Improve their

Health and Education." *The Atlantic*, April 22, 2014. https://www
.theatlantic.com/business/archive/2014/04/sanitary-napkin
-business/360297/.

Thompson, Clive. "How Khan Academy Is Changing the Rules
of Education." *Wired*, July 15, 2011. www.wired.com/2011/07
/ff_khan/.

Thrun, Sebastian. "Google's Driverless Car." Ted2011, March
2011. https://www.ted.com/talks/sebastian_thrun_google
_s_driverless_car?referrer=playlist-planes_trains_and
_automobiles.

————. "Leave the Driving to the Car, and Reap Benefits in Safety
and Mobility." *New York Times*, December 5, 2011. https://www
.nytimes.com/2011/12/06/science/sebastian-thrun-self-driving
-cars-can-save-lives-and-parking-spaces.html.

————. "What We're Driving At." *Google Official Blog*, October
9, 2010. https://googleblog.blogspot.com/2010/10/what-were
-driving-at.html.

Thrun, Sebastian, and Chris Anderson. "What AI Is – and Isn't."
Ted2017, April 2017. https://www.ted.com/talks/sebastian
_thrun_and_chris_anderson_what_ai_is_and_isn
_t?language=en.

Ummelas, Ott. "World's Most High-Tech Voting System to Get
Hacking Defenses." Bloomberg, July 18, 2017. https://www
.bloomberg.com/news/articles/2017-07-17/world-s-most-high
-tech-voting-system-to-get-new-hacking-defenses.

United Nations. "United Nations Dignitaries Hail Nobel Peace Prize
Winners in Special Tribute to Muhammad Yunus, Grameen
Bank." November 17, 2006. https://www.un.org/press/en/2006
/dev2610.doc.htm.

University of Michigan. "Carbon Footprint Factsheet." Center for
Sustainable Systems, Pub. No. CSS09-05, 2020. http://css.umich
.edu/factsheets/carbon-footprint-factsheet.

University of Utah. "The Evolution of Corn." Genetics Learning

Center, July 2015. http://learn.genetics.utah.edu/content
/selection/corn/.

Urstadt, Bryant. "Salman Khan: The Messiah of Math." *Bloomberg
Businessweek*, May 19, 2011. www.bloomberg.com/news/articles
/2011-05-19/salman-khan-the-messiah-of-math.

US Government Accountability Office. "Supply Concerns Continue,
and Uncertainties Complicate Planning." May 20, 2014. www
.gao.gov/products/GAO-14-430.

U.S. News and World Report. "Grace King High School." www
.usnews.com/education/best-high-schools/louisiana/districts
/jefferson-parish-public-school-system/grace-king-high-school
-8639.

Valimised. "Statistics about Internet Voting in Estonia." www
.valimised.ee/en/archive/statistics-about-internet-voting
-estonia.

Virta. "The Global Electric Vehicle Market in 2020: Statistics &
Forecasts." https://www.virta.global/global-electric-vehicle
-market.

Wade, Andrew. "Made in Space: New Production Frontiers." *The
Engineer*, February 8, 2016. https://www.theengineer.co.uk
/made-in-space-new-production-frontiers/.

Wagner, Alex. "Can Sal Khan Reform Education in America?"
Huffington Post, June 4, 2011. www.huffingtonpost.com/2011
/04/04/the-khan-academy-and-educ_n_844390.html.

Wall, Mike. "In-Space Manufacturing Is about to Get a Big Test."
Space.com, December 11, 2017. https://www.space.com/39039
-made-in-space-off-earth-manufacturing-test.html.

Walters, Helen. "Two Giants of Online Learning Discuss the Future
of Education." Ideas.Ted.com, January 28, 2014. https://ideas
.ted.com/in-conversation-salman-khan-sebastian-thrun-talk
-online-education/.

Wang, Brian. "Cheap Sanitary Pads Are Better Than Apple iPads for
Poor Women in India by Improving Lives, Improving Health and

Providing Thousands of Jobs." *Next Big Future*, March 5, 2014. https://www.nextbigfuture.com/2014/03/cheap-sanitary-pads -are-better-than.html.

Wattles, Jackie. "NASA Says Moon Rocket Could Cost as Much as $1.6 Billion Per Launch." CNN, December 9, 2019. www.cnn.com /2019/12/09/tech/nasa-sls-price-cost-artemis-moon-rocket-scn /index.html.

We Build Value. "Tokyo, the Earthquake-Proof City." June 27, 2018. www.webuildvalue.com/en/reportage/tokyo-the-earthquake -proof-city.html.

Wee, Sui-Lee. "Chinese Scientist Who Genetically Edited Babies Gets 3 Years in Prison." *New York Times*, December 30, 2019. https://www.nytimes.com/2019/12/30/business/china -scientist-genetic-baby-prison.html.

Winegard, Timothy. "People v Mosquitos: What to Do about Our Biggest Killer." *The Guardian*, September 20, 2019. https://www .theguardian.com/environment/2019/sep/20/man-v-mosquito -biggest-killer-malaria-crispr.

Wolman, David. "Before the Levees Break: A Plan to Save the Netherlands." *Wired*, December 22, 2008. https://www.wired .com/2008/12/ff-dutch-delta/.

Wong, Julia Carrie. "Elon Musk Unveils Tesla Electric Truck – and a Surprise New Sports Car." *The Guardian*, November 17, 2017. https://www.theguardian.com/technology/2017/nov/17/elon -musk-tesla-electric-truck-sports-car-surprise.

World Bank. "Bangladesh Continues to Reduce Poverty but at a Slower Pace." October 24, 2017. www.worldbank.org/en/news /feature/2017/10/24/bangladesh-continues-to-reduce-poverty -but-at-slower-pace.

World Economic Forum White Paper. "Meat: The Future Series; Alternative Proteins." 2019. http://www3.weforum.org/docs /WEF_White_Paper_Alternative_Proteins.pdf.

World Health Organization. "Drinking Water." June 14, 2009. http://
www.who.int/news-room/fact-sheets/detail/drinking-water.

———. "Mosquito Sterilization Offers New Opportunity to
Control Chikungunya, Dengue, and Zika." November 14, 2019.
https://www.who.int/news-room/detail/14-11-2019-mosquito
-sterilization-offers-new-opportunity-to-control-chikungunya
-dengue-and-zika.

World Watch. "Livestock and Climate Change." November/
December 2009. https://awellfedworld.org/wp-content
/uploads/Livestock-Climate-Change-Anhang-Goodland.pdf.

Wynne, Alexandra. "Special Report: Plugging the Floods Will Mean
Going Dutch." *New Civil Engineer,* June 3, 2014. https://www
.newcivilengineer.com/archive/special-report-plugging-the
-floods-will-mean-going-dutch-03-06-2014/.

Xinhuanet. "The First Trial of 'Gene Editing Baby' Sentenced He
Jiankui and Three Other Defendants to Be Held Criminally
Responsible" [in Chinese]. December 30, 2019. http://www
.xinhuanet.com/legal/2019-12/30/c_1125403802.htm.

Xolo. "10 Notable People Who Are E-Residents of Estonia." October
11, 2016. https://blog.leapin.eu/10-notable-people-who-are
-e-residents-of-estonia-c3b7dcd3c7d6.

Ya'ari, Sivan. "Africa: Is Good Enough?" TEDx Tel Aviv University,
February 15, 2016. https://www.youtube.com/watch?v=
tfgAexR5Z2w.

Young, Jeffrey R. "College 2.0: A Self-Appointed Teacher Runs a
One-Man 'Academy' on YouTube." *Chronicle of Higher Education,*
June 6, 2010. www.chronicle.com/article/College-20-A-Self
-Appointed/65793.

Yunus, Muhammad. "Grameen Bank at a Glance." Yunus Centre,
March 12, 2008. https://www.muhammadyunus.org/post/370
/grameen-bank-at-a-glance.

Zelaya, Ian. "Lighting a Continent." *Washington Jewish Week,*

November 13, 2013. http://washingtonjewishweek.com/7152
/lighting-a-continent/news/world-news/.

Zimmer, Carl. "From Fearsome Predator to Man's Best Friend." *New York Times*, May 16, 2013. www.nytimes.com/2013/05/16/science /dogs-from-fearsome-predator-to-mans-best-friend.html.

Interviews

Abe, Yoshiko, PhD – Sustainability Strategist, Kokusai Koygyo Co. Phone, March 31, 2020.

Adriaenssens, Sigrid, PhD – Professor of Civil and Environmental Engineering, Princeton University. Phone, April 16, 2020.

Ahlin, Christian, PhD – Professor, Michigan State University. Phone, May 29, 2020.

Allen, Mark, MD – CEO and cofounder, Elevian. Phone, March 23, 2020.

Anand, Sashi – Vice President, Coimbatore Women's Welfare Organization. Phone, March 30, 2020.

Ani, Karim – founder, Mathalicious. Phone, May 19, 2020.

Arison, David – Former VP of global business relations, Miya. Phone, March 30, 2020.

Arnold, David, PhD – Professor, Umass-Amherst. Phone, May 28, 2020.

Ayala, Alberto, PhD – Air Pollution Control Officer, Sacramento Metropolitan Air Quality Management District. Phone, May 6, 2020.

Barrangou, Rodolphe, PhD – Professor, North Carolina State University. Phone, June 16, 2020; October 12, 2020.

Eli Beer – Founder, United Hatzalah. Phone, June 10, 2020.

Beena, Sujithra, MD – Physician, Coimbatore, India. Phone, March 28, 2020.

Berman, Bradley – Advanced automotive journalist. Phone, May 4, 2020.

Bouzari, Ali, PhD – culinary food scientist. Phone, May 28, 2020.

Bruysten, Saskia – Cofounder and CEO, Yunus Social Business. Phone, May 6, 2020.

Burke, Andrew, PhD – Research Engineer, University of California Davis, Institute of Transportation Studies. Phone, May 4, 2020.

Burns, Lawrence, PhD – author of *Autonomy*; current advisor to Waymo, Google's self-driving car initiative, and former executive with GM. Phone, April 27, 2020.

Cagle, Yvonne, MD – NASA astronaut. Phone, July 21, 2020.

Cahn, Amir – Executive Director, Smart Water Network Forum. Phone, April 2, 2020.

Campbell, Doug – CEO, Solid Power. Phone, May 5, 2020.

Charo, Alta, JD– Professor of law and bioethics, University of Wisconsin, Madison. Phone, September 1, 2020.

Chowdhury, Dilruba – Khan Academy, Bangla Program Director. Phone, May 27, 2020.

Colucci, Lamont, PhD – Associate Professor of Politics and Government, Ripon College. Phone, May 8, 2020.

Cummings, Missy, PhD – Director of Humans and Autonomy Laboratory and Professor in the Department of Electrical and Computer Engineering, Duke University. Phone, May 4, 2020.

Cunningham, Tshaka, PhD – Scientific Program Manager for aging and neurodegenerative diseases, US Department of Veterans Affairs. Phone, July 10, 2020; October 8, 2020.

Danko, Eric – Director of Federal Affairs, Cruise. Phone, June 11, 2020.

Daver, Shernaz – former Chief Marketing Officer, Udacity. Phone, November 16, 2020.

Diamond, Robbie – CEO, Securing America's Future Energy (SAFE). Phone, April 17, 2020.

Dijkman, Jos – Engineer, Deltares Water Research Institute, The Netherlands. Phone, April 11, 2020.

Distel, Oded – former director of the Israel NewTech program, Israeli Ministry of Economy and Industry. Phone, March 12, 2020.

Dunn, Jason – cofounder, Made in Space. Phone, July 20, 2020.

Eberhard, Martin – Founder and former CEO, Tesla. Phone, November 23, 2020.

Eisele, Stephen – VP of Business Development, Virgin Orbit. Phone, April 28, 2020.

Ejiri, Norihiro – Structural Engineer, EJIRI Structural Engineers. Written exchange, April 20, 2020.

Figenbaum, Erik – Chief research engineer, Institute of Transport Economics in Norway. Phone, May 15, 2020.

Finette, Pascal – Chair for Entrepreneurship and Open Innovation, Singularity University. Phone, November 12, 2018.

Foster, Andrew, PhD – Professor of Economics and Health Services, Policy, and Practice, Brown University. Phone, May 18, 2020.

Frank, Andrew, PhD – Emeritus Professor, Mechanical and Aerospace Engineering, University of California Davis, Institute of Transportation Studies. Phone, May 6, 2020.

Garretson, Peter – Senior Fellow, American Foreign Policy Council, and former US Air Force officer. Phone, May 12, 2020.

Gasson, Christopher – Publisher, Global Water Intelligence. Phone, March 30, 2020.

Glas, Peter – Delta Program Commissioner, The Netherlands. Phone, March 26, 2020.

Goldberg, Jodi, JD – Associate, Wiley. Phone, May 14, 2020.

Goldberg, Lev – CEO, Aquify. Phone, March 16, 2020.

Goldstein, Carol, JD – satellite and space law expert. Phone, April 19, 2020.

Goldstein, Nir – Managing Director, Good Food Institute, Israel. Phone, June 25, 2020.

Gondal, Vishal – CEO, GOQII. Phone, April 8, 2020.

Grey, Aubrey de, PhD – Chief Science Officer, SENS Research Foundation. Phone, March 27, 2020.

Griffin, JT – Chief Government Affairs Officer, Mothers Against Drunk Driving (MADD). Phone, April 20, 2020.

Grinstein, Gidi – founder, Reut Group. Phone, December 17, 2020.

Hardman, Scott, PhD – Researcher, Institute of Transportation Studies. Phone, May 7, 2020.

Haskel, Gil, Ambassador – Head of Mashav, Israel's Development Agency. Phone, March 10, 2020.

Hays, Keith – Managing Director, Bluefield Research. Phone, April 4, 2020.

Hsieh, Fu-Hung, PhD – Professor, University of Missouri. Written exchange, May 30, 2020.

Hurt, Brett – CEO, Data.World. Phone, June 4, 2020.

Hwang, Roland – Managing Director, Climate and Clean Energy Program, National Resources Defense Council. Phone, May 15, 2020.

Ilves, Toomas Hendrik – former President, Estonia. Phone, March 27, 2020; April 3, 2020; November 9, 2020.

Ishiwatari, Mikio, PhD – former Senior Advisor, Japan International Cooperation Agency (JICA). Phone, April 19, 2020.

James, Anthony, PhD – Distinguished Professor of molecular biology and biochemistry and of microbiology and molecular genetics, UC Irvine. Phone, June 12, 2020.

Jonkman, Bas, PhD – Professor of Hydraulic Engineering, Delft University of Technology. Phone, April 14, 2020.

Joyce, Meri – Board Member, Peace Boat Disaster Relief (PBV). Phone, April 7, 2020.

Jurado, Jennifer, PhD – Chief Resilience Officer, Broward County, FL. Phone, April 15, 2020.

Kaevats, Marten – National Digital Adviser, Estonia. Phone, April 6, 2020.

Kaljulaid, Kersti – President, Estonia. Interview, Washington, DC, March 3, 2020.

Kaner, Avi – CEO, Morton Williams, and philanthropist. Phone, March 24, 2020.

Kaner, Liz – Member of the Board, Innovation: Africa. Phone, March 12, 2020.

Kelly, Tony – former CEO, Yarra Valley Water in Melbourne, Australia. Phone, April 1, 2020.

Kemmer, Aaron – cofounder of Made in Space. Phone, June 19, 2020; July 3, 2020.

Khadem, Ramin, PhD – former Chairman of the Board of Trustees, International Space University. Phone, April 27, 2020.

Khandker, Shahidur R., PhD – former World Bank Economist. Phone, June 1, 2020.

Kinnan, Cynthia, PhD – Professor, Tufts University. Phone, May 21, 2020.

Kirsh, Natie, PhD (honorary) – philanthropist and billionaire businessman. Phone, March 25, 2020.

Kockelman, Kara, PhD – Professor of Transportation Engineering, University of Texas at Austin. Phone, April 27, 2020.

Komino, Takeshi – Disaster Management Practitioner, Japan. Phone, April 13, 2020.

Korjus, Kaspar – Managing Director, Estonia's e-residency program. Phone, April 29, 2020.

Kornhauser, Alain L., PhD – Professor of Operations Research and Financial Engineering Director of the Program in Transportation, Princeton University. Phone, April 29, 2020.

Koseff, Stephen – former CEO, Investec. Phone, March 19, 2020.

Kotka, Taavi – first digital ambassador and Chief Information Officer, Estonia. Phone, August 1, 2019.

Kraft, Daniel, MD – Chair for Medicine and Neuroscience, Singularity University; founder and Chair, Exponential Medicine. Phone, February 19, 2020.

Kramer, William, PhD – Lecturer, International Space University; retired official of the US Fish and Wildlife Service. Phone, April 28, 2020.

Krimmer, Robert, PhD – Professor of e-Governance, Talinn University of Technology. Phone, April 8, 2020.

Kutter, Bernard – Chief Science Officer, United Launch Alliance (ULA). Phone, May 20, 2020.

LaRocco, Phil – Adjunct Professor, Columbia University. Phone, March 25, 2020.

Lieu, Chan – Senior Safety Program Analyst, Uber. Phone, April 23, 2020.

Lindt, John W. van de, PhD – civil engineering professor, Colorado State University. Phone, April 23, 2020.

Loss, Chris, PhD – food scientist and lecturer at Cornell University. Phone, June 4, 2020.

Lubi, Viljar – Deputy Secretary General for Economic Development in the Ministry of Economic Affairs, Estonia. Phone, April 4, 2020; November 6, 2020.

Mackey, John – founder of Whole Foods. Phone, June 15, 2020.

Mahadevan, Venkatesh – Chief Information Officer, Dubai Investments. Phone, April 2, 2020.

Maniam, Aaron – Deputy Secretary, Industry and Information, Ministry of Communications and Information, Singapore. Phone, April 15, 2020.

Margolis, Aleta – Founder, Center for Inspired Teaching. Phone, May 26, 2020.

Martens, Tarvi – National Electoral Committee's head of e-voting, Estonia. Phone, July 30, 2019.

Martinez, Sylvia – coauthor, *Invent to Learn*. Phone, May 19, 2020.

May, Scott – Head of MISTA at Givaudan. Phone, June 8, 2020.

Meri, Joyce – International Coordinator and Board Member, Peace Boat. Phone, April 7, 2020.

Metz, Tracy – Author, *Sweet & Salt*. Phone, April 6, 2020.

MohanaSundari, J., PhD – Managing Director, Sharp Electrodes. Phone, March 28, 2020.

Molavi, Afshin, PhD – Senior Fellow at the Johns Hopkins SAIS Foreign Policy Institute. Phone, March 16, 2021.

Morduch, Jonathan, PhD – Professor, New York University. Phone, May 27, 2020.

Morris, Dale – Economist and Director of Strategic Partnerships Water Institute. Phone, April 2, 2020.

Murphy, Robert, PhD – Former Senior Researcher, Rand Corporation. Phone, May 27, 2020.

Muruganantham, Arunachalam – innovator of low-cost sanitary pad. Phone, February 21, 2020.

Nishikawa, Satoru, PhD – disaster resilience expert; former senior Japanese Cabinet official. Phone, April 6, 2020.

Ogden, Timothy – Managing Director, The Financial Access Initiative, a research center based at NYU. Phone, May 26, 2020.

Ono, Yuichi, PhD – Assistant Director and Professor, International Research Institute of Disaster Science (IRIDeS), Tohoku University. Phone, April 16, 2020.

Ovink, Henk – Special Envoy for International Water Affairs, Kingdom of the Netherlands. Phone, April 1, 2020; October 28, 2020.

Peleg, Amir – CEO, Takadu. Interview, Washington, DC, April 2, 2019; Phone, October 22, 2020.

Pitt, Mark, PhD – Professor of Population Studies and Professor Emeritus of Economics, Brown University. Phone, May 16, 2020.

Potter, Michael, PhD (Honorary) – founder, Geeks without Frontiers; Space Policy Expert. Phone, April 17, 2020.

Rahmstorf, Stefan, PhD – Professor of physics of the oceans, Potsdam University. Phone, March 26, 2020.

Ramesh, S R – Hand-loom weaver, Coimbatore, India. Phone, March 28, 2020.

Reis, Evan – cofounder, US Resiliency Council. Phone, April 23, 2020.

Sallaberger, Christian, PhD – CEO, Canadensys Aerospace

Corporation; Chairman of the Board, International Space University. Phone, May 7, 2020.

Sato, Jun, PhD – structural engineer and associate professor, University of Tokyo. Phone, May 4, 2020.

Schwartz, Rusty, JD – founder, Kitchentown. Phone, June 2, 2020.

Sena, Michael – Telematics Expert. Phone, May 12, 2020.

Shaw, Rajib, PhD – Professor of Media and Governance, Keio University. Phone, April 20, 2020; December 15, 2020.

Siegel, Seth M. – author, *Let There Be Water*. Interview, New York. October 28, 2017.

Sperling, Daniel, PhD – Founding Director, Institute of Transportation Studies at the University of California, Davis. Phone, May 11, 2020.

Stager, Gary, PhD – Veteran teacher of education. Phone, May 22, 2020.

Steenhuis, Marinke, PhD – founder, SteenhuisMeurs. Phone, April 14, 2020.

Stive, Marcel, PhD – Civil Engineering and Geosciences Professor, Delft University of Technology. Written exchange, March 28, 2020.

Stott, Chris – founder, MANSAT; and space entrepreneur. Phone, April 20, 2020; May 8, 2020.

Stott, Nicole – former astronaut, STEM advocate. Phone, May 11, 2020.

Takeuchi, Toru, PhD – Professor of Architecture and Structural Engineering, Tokyo Institute of Technology. Phone, April 17, 2020.

Tarpenning, Marc – cofounder, Tesla. Phone, November 17, 2020.

Tepper, Steve, JD – General Council, Selfhelp Community Services. Phone, March 16, 2020.

Theo, George – CEO, Unitywater of Queensland Australia. Phone, March 30, 2020.

Thirugnanam, Natarajan, MD – plastic surgeon, Sri Ramakrishna Hospital, Coimbatore, India. Phone, March 22, 2020.

Tripathi, Supriya – Hindi content creator at Khan Academy, Khan Academy India. Phone, May 23, 2020.

van de Lindt, John W., PhD – Professor of Civil and Environmental Engineering, Colorado State University. Phone, April 23, 2020.

Venkatesh, Rangaraj, MD – Chief Medical Officer, Aravind Eye Care System. Phone, March 18, 2020.

Viik, Linnar – Programme Director, Estonian e-Governance Academy. Phone, August 20, 2019.

Waggonner III, J. David – Founding Principal, Waggonner & Ball. Phone, April 13, 2020.

Wang, Yunshi – Director of the China Center for Energy and Transportation, UC Davis Institute of Transportation Studies. Phone, May 12, 2020.

Watkins, Todd – Economics Professor, Lehigh University. Phone, May 22, 2020.

Weeden, Brian, PhD – Director of Program Planning, Secure World Foundation. Phone, April 30, 2020.

Weintraub, Seth – Founder, Elektrek. Phone, May 12, 2020; May 18, 2020.

Whittaker, William (Red) L., PhD – Director of the Field Robotics Center, Carnegie Mellon University. Written exchange, April 28, 2020.

Williams, Peter – industry expert; IBM Distinguished Engineer (retired). Phone, March 11, 2020.

Winetraub, Yonatan – cofounder, SpaceIL. Phone, April 24, 2020.

Wydick, Bruce, PhD – author, *Shrewd Samaritan*; Program Director of International and Development Economics, University of San Francisco. Phone, May 14, 2020.

Yaari, David – Chairman, A.B. Yaari Holdings. Interview, Washington, DC, March 3, 2020.

Yaari, Sivan – Founder, Innovation: Africa. Interview, Herzliya. August 8, 2019; Phone, October 27, 2020.

Yogeswaran, Babu – director and filmmaker. Phone, March 26, 2020.

Zakai, Shira – Head of Communications, Beyond Meat. Phone, January 27, 2020.

Zellner, Debra, PhD – Montclair State University. Phone, June 4, 2020.

Zheng, Jenny – Khan Academy Simplified Chinese Text Translation Advocate. Written exchange, June 3, 2020.

Zingher, Tally, JD – CEO, Dawsat. Phone, February 27, 2020.

About the Author

Avi Jorisch is a Senior Fellow at the American Foreign Policy Council and bestselling author of *Thou Shalt Innovate: How Israeli Ingenuity Repairs the World*, which has been translated into over thirty languages. He holds a bachelor's degree in history from Binghamton University and a master's degree in Islamic history from the Hebrew  University of Jerusalem. He also studied Arabic and Islamic philosophy at the American University in Cairo and al-Azhar University. He has lectured around the world, and his articles have appeared in influential outlets including the *New York Times*, the *Wall Street Journal*, *Foreign Affairs*, *Forbes*, and Al-Arabiya.net. He has also appeared on CNN, CSPAN, Fox News, and MSNBC. He is a member of the Council on Foreign Relations and the Young Presidents' Organization (YPO).

Made in the USA
Columbia, SC
29 April 2023

5ed94770-a048-4cbe-8be6-6cc1e24cc098R01